ESSAYS & OPINIONS

ESSAYS
& OPINIONS
1921–1931

by Edgell Rickword

edited by Alan Young

A CARCANET NEW PRESS PUBLICATION

TO
DAVID HOLBROOK
Friend of Many Seasons

SBN 85635 071 0

Copyright © Edgell Rickword 1920, 1921, 1922, 1923, 1924,
1925, 1926, 1927, 1928, 1929, 1930, 1931, 1974 (Text)
Copyright © Alan Young 1974 (Introduction)

First published in 1974
by Carcanet New Press Limited
266 Councillor Lane
Cheadle Hulme, Cheadle
Cheshire SK8 5PN

Printed in Great Britain
by W & J Mackay Limited, Chatham

CONTENTS

Introduction

The decade, 1921–1931, during which all the criticism in the present volume was written, was one of the most crucial periods in twentieth-century English literature. If our literature and criticism of the nineteen-twenties failed to manifest anything approaching those inventive and destructive extremes which were to be found then throughout the Western world, from New York to Berlin and beyond, it was not because English artistic life settled down again complacently or apathetically to the attitudes and standards of pre-war artistic activity. The critical and creative revolution which had begun in London before World War I was given an extra boost by a younger generation of artists returning from the trenches. In literature, the moribund standards of late-Victorian, Edwardian, and even Georgian criticism, against which Eliot and Pound had fought their apparently lonely battles, were now to be the object of concerted attack by this new generation whose angry awareness of the inadequacy of the accepted norms of the pre-war Establishment was reinforced by a more confident knowledge of what modern writing might achieve. An age which had already produced some of the finest poetry of Yeats, Eliot, Pound, and Wilfred Owen, and the prose of Conrad, Lawrence, Joyce, Wyndham Lewis, Katherine Mansfield, Ford Madox Ford, Virginia Woolf, E. M. Forster, Lytton Strachey, and many others, had no necessity to feel overawed by even the most formidable achievements of the Victorians.

First shoots of a criticism which could match the undeniable creative achievements of modern literature had already emerged before and during the War. The sharper judgements and more sensitive, intelligent, and informed response to literature of critics such as T. S. Eliot, Ezra Pound, F. S. Flint, and Harold Monro had created a distinctive new tone in such periodicals as *The English Review*, *Poetry and Drama*, *The Egoist*, and *Art and Letters*. After the War, the position was consolidated in *The Monthly Chapbook*, *Coterie*, *The Tyro*, *The Athenaeum*, *The Adelphi*, and *The Criterion*, and the new critics of the Post-War included Richard Aldington,

Aldous Huxley, J. Middleton Murry, I. A. Richards, Robert Graves, Herbert Read, and Edgell Rickword himself.

The task for criticism during the Twenties was far from easy. These younger writers knew that the prevailing standards of most of their immediate literary forebears were totally inadequate, but not because they themselves participated in any general cultural consensus. Delayed but always unavoidable reaction to the horrors experienced during World War I, the challenge of new ideas (especially in the behavioural sciences) which intensified rather than clarified the intellectual bewilderment, the slow breakdown of democracy in Europe and the growth of totalitarian regimes, the General Strike and the Depression, and, not least, the increasing awareness of the artistic insufficiency if not impotence of stylistic modernism – Parisian or Bloomsbury varieties – all these meant that no simple and sure artistic creed or methodology would emerge. All the greater credit, then, that the period produced in so much of its literary criticism a determined *will* to abide by the highest possible standards of critical intelligence. As the work in this volume shows, Edgell Rickword's contribution to the setting of such critical standards was of central importance.

In the wide range of interests revealed in Rickword's reviewing there is a kind of pattern which the thirty earlier 'apprentice' pieces selected for this volume echo: the word 'apprentice' is used with caution because of a maturity which is manifest even in the earliest work. From the beginning, the principal interest is poetry, or, rather, language and form taken seriously. Contemporary work is tested against what is vital in the English literary tradition, and, in its turn, the work of Marlowe and Chapman, Donne, and Dekker, for example, is tested against the thought habits of their own time. In a short review of Sampson's *The Cambridge Book of Prose and Verse* (1925) Rickword suggested that the word 'barbarous' is most appropriately applied to those writers of any age who break their artistic trust:

> who treat language, not as the habit of thought but as a lifeless substance which can be built up into patterns independent of the rhythm of contemporary life.

Rickword's concern with standards of linguistic usage is evident as much in the sharply focused criticism of the new verse of his contemporaries as in his mourning over the general debasement of linguistic values in comparison with Dekker's time:

One cannot help wondering what sort of a journalist Dekker would make today, when so much of the vitality of the wonderful language he was born to has been dissipated.

Accurately directed attention to detail and a general social concern are ever-present in these early pieces. At times, though rarely, the books he reviewed were hardly worth the effort, but they all underwent his customary clear and penetrating examination or, rather (to use the word which Rickword chose to characterize the right approach to works requiring or deserving proper examination), *scrutiny*. Thus, for example, in 1921 he writes that 'the test of the consideration due to a contemporary lies in the examination of his style' and cites Robert Graves whose words are 'young and vigorous, carrying no more than their own weight of flesh. His rhythms, always apparently simple, possess those subtle variations which a poet alone can introduce, making of a stock metre a personal instrument.' He illustrates his description by quoting from Graves's 'Morning Phoenix' ('a poem with a sound core'). In the same review he shows how, by contrast, Maurice Baring's verse can be derivative, with 'neither imaginative perception nor direct observation'. That he was quite capable of making telling observations some years before *The Calendar of Modern Letters* came into being is seen also in an otherwise relatively polite notice of J. C. Squire's *Selections from Modern Poets* (1921):

> One may feel that the merits of Mr. Eliot and other new poets entitle them to inclusion, but it would have been false hospitality to immerse them in that particular atmosphere.

In relation to Eliot (whose critical attitudes and methods Rickword greatly admired), Rickword's well-known review of *The Waste Land* for *The Times Literary Supplement* is a typical mixture of honest response and intelligent perplexity. Though later Rickword was to admit that he had underestimated Eliot's poem and made amends in a fine review of Eliot's *Poems, 1909–1925* in *The Calendar*, even now not all the awkward questions which he asked about *The Waste Land* in 1923 have been satisfactorily answered.

As we would expect from a man who later became a Marxist critic and editor of *Left Review*, several of the early reviews go beyond creative literature into general aesthetics, and also into psychology and anthropology. Some of the *New Statesman* pieces reveal his lifelong preoccupation with social and political issues. There are comments on French literature which reveal a deep knowledge of modern and contemporary French writing especially. Here too he applies the same standards of polite but incisive scrutiny, expecting from French writing no less a respect for traditional (though never dull and merely respectable) standards of literary and human values. Of the two, as he suggested in relation to a translation by Richard Aldington of Cyrano de Bergerac's *Voyages to the Moon and the Sun*, human values – especially those of a free and reasonable life – are of greater importance than merely literary ones:

> These voyages, though it cannot be said that they are as fresh as when they were first written, are still very much alive and likely to retain their interest for an indefinable period. This perennial attraction is due not so much to his fantastic invention . . . as to the freedom of his intellect from the prejudices which in one form or another are a continual menace to the cultivation of a reasonable life. This emancipation is evidently a thing of the personality and has nothing whatever to do with literary achievement. We are as likely to find it in a farm labourer's cottage as in a university common room.

His concern with the struggle in art and in society between the free intellect and dead convention led Rickword to the remarkable life and equally remarkable work of Arthur Rimbaud. Writing in the Rimbaud issue[1] of *Adam* in 1954, Dr. Enid Starkie – herself a fine Rimbaud scholar – asserted that Edgell Rickword's study *Rimbaud: The Boy and the Poet* of 1924 was the best book on Rimbaud to have appeared up to that date in any country, even in France. Rickword's pioneer attempt to give a psychological interpretation of Rimbaud's life and work came to the original and interesting conclusion that the French poet's abandonment of poetry was only a stage on the road to greater 'poetic' maturity which was reached when Rimbaud became man-of-action, trader and explorer in Abyssinia. The extracts from the book reprinted here demonstrate Rickword's sympathetic understanding of the work of a poet whose reputation in England was still to be established. As Dr. Starkie suggested, *Rimbaud: The Boy and the Poet* has continued to hold an interest for modern readers, and there is no doubt that it has inspired much of the enthusiasm for Rimbaud which began in this country during the mid-Twenties. Rickword's own translations of some of the poems from *Les Illuminations* are given in a short appendix to this section.

[1] *Adam*, Nos. 244–246, 1954.

During 1924 Edgell Rickword collaborated with Douglas Garman and Bertram Higgins to plan the launching of a new literary periodical which made its first appearance in March 1925 as *The Calendar of Modern Letters*. Rickword has said[1] that the editorial committee were 'a sort of discontented club' whose members disliked the pseudo-classicism of T. S. Eliot's *Criterion* as much as they abhorred the literary coteries and cliques which were so much a part of London literary life in the early-Twenties. Above all, they despised the Establishment critics who dominated the popular literary press. *The Calendar of Modern Letters* in both its creative and its critical work represented a full-scale assault on timid, enclosed and conventionally dull literary attitudes. Among the writers published in *The Calendar* were D. H. Lawrence, E. M. Forster, A. E. Coppard, Edwin Muir, Robert Graves, Liam O'Flaherty, Mary Butts, John Crowe Ransom, Hart Crane, and Allen Tate. Some of his contributors became better known abroad, as for example Iris Barry, protégé of the earnest Ezra Pound. Translations of several French and Russian writers (including, for example, the whole of Chekhov's *The Wood-Demon* as well as recent work by young Soviet writers) gave *The Calendar* a richer quality and wider scope than any other English periodical of the time. Joyce's '*Anna Livia Plurabelle*' would have graced the *Calendar*'s first issue if the printers had not appointed themselves literary censors.

Rickword's own contributions typify the intellectual vitality and range of the whole venture. In addition to poems and stories, he provided essays, reviews, and much of the editorial comment. His continual concern with the renewal and maintenance of linguistic vigour in literature is balanced by the consciousness that this could not be easily achieved. His essay 'The Returning Hero' (1925) was an illuminating analysis of the plight of poetry in the Twenties, an analysis which has much relevance to the cultural life of a half-century later. Rickword's statement that he could not imagine modern English poets 'remaining content to cultivate the drugget-fields of genteel discontent' should make us aware that we, too, are still waiting signs of the approach of the new artistic Hero who would be

[1] 'A Conversation with Edgell Rickword', *Poetry Nation*, No. 1, 1973, pp. 73–89.

an exhaustively disillusioned Hero (we could not put up with another new creed) who has yet so much vitality that his thoughts seize all sorts of analogies between apparently unrelated objects and so create an unbiased but self-consistent, humorous universe for himself.

The modern writer's predicament, Rickword argued, could not be separated from that of his society, and the necessary task was a formidable one involving both the will to create and the need to tell the whole truth, no matter how painful.

Reviews in *The Calendar* of poets such as T. S. Eliot and Carl Sandburg who had attempted this dangerous and difficult task are always more sympathetically encouraging than those of poets such as Laurence Binyon, Alfred Noyes, and Humbert Wolfe who always failed to acknowledge their artistic responsibility in a new age. Books by other critics, too, tend to be divided into sheep and goats. For example, praise for volumes by I. A. Richards, Robert Graves, and Virginia Woolf (all of whom are seen to be trying to perform the essential critical task of relating literature to the needs of a contemporary mind) is contrasted with a devastatingly argued dismissal of F. L. Lucas's *Authors Dead and Living* which lazily failed to take either literature or life seriously.

Inclusion of 'foundation' texts in the behavioural sciences among the books selected for review by Rickword in *The Calendar* underlines his determination to establish the necessary links between literature and all the activities of the modern intellect, while the remarkable 'Notes for a Study of Sade' was among the first attempts in English to treat with due seriousness the work of an influential French writer who had been largely ignored here, probably, as Rickword suggested, because a proper reading of de Sade would make us ask too many painful questions about ourselves:

> there is abundant evidence, in literature and in experience, for the view that the impulse which in him was developed to the degree of mania, is an essential component of the most commonplace, as well as the most exceptional, expressions of vitality. Such a conclusion can only be accepted or rejected finally by a scrupulous examination of personal motives; 'instinctive' revulsion is no argument against it.

Fiction, like poetry, was assessed in *The Calendar* according to the writer's ability to forge appropriate language-structures. One of the most famous and valuable pieces to appear in *The Calendar* was by C. H. Rickword, Edgell Rickword's cousin. 'A Note on Fiction' (which has been reprinted in the present volume) was published in two parts in 1926. As Malcolm Bradbury has claimed, this essay marks 'the transition of modernism into literary criticism of the novel'.[1]

Perhaps the best-known of all the contributions to *The Calendar* were the 'scrutinies' of established writers of the day. Edgell Rickword wrote the first of these, on Sir James Barrie, and he edited two collections, the second of which was intended to include assessments of contemporary writers' achievements to date and not, as in the earlier volume, deliberate attempts to puncture the reputations of Establishment writers. As Rickword wrote in the Foreword to the second of these collections (1931), the attack on 'national figures in the sense that Wells, Shaw, Kipling, and the others were, each expressing the "conscience" of some numerically important group' had aroused a great deal of hostility against the critics of *The Calendar* and *Scrutiny I*. Rickword refused to be intimidated by the resultant indignation and anger. Replying to *The Times Literary Supplement*'s charge of a 'low standard of literary courtesy' in the 'scrutinies' Rickword was aggressively unrepentant:

> To a paralytic, I suppose, any man who walks with ordinary freedom must seem to be executing a violent and gratuitously offensive gesture.

But if the 'scrutinies' appeared to be the most radically exciting of the ventures introduced in *The Calendar* it would be an error to view them as being different in kind or even degree from the general critical concerns of the periodical or, indeed, from those found in Rickword's own criticism from the earliest reviews.

The influence of this work of the Twenties cannot be over-estimated. When, in 1933, F. R. Leavis presented his selection[2] of critical essays and reviews from *The Calendar* he suggested that the periodical's greatest achievement had been to bring to life and to sustain a spirit of open critical intelligence in response to literature. This response had been a cultural landmark in a period of intellectual disintegration, a time when the taste of the English reading public was being seriously misled and even increasingly undermined by many established literary pundits. As we have

[1] Malcolm Bradbury, 'The Novel in the 1920s', in *Sphere History of Literature in the English Language*, vol. 7, ed. Bergonzi, Barrie & Jenkins, London, 1970, p. 220.

[2] *Towards Standards of Criticism: Selections from The Calenda of Modern Letters, 1925–27*, chosen and with an Introduction by F. R. Leavis, Wishart & Co., London, 1933.

seen, *The Calendar*'s editors were themselves quite aware of their social responsibilities in an age of cultural crisis:

> We have the small body of educated sharp-witted readers from whom a small spark of intelligence sometimes flickers; but being passionate, if at all, only about values and not experience, ultimately uncreative; and themselves so frequently practitioners as to be unsatisfactory even as audience. Beyond lies the vast reading-public which is led by the nose by the high-class literary journalist-poet type; and its tail tweaked by the paragraphist with pretensions not rising above personal gossip.

This statement by Rickword (taken from his review of Virginia Woolf's *The Common Reader*) defines his ideal requirements for the role of literary critic – a sustained intelligence, one passionate about real experience, and responsibly devoted to the foundation of a common standard of creative criticism. Nothing less than this ideal is to be found in Rickword's own criticism or in that of the periodical which he edited. The successful establishing of such a standard of criticism meant that a new generation of readers was able to develop in and for itself what Dr. Leavis termed 'mature intelligence'. By 1933, for example, according to Dr. Leavis, one major definite result of *The Calendar*'s work had been to lay down 'the grounds of criticism upon which Mr. Eliot was to be duly appraised, so that recognition of his significance came as a matter of course'. The appearance of *Towards Standards of Criticism* only a few months after the first issue of the critical review *Scrutiny* should remind us how much, in addition to its title, the major English critical journal of the Thirties and Forties itself owed to the forthright, responsible, and clear-minded courage of *The Calendar*, though, alas, *Scrutiny* was never to achieve the remarkable, civilized balance of the critical and the creative found in the earlier periodical.

In 1928 Rickword published a translation (with Douglas Garman as co-partner) of François Porché's *Life of Baudelaire*. At the end of that year he made the acquaintance of E. Hayter Preston, a man of the pre-war generation who had known Ford, Pound, and Aldington. Preston was free-lancing in Fleet Street, but at the end of the year he took a full-time job as literary editor and much else on the *Sunday Referee*, a paper incongruously devoted to show-biz, since its owner was the impresario Isidore Ostrer, of the Stoll Theatre and other interests. He immediately took steps to raise the standard of the paper's literary pages, and at once invited

Aldington to write the main review or literary feature each week. This Aldington fulfilled for some two years, doing much excellent work, notably on French writers. Preston was on friendly terms with Edgell Rickword and asked him to take a share in the page, particularly on new poetry publications. The literary pages of this popular Sunday newspaper are a model for serious journalism. The short selection of reviews by Rickword from the *Sunday Referee* is further confirmation of his constant aim to create bridges between the general reading public and the best writing of his time. No modern literary critic has done more to create such bridges while refusing to relinquish the highest literary values.

Alan Young

A Note on the *Appendix*: Articles from the *Daily Herald*, 1920: Early contributions by Edgell Rickword to the 'Books of Today and Tomorrow' page of the *Daily Herald* were discovered only after this book had passed the page-proof stage. Among these were reviews of contemporary poetry and criticism, as well as short bibliographical introductions in the *Herald*'s 'Great Names' of English literature.

The pieces chosen for inclusion in the *Appendix*, all published in 1920, confirm the remarkably early maturity of Rickword's critical mind. His support for the new critical standards represented by T. S. Eliot's *The Sacred Wood* and J. Middleton Murry's *Aspects of Literature*, for example, is underlined by sensitive response to the poems of Edward Thomas and Edmund Blunden as much as by his shrewd questioning of F. S. Flint's latest theories about *vers libre* and Edith Sitwell's most recent display of verbal fireworks.

Essays and Reviews from
the *New Statesman* and
The Times Literary Supplement
1921–1925

HERO AND LEANDER

Hero and Leander. By Christopher Marlowe and George Chapman
(The Haslewood Reprints No. 2)

There were ten editions of *Hero and Leander* within the forty
years which followed its publication: and from the scarcity of
surviving copies it is likely that they were mostly read to rags. I
could wish a similar heroic destiny to this edition, though it is so
attractively produced that it must be numbered among those books
which are not lent willingly. It is a page for page reprint of Linley's
1598 edition, which was the second edition of Marlowe's work,
but the first to contain Chapman's completion of the poem. If anything could add to one's enjoyment of such glorious poetry, it
would be to read it in this simple and dignified form, which reproduces as far as it is possible for us the original appearance of the
poem. We may think that this is how Shakespeare read it, and
Donne, and the hosts of obscure great men who found no divorce
between its vigour of imagination and their passionate experience,
in that age when life was poetic and poetry not less but more than
lifelike.

Putting aside *Paradise Lost,* it would seem impossible to find a later
rival to *Hero and Leander.* Certain passages of the *Excursion* are
far above it in philosophical significance, but Wordsworth's poem
as a whole does not reach near it in artistic unity. In other narrative
poems one quality or another has been developed to a greater
intensity, but in none is so perfect and consistent a balance maintained between the natural world and the world of poetic imagination. It is the most classic of English love poems, if classic means
that the emotions are represented in their natural proportions, their
significance revealed by selection, not by elaboration, and the whole
human spectacle worked out against a background of destiny
which the reader is brought to realize by purely aesthetic means. It
affects us as a vision, as a revelation of ideal beauty, but not as
one which is above all 'breathing human passion'; and though inestimable things have been done since, the poet and the man of
this world have not again composed in such perfect unison.

I have written as though the whole poem were the work of one
individual; but indeed the break at the end of the second Sestiad is
such as to make the development of the tragedy fall to Chapman's

share. Nothing in his treatment of its moral significance is implied in Marlowe's commencement, and this lack of coherence is only not fatal because of a common quality in their inspiration, their loving comprehension of life. Their preoccupations, though, are very different. There are some significant lines in the opening of Chapman's work:

> Love's edge is taken off, and that light flame.
> Those thoughts, joys, longings that before became
> High unexperienced blood, and maids' sharp plights
> Must now grow staid, and censure the delights,
> That being enjoyed ask judgement . . .

Fortunately Chapman's censure does not come to much once it is under the spell of Hero's foredoomed beauty; but the addition is characteristic. His Leander is quickly filled

With sense of his unceremonious part,

and sets about the preparations which will enable him to marry Hero. It is unfortunate that we cannot know whether Marlowe was accidentally prevented from finishing the story, or whether he had paused at a point where he could not see his continuation clearly. His Leander is so personal a projection, so keen a lover of beauty, and so swift and fine in his movements to enjoyment that beside it a regard for ceremony, other than that of personal integrity, must seem to hobble his Attic grace. Had Marlowe gone on to relate the tragedy in the same condition of mind, he would have been faced, as in *Dr. Faustus*, with a power which could limit and punish individual ambition, against which, as his plays show, his nature was in rebellion. As it is, the fragment he left is complete in itself, the perfect expression of his youthful spirit in his maturest manner.

But for Shakespeare and Jonson, there was no one living who might have finished the poem on the level at which it began; but, if Chapman had not devoted his work to the memory of his greater friend, his poem might be valued at an estimation much higher than that in which it is generally held. Chapman is a thoughtful poet, using the phrase with rather a slang meaning. He does not understand more profoundly than Marlowe, but his thought processes are nearer the surface, and interfere with its crystallization, first into imagery and then into formal expression. There is not to be found in him anywhere such an expansive utterance as Marlowe's:

A stately builded ship, well-rig'd and tall
The Ocean maketh more majesticall:
Why vowest thou then to live in Sestos here,
Who on Love's seas more glorious wouldst appear?

But his vigorous, masculine versification is continually breaking into such felicities as

Graceful Ædone that sweet pleasure loves,
And ruff-foot Chreste with the tufted crown.

and it is he, of course, who found this miraculous compliment –

Leander into Hellespontus throws
His Hero-handled body, whose delight
Made him disdain each other Epethite.

It would be a pleasant task to go on quoting from Chapman, if only to disprove the momentary lapse of that sensitive critic Edward Thomas, when he wrote that 'Marlowe died, and Chapman knew not the incantation'. I might choose the beautiful conclusion to the whole poem, but because it raises an interesting point in comparative criticism I would refer to the closing lines of the third Sestiad. It would be strange if the 'scientific' imagery, the psychological preoccupation, even the emphasis in the expression, did not recall Donne, and bring in question the isolation which has generally been considered to surround his style. These are the concluding lines of Hero's address to the bed in which her lover has lain:

This place was mine: *Leander* now 'tis thine;
Thou being myself, then it is double mine:
Mine, and *Leander*'s mine, *Leander*'s mine.
O see what wealth it yields me, nay yields him:
For I am in it, he for me doth swim.
Rich, fruitful love, that doubling self estates
Elixir-like contracts, though separates.
Dear place, I kiss thee, and do welcome thee,
As from *Leander* ever sent to me.

If what was once known as wit had never been raised to poetry by Chapman's greater contemporary, Donne, at least this would have told us plainly of the possibility. In its combination of sweetness and strength it is personal to Chapman at his best; and in the breath-taking naturalism of the last couplet it recalls a time when flesh and blood did inhabit the poetic world. What an example for our distracted poetry, which so often now strikes at the absolute and achieves the commonplace! These poets lived life from the ground upwards; and with such roots 'Hero and Leander' enjoys a perpetual spring, which the miracle of art enables us to share.

NEW POEMS OF SHAKESPEARE?

The Poems of Edward de Vere. By J. Thomas Looney (Cecil Palmer)

' "Shakespeare," ' says Mr. Looney in a note, 'is here used as the pen-name of the poet. The Stratford man's name was Shakspere (Shaxper).' The modified form is, he holds, 'suggestive of Oxford's fame as a spearsman'.

Mr. Looney is so sensitive to the subtlest suggestions that he might have felt in the atrocious sound of 'Shaxper' a motive sufficient to explain the Stratford man's adoption of a more euphonious spelling. That, however, would have rallied the disintegrating ranks of the Stratfordians, who, after suffering the ravishment of the plays and sonnets, must now submit to further encroachments on the work of traditional poets. Lyrics of Raleigh, Fulke Greville, Richard Barnefield, and the better parts of Anthony Munday, are here transferred to the credit of the mysterious Earl of Oxford. Dr. Grosart considered twenty-two poems as genuine work of de Vere, and even one of these he snatched from the grasping ambition of Queen Elizabeth. That was a paltry effort in the cause of Justice compared to the ramifications of Mr. Looney's tentacular genius. Everything that he touches turns to honey, or rather, all the honey that he gathers in the luxuriant flowering of Elizabethan literature is transferred with bee-like, automatic industry to the hive of Edward de Vere.

I have mentioned some of the poets he leaves the poorer for his visitation. Campion, besides, is only temporarily safe; evidence collects against him. There is a poem by Lyly (another pen-name, beyond all doubt if it could be discovered that Oxford was noted for the pallor of his complexion) in which this line occurs:

> On Daphne's cheek grow rose and cherry . . .

which is obviously an early draft of Campion's:

> There is a garden in her face
> Where roses and white lilies grow ...

The mention of lilies, the fact that campions grow abundantly wild, and the pastoral nature of some of de Vere's poetry should prove beyond dispute a common authorship hidden under three personalities.

Mr. Looney sets us the example of this kind of reasoning. He says that the line:

> Other help for him I see that there is none

almost reproduces Oxford's 1576 line:

> And help for me there is none sure.

This is ingenuity playing with ductile material. The intractable evidence of Jonson is a very different matter, but Mr. Looney is more than equal to the occasion. He undermines the obstacle, blows Jonson sky-high, and waves defiantly in the direction of Stratford:

> A pretension was made that the works (First Folio) had been gathered together by two actors, Heming and Condell, who signed certain of the prefatory pieces. Their claims are now recognised as false, making it clear that there was subterfuge in the publication, and to these false pretensions Ben Jonson was a party, thus destroying the value of his testimony on the question of authorship. Under these circumstances there is something humorous in the serious way in which Jonson's 'camouflage' has been put forward in support of the traditional authoship.

In his early days, in the intervals of spear-shaking, before he had become model to 'the secret poets of the Oxford school', Edward de Vere found time to write very reasonable poetry. His place is secure in any limited anthology, say, one of sixteenth-century verse, but he seems never to achieve the necessary concentration, the firing-out of dross which usurpers of his fame occasionally do. He can fill the eternal commonplace with a measure of new breath:

> A doubtful choice of these things which to crave,
> A kingdom or a cottage or a grave.
>
> .   .   .   .
>
> If woman could be fair and yet not fond ...

He has a rather bitter insight into the psychology of Desire, on which he writes some of his best poems. He ends one of them:

> Nor greater joy can be than this:
> That to enjoy that others miss.

There is another poem which, though apocryphal, has definite links with a part of Oxford's work. It begins as a pleasant pastoral, of a shepherd's dream in 'peascod time',

> When little boys with pipes of corn
> Sat keeping beasts afield.

It continues in a conversation between allegorical figures, Good Sport, Wit, Honest Meaning, etc., racily done but a little diffuse. At last Venus becomes angry, and the crowd scatters:

> Then Lust fell cold, and Beauty white
> Sat babbling with Desire.

By means of the three words, cold, white and babbling, he animates these hollow forms with a perverse and shuddering vitality. He does not do it again, and after all, it may not be de Vere's poem.

In a certainly authentic poem he speaks of women as

> These gentle birds that fly from man to man . . .

It is the limit of his power, that of a man driven despairingly into a position, rather than one merely using current cynicism. Generally, he writes directly from experience, and his poetry rarely passes beyond criticism of that experience.

A STUDY OF DONNE

John Donne: A Study in Discord. By Hugh I'Anson Fausset (Cape)

'The Life of Donne', Campbell remarked in his *British Poets*, 'is more interesting than his poetry.' That evaluation is given a new meaning by Mr. Fausset, who traces throughout Donne's life a conflict between the physical and the spiritual impulses of his nature. In his estimation, the fact that neither as a poet nor as a preacher did Donne permanently resolve these discords into a harmony deprives him of a place among the poets who have achieved the expression of beauty in its purest form.

This view is argued with the idealistic fervour which characterized Mr. Fausset's *Keats: A Study in Development*; but, as he finds himself in antipathy to the realistic strain which is inherent in Donne's character, there is a turbulence in his exposition and a harshness in much of his comment from which the earlier work was free. The kind of criticism he practises, the estimation of a poet's creative value rather than his literary eminence, is of the highest importance, for as Browning says: –

> In the hierarchy of creative minds it is the presence of the highest faculty that gives first rank, in virtue of its kind, not degree; no pretension of a lower nature, whatever the completeness of development or variety of effect, impeding the precedency of the rarer endowment though only in the germ.

The faculty which distinguishes the noblest poets from the interesting majority of writers and artists is the gift of perceiving the universe, not through the disparate evidence of the senses or through the conceptual entities of the intelligence, but as a unity in which all the dualisms are extinguished. But once the evidence for the possession of this gift has been received we are not to demand that the poet shall testify incessantly to a unity, 'like an angel out of a cloud', which manifestly is not a constant attribute of human experience. Rather we should be glad that he descends to illuminate the dualistic world in which we pass much of our time; and it is then the delightful task of aesthetic criticism to reveal the form and pattern in the poet's creation. For it is this æsthetic whole, the poem concrete in rhythm, rhyme and imagery, which, whatever its subject, constitutes the body in which and through which we can perceive the idea of beauty. How else, indeed, can we perceive beauty? In other words, beauty of idea can only be apprehended through beauty of expression: –

> So must pure lovers' souls descend
> T' affections, and to faculties,
> Which sense may reach and apprehend,
> Else a great Prince in prison lies.

So, too, must the good critic humble himself to a consideration of the poet's technique, renouncing the temptations of a moral judgement relevant only to his own sensibility, but attempting to share imaginatively the experiences the poems record. For though a man may not achieve absolute harmony in his life as a whole (indeed, he will hardly be able to do so since he must express his life in a medium which is material and, in the philosophic sense, real), he may, through the function of art perpetuating the moment of vision, achieve ideal and absolute expression. It is because Donne's personality was discordant, Mr. Fausset says, that his style

> whether as poet or preacher, never achieved either the fresh, effusive gaiety or the assured serenity of Absolute Beauty. He could not create beauty out of life, he could not even see the beauty in which the limbs of life were veiled, which flowed through and over the bleak anatomy of fact, consecrating the perishable dust and redeeming it of squalor and grossness.

That is Mr. Fausset's astonishing verdict on the poet who wrote 'The Relic', 'The Autumnal', 'The Second Anniversary' (which he praises highly) and, to mention a less familiar poem, 'Sapho to Philaenis', and not a few others of the same excellence. If the stricture were a technical one it could at least be understood though one should expect even a Ben Jonson of the present day to quash the finding that 'Donne for not keeping of accent deserved hanging.' Our ears have been opened; and it would be profane now to think of Donne as less than a master of English verse. If any demonstration were needed other than the reader's own sense of rhythm, Professor Grierson has shown how Donne weaves speech rhetoric and metrical stress into his stanzas and so procures their unique melodic coherence. If this Absolute Beauty, (by comparison with which Donne's style is so diminished in Mr. Fausset's judgement), has received any literary expression, his condemnation should have given more particular instances of it than by saying that 'it is plain to read not only in a modern like Tchehov, but in the purest utterance of almost every great artist in the past.' If we are to compare 'purest utterances', those of Donne on sacred and profane love are, it has been granted, excelled by no poet in the language. If we are to consider the work as a whole, then Donne's early grossness and cynicism may be matched with Keats's early sensuality or Wordsworth's long and piteous complacency. Mr. Fausset has shown that there is in Keats a steady development of the tendency to harmonize the discordant strains in his character and argues that Donne remained distraught to the end. Here is, admittedly, a real basis for judgement; but it is one of personality not of poetry. Mr. Fausset is primarily and most interestingly a critic of personality, but since he works on literary subjects we must first consider his treatment of his literary material before we can assess the justice of his conclusions.

Very few facts are known about Donne's life between his entering
Lincoln's Inn when he was nineteen and his appointment as secre-
tary to Sir Thomas Egerton when he was about twenty-six. In this
period all the Satires and most of the 'Songs and Sonets' and
'Elegies' appear to have been written; and from the experiences they
reflect Donne must have been at this time a curious and energetic
lover, passionately interested in sexual relationship, and even from
the beginning demanding from his mistress very much more
than sensual pleasure. It is, however, part of the mystery we call
love that, except between chosen individuals, sex cannot be transcended. This is the complaint of Donne's earliest cynicism. It is
plain, however, from the acuteness of his analysis of symptoms,
that he very quickly discovered the meaning of love and that he
found, before he met the girl who was to be his wife, at least two
women who for the time absorbed all his emotional energies.

So much may be read in the 'Elegies'; but there is no bridge
from them to the lyrics, with the exception of two valedictions
which Walton leads us to attribute to Donne's married years. Sir
Edmund Gosse made some discreet speculations in which he
suggests that 'The Apparition' may represent the dissolution of the
intimacy with the married woman addressed in Elegies 1, 7, and 13.
In his *Life and Letters of John Donne* this is clearly regarded as at
best a plausible supposition; Mr. Fausset takes it to be canonical
and uses it as the theme for a novelette. He pleads like a barrister
for his client in a divorce suit. So much righteous indignation expended in defence of a woman whose character we cannot know,
against a poet whose intimacy is a noble privilege, would be in any
case unbalanced; when it rests on a mere hypothesis and is re-
deemed neither by style nor by wit it becomes a little ridiculous. Mr.
Fausset arranges the chronology of the 'Songs and Sonets' to
illustrate the tale he has to tell. No doubt he has chosen with discrimination, but he has chosen so that his quotations work up to a
climax which can never be more than speculative. Of that climax
he writes in a style which is typical of too many passages of conventional eloquence in his work:

> So at last in a savage frenzy he turned upon the poor woman, whom
> so short a time before he had bent to his purpose with a militant
> ardour and a shameless licence. The cold and cruel cynicism, the
> elemental spite of this last farewell to one who must at least have given
> as much as she received, has no parallel in our literature. In truth

no one is so ruthlessly vindictive, so callous to every claim of sentiment and generosity, as the moralist newly risen from the ashes of the brute.

The poem which calls forth this indictment, 'The Apparition', is written in a very different tone from the elegy beginning: –

> Nature's lay idiot, I taught thee love

with which it must be linked if Mr. Fausset's chronology is followed. In a poet of Donne's character the first line of 'The Apparition': –

> When by thy scorn, O murd'ress, I am dead

would sound more plausibly addressed to a mistress whose heart he had hoped 'by long siege to bow', than to a woman whom he had enjoyed and by whom he had been deceived. It is even possible that she had asserted her chastity as a defence against his solicitations, since in the fifth line he addresses her as 'feign'd vestal', an appellation not at all appropriate to a woman with whom he had had a lengthy liaison, and hardly more so to a married woman. His rage then would be due to her use of her honour as a means of deceiving him with another lover, and not the reprehensible lack of gratitude of which Mr. Fausset accuses him; or simply to his disappointment.

Donne loved playing with an idea for its own sake and for the delight he wrung from his audacities of expression. Poems like 'The Curse' and 'The Will' are warnings to walk carefully when looking for biographical facts in lyrics. It is probable that in its particulars Donne's early life must remain a mystery. There is, however, a very great deal of biographical material relating to the period from his marriage onwards, which is readily available in Gosse's admirable work on the poet. As was inevitable, Mr. Fausset has followed the lines there laid down, elaborating in one place and emphasizing in another in order to bring out the full effect of his conception of Donne as one who 'through the agonized errors of sex rose to the sublimities of religion'.

Where the material is more plentiful Mr. Fausset's portraiture becomes less rhetorical and more dramatic. It is at its best in the last section, in which he paints the preacher, having passed through the three stages of pagan, penitent and pensioner, still wrestling with his divided nature. It was not in the 'pretty rooms' of love-poems that the duel continued, but on the Church's impressive stage and in sight of a great congregation. For evidence as to the condition of his spirit, Mr. Fausset analyses the divine poems and, more particularly, the sermons. The result is a vindication of his view that Donne never achieved a harmonious conscience; for even in the bosom of religion he was dependent on moments of intuition for his faith, and though he magnificently maintained the attitude of the priest, the dread of death and the doubt of God's mercy tormented him till he lay on his last sick-bed.

After his long hesitation to take Orders it has seemed to some critics that Donne's final decision was a compromise with his conscience. In a superficial way it may have been; but it is obvious that the God of whom he preached was to him as personal pure, and non-sectarian an inspiration as that of his poems. If Mr. Fausset seems less than just to Donne as a poet, he grudges him no extreme of admiration for his spiritual integrity. Donne has been too long regarded as an eccentric, as an outsider to the tradition of English poetry and English theology, in spite of the idolatry of the literary chapels. Mr. Fausset describes him as an individual in whose unrest we may see an image of our own, so that he wears the air of a god in exile, still. Another generation will probably find it strange that he should have been perversely honoured for so long and yet held a little at bay.

DONNE THE DIVINE

The personality of Donne is necessarily the object of the keenest curiosity to his readers. His work as a whole is not self-sufficient in the sense in which *Paradise Lost* is, which would express as much if we knew no more of Milton than that he was blind when he wrote it, a fact which has both its statement and its significance in the poem itself. On the other hand, there is between the Donne of the secular poetry and the great preacher a gap so pronounced that there is a temptation to simplify the problem by supposing a change to have occurred in the man himself. It is plain that such could be only a makeshift interpretation; for, however much men may grow, and the greatest men grow so long as they are alive, no one has ever changed the fibres of his character. A contemporary elegist admirably stated the coherence of Donne's development:

> He kept his loves, but not his objects; wit
> He did not banish, but transplanted it,
> Taught it his place and use, and brought it home
> To Pietie, which it doth best become.

Piety is not now generally associated with wit, either in its narrower meaning or as a term for real intellectual subtlety. In both senses Donne was a witty preacher, as he was a witty poet. He punned even with God, and inserted wit among the attributes of divinity.

For Donne, entering the priesthood meant a pure addition to his vital faculties, and implied no subtraction from humanity. It is the manliness, frankness, and passion of his devotional writings which keeps them undiminished, alive, in spite of the quantity of obsolete scholarship which accompanies them. His humility and contrition are the natural expressions of a man who measures his own inconstant and imperfect aspirations by the terrible and sublime candour of the Absolute. He does not surrender the magnificent arrogance of his youth, for that too has its part in the imagination of the Divine. When a man has perceived God his passions are not altered but sanctified (to use the Dean's own phrase), and the man timid, generous, or distrustful in his ordinary life will put his fear, his abundance, or his suspicion into his religion.

The ambiguity of Donne's emotional attitude, which cannot be summed up in any simple definition, is due partly to his agility in the intellectual debates which he carried on within himself, but more fundamentally to his constitutional complexity. His temperament was made up of two antagonistic tendencies, of the two modes of feeling which in his day were known as the sanguine and the bilious humours. His poems range from physical and idealistic exuberance to disgust both with the physical and with the ideal, expressed in satire which follows a similar range of mental delicacy, from the vast grossness of the 'Julia' elegy to the self-pitying irony of 'Love's Fool'.

So in the years preceding his ordination the fervid idealism of the 'Anniversaries' and 'Verse Letters' is balanced by the laborious compilation of 'Biathanatos' – which asks 'whether Self-Homicide is so naturally sin that it may never be otherwise'. It is a learned and not generally interesting discussion of a problem which had certainly presented itself to him in no such respectable disguise, for he confesses that he had early become aware in himself of 'sickly inclinations' to suicide. The same dualism is apparent in the sermons:

in his disgust with his own spiritual declensions, which sink him into periods of despondent meditation among almost tangible representations of the horrors of the grave and of hell. His weakening of faith in the Divine mercy is only momentary, for he measures the certainty of God's love towards him by the amplification of his own love towards God.

Donne's temperament was predominantly enthusiastic; its natural inclination was to seek an object outside the self; and the long history of his hesitation in taking up an unequivocal position was due to his genius for the analysis of motives and emotions – he could not accept a doctrine based on faith till he had satisfied his subtle conscience that faith was not less but more than reasonable. It was not till then that he was able to exercise fully the deep craving of his nature, the necessity of adoration. Adoration is the impulse behind all the lyrical passages of Donne's verse and prose. It is an essentially lyrical mood and one very susceptible to splenetic reactions, but its dominance determines all the radical movements in Donne's spiritual progress.

The audacious poet of the *Songs and Sonets* scandalized even his own age a little; and critics in our more censorious times have seen fit to shake reproving fingers at some of his vigorous expressions of disillusionment. In his worldly days Donne must have been a most fascinating acquaintance. His mingling of the 'melancholy and pleasant humours', his blend of irony and passion, enthusiasm and incisive scorn, would have made his friendship a continual adventure. His intense enjoyment of the spectacle of London life, of Elizabethan London life, is reflected directly in his poems, and, what is more, it was coupled with a fastidiousness of mind which became an instrument of his moral development. He is to be seen very clearly in this rapid sketch by a contemporary:

> Mr. John Dunne, who leaving Oxford, liv'd at the Inns of Court, not dissolute but very neat; a great Visiter of Ladies, a great Frequenter of Plays, a great Writer of conceited Verses.

The splendid novelty of the new drama, the bewildering speculations of the new science, the intoxication of a brilliant Court, and the not then legendary company of the Mermaid combined to nourish most richly one of the acutest minds of any generation. By means of these varied contacts with the world he became sophisticated as few of our poets have been since the eighteenth century, since the rural revolution seized even the metropolis. 'The barbarouseness and insipid dullness of the Country' was not to Donne's mind. Although with no illusions as to the intellectual level of the aristocracy, yet, like all artists whose genius resides partly in their personality, he loved to see himself in a brilliant setting. He despised the courtiers, but he revolved round the same centre because, as he writes to Wotton, 'I will not be utterly out of fashion and unsociable.' When, later, in one of his sermons he said 'Company is the Atheist's Sanctuary', he no doubt remembered the long and isolated struggle against penury in his 'Hospital at Mitcham', where his worldly pride and desire were first broken. In the earliest of his letters to survive, written when he was twenty-four, and lying at Plymouth with the storm-battered fleet which had been fitted out for the Islands Voyage, he writes very much in the manner of the witty gallant, but at least one of his witticisms betrays the 'intellectual' beneath the fashionable adventurer. He complains of Plymouth as a wretched billet, and adds, 'but for the much gay cloths (which yet are much melted) I should think we were in Utopia; all are so utterly coinless.' His kinship with Thomas More is no doubt relevant here.

In all his familiar letters he professes most fervently the religion of friendship. But we note, too, his growing impatience with the corruptness of the courtier's life, for whom advancement was the fruit of astuteness in intrigue. Donne several times makes a distinction between being at Court and being a courtier, and finds it a 'continual battle' to maintain his reputation for honesty. His references to his integrity, which judged by modern custom seem strangely affected, would have been only natural in those times and circumstances when men's words were often blatantly for sale. From being a conventional satiric subject, the corruption of Court life became a bitterly intimate part of Donne's experience. The impeachment of the Earl of Essex must have been a shock to him, and his reference to it is of particular interest. His comment is singularly delicate 'that he [Essex] understood not his age, for it is a natural weakness of innocency, that such men want locks for themselves and keys for others'.

It has never yet been fully explained why a man of Donne's admirable parts was not chosen for secular preferment. His clandestine marriage seems an insufficient reason for more than twelve years of neglect; and it may be that his being known as a man who could be relied upon not to compromise with his conscience had more than a little to do with it.

A writer survives in each generation, otherwise than as a figure in literary text-books, precisely to the extent that he interests us as a contemporary; one of the qualities of the classics is a perennial modernity. The psychological acuity of Donne's poetry accounts largely for the eagerness with which it was seized upon by an analytical generation early in this century. But the theological writings, though they too have much of this same acuity are enclosed in a husk of obsolete learning which makes their appreciation often difficult. Much enlightenment is to be found in Mary Paton Ramsay's richly documented dissertation, *Les Doctrines Médiévales chez Donne* (Oxford University Press). This invaluable work enables our sympathy to flow almost as readily to the Divine as to the Poet. It reveals the way in which the Neo-Platonic doctrines on which Donne's thought was based, led naturally to his passionate conception of the Christian Church as the revelation and representation of the eternal beauty. His conversion was not a sudden emotional revulsion from sensuality, nor the despairing surrender of an untenable outpost of scepticism. The great struggle was not between materialism and mysticism, but between idealism and Christianity. The brilliant casuistry of the 'Problemes and Paradoxes' did not long delude him, though such delightfully insolent inquiries as 'Why hath the Common Opinion afforded Women Souls?' or the assertion 'That the gifts of the Body are better than those of the Mind', are no doubt the sincere expressions of his reaction to youthful experiences. Unmitigated idealism is, in a young man, a sign of a very limited sensibility, leaving little opportunity for that growth by and through experience which is the only valid test of any attitude to the universe.

A passage from the paradox 'that the gifts of the body are better than those of the mind' provides a rare glimpse of the younger Donne, eager for emancipation from the ethical idealism which would humiliate his sensuous and intellectual pride: –

> Now if my Soul would say, that she enables any part to taste these pleasures, but is herself only delighted with those rich sweetnesses which her inward eyes and senses apprehend, she should dissemble; for I see her often solaced with beauties, which she sees through mine eyes, and with musicke which through mine ears she hears. This perfection then my body hath, that it can impart to my mind all his

pleasures; and my mind hath still many, that she can neither teach my
indisposed part her faculties, nor to the best espoused parts show it
beauty of Angels, of Musicke, of Spheres, whereof she boasts the contemplation. Are chastity, temperance, and fortitude gifts of the mind?
I appeal to Physitians whether the cause of these be not in the body . . .

It was in the early years of his marriage, when penury and disappointment had cut him off from social esteem, that the fascination of philosophy led him to examine his ideas more closely. The
research work which he did for Thomas Morton in his controversy
with the Romanists led him to read closely the theological works of
the authorities of the Church and, no doubt, to familiarize himself
more deeply with the early Fathers. He found in these great men
of the past not merely the discussion of Church doctrine, but a
current of philosophy flowing right back to the great age of Greek
thought. Though the tradition became in places corrupt, Plato
evidently stands behind the immediate source of Christian theology,
which, as Dr. Inge has said, is so fundamentally Neo-Platonic that
if a writer is not dealing with either the Incarnation, the resurrection
of the body, or the creation of the world in time, 'it is probably
impossible to tell whether he is a follower of Plotinus or a Christian.'

In most of Donne's work written during the first ten years of his
marriage, the first decade of the seventeenth century, the idealist
philosopher has the upper hand. The change in tone of his poems
is most marked; they are hardly ever critical, but securely devout.
He adores the virtues and beauties of his women friends; his sarcasm
is practically extinct. The culmination of this mood is reached in
the 'Anniversaries' which celebrate the death of Elizabeth Drury.
As it happened, he only celebrated two of these occasions; but there
is a point in connexion with the mutation of his philosophic idealism
into the religious, which is suggestive. In 'The First Anniversary' he
writes that there are two births of the soul:

> for though the soul of man
> Be got when man is made, 'tis born but then
> When man doth die; our body's as the womb,
> And as a mid-wife death directs it home.

But a year later death has become the soul's third birth:

> Creation gave her one, a second, grace . . .

and from this time his didactic acceptance of religion is shattered
as if he had himself experienced the gift of grace. It was certainly

not through philosophy that his conversion took place, though it may have prepared his mind, but through the contemplation of the person of Christ. The 'Holy Sonnets' are evidence of his passionate desire to be forced to believe.

It is not remarkable that Donne should have moved over from the Neo-Platonists to the Christians because of his realization of the significance of Christ. St. Augustine said of them, 'Only the Word made flesh, that found I not among them.' Similarly, Donne says that it is useless to believe that Plato can teach us to believe in God, for in him, though we certainly find a God, we find no Christ. Miss Ramsay, in her admirable exposition of Donne's philosophy, has not sufficiently emphasized his incalculable distance from the Neo-Platonists. For him the whole of existence was bound up with the knowledge and love of God; and, since he was too keen a metaphysician to believe that there can be direct communication between our relative world and the Absolute, God's mercy in providing the Incarnation as a means of salvation from the ruin of the natural world became the focus of Donne's raptest adoration.

*

Enormous cycles of years must have revolved before primitive man conceived the idea of God. In summer he was borne up against the threat of winter by the sensuous beauty of the season; in winter he was protected against despair by his faith in the return of spring. Out of the memory of these innumerable alterations an idea was abstracted, that of Time. With the conception of the world in time a great misery settled over mankind, like that which comes to a child when it loses the innocence of timeless play and realizes that enjoyment has a period. Joy, which was an eternal ecstasy, becomes pleasure, which is a finite excitement. Material civilization is the effort of a fallen humanity to prolong pleasure. The best Utopias of this kind offer no more than the absence of discomfort; and the refinement of luxury, as the literatures of the past show, leads only to pessimism or melancholy. Man, in Time, is faced with the gloomy alternatives of annihilation or eternal recurrence, unless he believes in the perfectibility of the physical universe. Donne has a most eloquent passage in the 'Devotions upon Emergent Occasions', in which he says that our happiness cannot be part of the spatial and temporal world. He has the mystical belief that eternal joy, the only reality, is to be found in that which does not *exist*, since that alone is real, the immanence of God:

This is Nature's nest of Boxes; the Heavens contain the Earth, the Earth, Cities, Cities, Men. And all these are Concentrique; the common centre to them all is decay, ruin; only that is Excentrique, which was never made; only that place, or garment rather, which we can imagine but not demonstrate. That light which is the very emanation of the light of God, in which the Saints shall dwell, with which the Saints shall be apparelled, only that bends not to this centre, to Ruin; that which was not made of Nothing, is not threatened with this annihilation.

Donne, it must be noted, did not turn from the enjoyment of this life to a rabid asceticism such as often overtakes converts. He was not in the ordinary sense a convert, having always felt that there was a world of imagination, a world of God, interpenetrating the world of humanity. To deny the pleasures of the body would have been to him as great a blasphemy as to abuse them. The birthday of Christ is a day of rejoicing, not of mortification; and the celebration of Christmas as a feast is symbolic of the eternal joy to which humanity is admitted through the Incarnation. Yet Donne makes it perfectly clear that the quality of eternal joy is not a multiplication of sensuous pleasure, like some pagan paradise, but the perception of a beauty to which we can only give names which limit what is the abstract of all qualities:

But here, in Eternity, the Holy Ghost proceeds not that way; by improvement of things, which we have and love here; riches or beauty, or musicke or honour, or feasts; but by an everlasting procession of that, which we hunger and thirst, and pant after, here, and cannot compass, that is, Justice and Righteousness.

Christianity has this advantage over the noble philosophy of Plotinus, that whereas in his system the soul returns to the Absolute by the gradual elimination of the unwilled, in Christianity it is by a movement of the Absolute towards mankind that we are released from the miseries of the finite world. The Christmas festival is the most beautiful and moving creation of the human imagination. Its ineffable consolation was perhaps felt more deeply by the people in the Middle Ages than ever since – at least their carols express it more poignantly; but always, since men must be always subject to seasonal vicissitudes, to the antagonism of matter, the birth of a Saviour in the dread mid-winter, poor as the most miserable peasant, must fill the imagination with new life. The suffering

humanity of the Divine Child did not escape Donne's long medita-
tions on all the aspects of the Trinity, for he writes:

> He found a Golgotha (where he was crucified) even in Bethlem,
> where he was born. For, to his tenderness then, the straws were almost
> as sharp as the thorns after; and the Manger as uneasy at first, as his
> Cross at last.

The sophisticated literary style, the forcing of congruities which is so
characteristic of Donne's turn of mind and the source of the loveliest
as well as of the most crabbed passages of his work, contrasts most
curiously with this fourteenth-century poem which the Virgin sings
to placate her child for the misery of His birthplace and her lack of
blankets to keep Him warm:

> Jesu, swete, beo noth wroth,
> Thou ich nabbe clout ne cloth
> Thee on for to folde,
> Thee on to folde ne to wrappe,
> For ich nabbe clout ne lappe;
> Bote ley thou thi fet to my pappe,
> And wite thee from the cold.

Yet there is this in common between the unknown minstrel and the
famous Dean of Paul's: that both are drawn to God by the mystery
of this condescension; for without this Divine assistance, as the
proudest man must see – and Donne was as proud as any – the
appalling infinity between the Absolute and man cannot be bridged
by human will.

Far from diminishing Donne, under the influence of his religious conception of the universe his genius expanded and took
wings. We may regret that he left no monument of pure art equivalent to the greatness which we feel in the sermons; but his æsthetic
gift was not adapted to constructions on a large scale. He had not
the architectonic faculty to a high degree; the wealth of images in
which his thoughts flowed are derived from the extraordinary
sense of congruities of which we have spoken and which enables
him to give plastic expression to the subtlest of his analyses. The
scholastic arguments in the sermons must prevent the bulk of them
from being generally read; but some, which are almost entirely
personal, like 'Death's Duel', his last, are masterpieces of sustained
eloquence. The others, too, are rich in passages in which he is inspired by some metaphysical or religious meditation, and these are

as truly poems as anything written in verse. The harmonizing of the cadences, which are always proper to pure prose, is often most exquisite, and though in reading his repetitions may appear sometimes too deliberate, it must be remembered that prose spoken to large audiences must linger over those ideas which it wishes to emphasize; the voice alone cannot beat much into the mind through the ears. Besides, Donne despised the crude rantings of the Puritans, and thought God's service worthy of all the art he could bring to it. In his style, whether as a lover, a poet, or a divine, that phrase of an early acquaintance is most descriptive, 'not dissolute but very neat'. His prose may seem at first to have a Gothic vastness and obscurity; but it is a continual revelation of form, since it is the expression of a great mind which, through its perception of divinity, realized more fully the intellectual and emotional passions of its humanity.

EDWIN ARLINGTON ROBINSON

Collected Poems. By Edwin Arlington Robinson (Cecil Palmer)

Sometimes, neglectful of the metaphor involved, we speak of the body of a nation as of a mere bulk. This is to ignore a complex organization which passes through health and sickness, exuberant and exhausted periods, on its way from youth to senility, and has each condition reflected in the character of the individuals produced, as a fever makes itself known by a rash on the skin. But a metaphor is not an explanation, and often, as in the present instance, it is applicable from only one point of view; we are led astray if we attempt to interpret history in terms of physiology. Yet even a star, most isolated of things, moves to a tug from our hands like a kite on a string, and it is not good to forget, even if we cannot explain, the dependence of the artist, most star-like of men, on the efforts of the people to which he belongs. Every nation endeavours to be self-supporting, for its cultural as well as for its grosser needs; yet to ensure continuous fertility it is obliged to accept stimulation from outside, and the strongest impulse is generally received from a discordant union.

It may seem improper that such considerations should be allowed to influence æsthetic criticism. Such criticism is an art in itself, and has its heroic artists, but for the majority our acceptance of a work of art depends on our national appetite. The relativity of criticism is absolute, and as we all hunger after strange fruits, we are likely to absorb much more readily a minor Latin than a minor Teutonic poet. We have seen the process occur in the last century in France, where the reverberation of a few American writers went much deeper, though on a small surface, than in this country. By a number of his countrymen which includes some of the most competent judges, Mr. Robinson is esteemed not only as a poet, but as the most representative of the living American poets and as one whose work has most surely the qualities of endurance. This collected volume represents the work of about thirty years in nearly 600 pages, and argues for a fair though not extraordinary fluency.

One of the first, not insignificant, details to catch the eye is the great number of proper names, standing either as titles or used in the body of the poem, in the early as well as in the later work; showing that the need for a dramatic protagonist has been a continuous part of this poet's character. With other poets, when used, it has generally been a feint, and hardly at that diverting the reader from the real subjectivity of the poem. As an instance to the contrary one thinks of Browning, whose persons do not occupy a stage, and even when the poet is beside them and monopolizing the conversation, heighten the emotions by their presence. In many of his pieces Mr. Robinson entertains his audience from behind a screen, and the voices that penetrate to us have a peculiar shrouded tone, so that we hardly recognize the emotions to which they belong, and regret that the information on the programme is so scanty. It is not mysterious, like a Maeterlinck drama, but mystifying.

Robinson really is interested in the relations of men and women to one another and to the general scheme, and not, or hardly, in the way they affect him. This distinguishes him from most poets, who frankly or under a mask rhyme their own sentiments. It is perhaps merely a distinction of the surface; underneath he must be narrating his own experiences, though the way in which he does it is affected by this absence of an egotistical motive. The long colloquies, such as 'Captain Craig' and 'The Book of Annandale', in which someone worries over a past gradually but not very definitely built up, do not show Mr. Robinson at his best. They are diffuse, and we cannot help feeling that this lack of concentration is a defect, or, rather, that it springs from a deeper defect. However definite his intention may have been, he does not communicate to us the certainty, not even the certainty of uncertainty, which the words lead us to suppose he intended.

> For what was his to live lives yet:
> ' Truth, quarter truth, death cannot reach;
> Nor is it always what we know
> That we are fittest here to teach.

Such a stanza alone would mark Mr. Robinson as being in the main line of American tradition, the tradition of a serious pre-occupation with ethical values, and the insistence on the superiority of transcendental experience. It is the instinct which has canalized into the great religions and for which such men as Emerson and Whitman attempted to drive other channels. Yet rather than a canal, such bodies as the Church are vast reservoirs of mystical experience into which one may dip one's cup of words certain to bring it up brimmed with meaning. The bulk of a nation's poetry when it is rich in this mystical or poetical experience answers the same purpose, for what a man can do with words depends so much on what has been done with them before him.

In the poem called 'The Man against the Sky,' which attracted attention when it first appeared in a volume with that title (1916), Mr. Robinson more definitely lays down his position and sketches the process of thought which leads him to repudiate a planless and indifferent universe:

> If after all that we have lived and thought,
> All comes to Nought, –
> If there be nothing after Now,
> And we be nothing anyhow,
> And we know that, why live?
> 'Twere sure but weakling's vain distress
> To suffer dungeons where so many doors
> Will open on the cold eternal shores
> That look sheer down
> To the dark tideless floods of Nothingness,
> Where all who know may drown.

In other pieces in that volume, and in the shorter pieces in the subsequent one, he seems to grip his material more tightly, as if he had hold of something tangible. However futile and trivial the circumstances of life may seem, the poet is assured of a purpose, not clearly defined nor to men themselves apparent, but pervading life like a faith which inhibits him from condemning that which may seem absurd or even subversive at the ground level of his view.

Never uncharitable, this poet's compassion comes nearer to the surface in such poems as 'The Poor Relation', 'The Voice of Age', and many others of which the subjects are among the despised and rejected, or merely the overlooked. 'Veteran Sirens', is another such, of which the title should be sufficient description, and it contains one line which is a flash of revelation:

> The patient ardor of the unpursued.

Mr. Robinson is not a writer from whom one can quote readily. His happiest effects, pictorial as well as verbal, are too intimately bound up with the poem to permit separating them alive. Perhaps this stanza, most fitting in its place, will yet stand by itself: –

> And all his wisdom is unfound,
>   Or like a web that error weaves
> On airy looms that have a sound
>   No louder now than falling leaves.

That, written of the Unseeing Man, has the gentle melancholy characteristic of his later attitude. It is the sadness, not of despair, but of a man who probes too deep to hope greatly. His work lingers in the memory like something observed, something experienced in reflection; not less real but less insistent than the direct impact of the poetic giants.

NEW POETRY

The Pier-Glass. By Robert Graves (Secker)
Poems 1914–1919. By Maurice Baring (Secker)
Outlaws. By Nancy Cunard (Elkin Mathews)
The Farmer's Bride. By Charlotte Mew (Poetry Bookshop)

If one considers the rise and fall of literary movements as organic processes and not as professional abstractions, there can be observed at the source of each a renovation of the current poetic diction. Old words put on a ramping youth in their unaccustomed surroundings till, grown sober with long customary travail, their vitality drained away, they lead a merely posthumous existence as commodities, done up in thousands or arranged as verse, for consumption by the reading public.

It is not that there is any virtue in out-of-the-way words and turns of speech, but the serious writer seeking body for his conceptions will be more hindered than helped by the usages fashionable in his time. The burden of association which renders idiom possible and useful in practical life, is to the poet a constant danger, by arousing sensations which will taint the freshness of those he is trying to create. So, not forgetting the legitimate use of a predecessor, the test of the consideration due to a contemporary lies in an examination of his style.

The cleanness of Mr. Graves's technique was from the first remarkable. His words are young and vigorous, carrying no more than their own weight of flesh. His rhythms, always apparently simple, possess those subtle variations, which a poet alone can introduce, making of a stock metre a personal instrument.

They have, too, an austerity, a renunciation of the garland-fetters of surface decoration (though he is not free from an occasional lapse) which can only be practised successfully in a poem with a sound core. 'Morning Phoenix' justifies this reliance on the bare essentials:

> Who could keep a smiling wit,
> Roasted so in heart and hide,
> Turning on the sun's red spit,
> Scorched by love inside?

The delicate, and humorous, fantasy of his early work is still present, though not predominant as it was once. It has assumed a grimmer tune; the fairies have turned goblins, and the fusiliers undergo sinister metamorphoses. A vein of satire crops up now and then. A sadder questioning approaches the mystery of the night-side of the spirit:

> Your grieving moonlight face looks down
>   Through the forest of my fears,
> Crowned with a spiny bramble crown,
>   Dew-dropped with evening tears.
>
>   .   .   .   .
>
> The black trees shudder, dropping snow,
>   The stars tumble and spin.
> Speak, speak, or how may a child know
>   His ancestral sin?

This volume has less homogeneity than *Country Sentiment*, and that had less than its forerunners. Mr. Graves is not content with a limited perfection, and a new direction is marked by the presence of a number of sombre pieces where the human mind is presented in circumstances of abnormal emotion. Though they suppose a history, they are not dramatic; rather, deliberations after the event, footnotes to the irrevocable: in 'The Gnat', the sins of youth and in 'The Pier-Glass', murder.

Those are not perhaps his most successful poems, but they raise the most speculation as to what he may do next. In the blank verse which he uses he is rather self-consciously at his ease, missing the supporting discipline of couplet or stanza. At his best, though, he can use it very well, as these lines will show:

> A sullen pier-glass cracked from side to side
> Scorns to present the face as do new mirrors
> With a lying flush, but shows it melancholy
> And pale, as faces grow that look in mirrors.

This has, besides, a suggestiveness, a reaching out beyond the mere statement which is not common in his work. Sometimes he even tells more than the reader wishes to know, but it is very rare to find any flaw in his good poems. When he fails, the failure is complete, and not due to any weakness of execution. In 'The Treasure Box' it results from the excessive indulgence of a taste for the *bijou*; in 'Fox's Dingle' from conceiving the poem in a convention too small for him – that of rural simplicity devised by some urban poets to their eternal damnation – in which economy becomes miserliness and restraint superfluous, because there is nothing to restrain:

> Now over the rough turf
> Bridles go jingle,
> And there's a well-loved pool,
> By Fox's Dingle ...

Mr. Baring relies very much upon the ornamentation of his verse. It is done with a gentle good taste most effective in a languorous way.

> Your eyelids drooped like petals wearily,
> Your face was like a lily of the vale.
> You had the softness of all summer days,
> The silver radiance of the twilight hour ...

But one cannot avoid calling it derivative. There is neither imaginative perception nor direct observation. He attempts the former and says: 'The moon is pallid as the phantom of a shell'; the latter and risks: 'The nightingale begins a liquid trill.' To these I prefer his less ambitious but satisfying line:

> And now the nightingale begins to sing.

A typical stanza from the dignified lament 'Diffugere Nives' sums up all that is to be said for and against his verse. One cannot deny the inspiration, nor that something has come between it and the expression of it – perhaps the 'souls of poets dead and gone':

> Now spreads the month that feast of lovely things
>   We loved of old.
> Once more the swallow glides with darkling wings
>   Against the gold.

To deny the charm of this, and of his earlier poems, and the larger utterance of some of the later ones, would be barbarous, but greater praise would show a failure to discriminate between a truly creative mind and a fine mind, cultured, noble and responsive to the many manifestations of the spirit, voicing his appreciations in pleasant and melodious phrases.

Both Miss Mew and Miss Cunard display a very definite personality in their poetry, which is nevertheless not entirely satisfying. Often in *The Farmer's Bride*, one feels that one has come upon a good poem, then it wavers, becomes argumentative, or conversational with some undefined 'you,' and loses itself finally in the morasses of the confessional.

Sometimes Miss Mew uses a rather watery dialect, or perhaps rustic syntax would be a more precise description of it:

> Out 'mong the sheep, her be, they said,
>   Should properly have been a-bed.

This gives a pleasing air of quaintness to the poem, but for its success depends entirely on the denial of all one's educated relatives, to whose sophisticated speech Miss Mew reverts with a disastrous rush:

> Shy as a leveret, swift as he,
> Straight and slight as a young larch tree . . .

While Miss Mew soliloquizes on emotional complications, Miss Cunard meditates among the abstractions:

> I sometimes think that all my thoughts are wheels
> Rolling forever through a painted world . . .

The idea is well carried through, but one feels that it is one of fancy's devices rather than an imaginative presentation of the truth. She treats her emotions intellectually and discusses with vigour where Miss Mew rambles, but too often it is just discussion and not that embodiment of a momentary certainty from which the lyric springs. But, in spite of her frequent lack of success, one can feel the pulse of an original mind beating through a rather uncongenial medium. The language, though often striking lacks that essential rhythm, that dominant note which absorbs and unifies the diverse elements of a poem, drawing them to an inevitable conclusion.

I like best the poem 'Voyages North', where she makes a half-humorous escape from the conventionalities that beset her. She is travelling out of London to some quiet provincial destination:

> But if I were free
> I would go on, see all the northern continents
> Stretch out before me under winter sunsets;
> Look into the psychology
> Of Iceland, and plumb the imaginations
> Of travellers outlandish, talking and drinking
> With stern, strange companies of merchants . . .

MODERN VERSE

An Anthology of Modern Verse. By A. M. (Methuen)
Selections from Modern Poets. By J. C. Squire (Secker)

It is necessarily more impertinent to criticize anthologies than any other kind of book. In so far as these are the expression of personal preferences, one can but state the agreement or disagreement of one's own negligible opinion. Had there been no war with Germany, and none with Ireland, it would have been reasonable to expect all the poets in Mr. Squire's anthology to be alive today. With great skill and delicacy of judgement he has detached the contemporary

organism, which in Sir Algernon Methuen's selection is embedded
in the corpses of its more immediate progenitors and harassed with
still-suckling offspring. The *Selections* is complete in this sense,
that whatever remains of the poetry of the first twenty years of this
century will be the work of poets in that volume. Mr. Squire may
have included a few ugly ducklings, but he passes by no swans.
One may feel that the merits of Mr. Eliot and other new poets
entitle them to inclusion, but it would have been false hospitality
to immerse them in that particular atmosphere.

It is only for a few of the poems Mr. Squire includes that one
fears the fate of Barton, Opie, Barbauld, and such others whom one
meets in old collections with an unenthusiastic curiosity. A. M.
has no such accurate discrimination; of his choice leaves, many are
already sere. Piety and rollicking sea-fights were at one time a
source of much emotion, but are now altogether too faded to rouse
the interest of a modern. Certainly his catholicity of choice justifies
his hope that the spirit of the new poetry inspires his book, but
I should be readier to turn his hope to certainty if there were any
evidence of a selective process. Dowson, Dobson and Drinkwater
follow De la Mare, and then the inexorable limitations of the alpha-
bet bring in Eden's 'Afterthought on Apples':

> And yet, O God,
> Tumble me not at last upon the sod, . . .
> Give Thou Thyself my stalk a little twist,
> Dear Lord, and I shall fall into Thy hand.

In the eternal order, that is contemporary with T. E. Brown,
H. C. Beeching, George Herbert, even. It is of a different age from
the poem which follows it, having no tone in common with the
dandyical scepticism of Mr. Eliot. Though one may find much to
carp at in A. M.'s collection, there is also a mass of indubitably fine
poetry, and some hitherto neglected. Mr. Ford Maddox Hueffer's
four poems more than compensate for Sir Henry Newbolt's
paternal moralizing in Clifton Chapel. It was perhaps better that
Gerard Manley Hopkins should be represented by a lucid poem,
but a bolder taste would have included more than one – even at the
sacrifice of Mr. Kipling's 'If – '. The three poems by Mr. Squire
are a good choice – particularly 'Winter Nightfall', which is a most
candid and original poem. There is, in Squire's best work, a freedom from conventional eloquence on which he might have insisted more strongly when compiling his own anthology.

To Mr. Squire's choice of poets, within his self-imposed limits, only a few additions suggest themselves. As regards the poems themselves, one or two which have had a wide circulation might have been replaced, where others equally good are available, to increase a just appreciation of the poet's work. Such redundencies are Mr. Belloc's 'South Country', Mr. Sturge Moore's 'A Duet' and Mr. Turner's 'Romance'; though it should not be forgotten that Mr. Squire's editing is responsible for the familiarity with which we regard them and many of the poems in this volume.

The unexpected, the rare poem or poet unaccountably missed, remains the opportunity of the anthologist, and here Mr. Belloc's 'Tarantella' is a most pleasurable surprise. Praise of Sussex is very well, but this goes deeper. It has a particular excellence of mellow, but passionate, manliness. Robin Flower (a name with a delicate bouquet that courtesy would ruin) is released from an undeserved obscurity. Miss Macaulay has a fierce imagination and a strong but subtle sense of rhythm.

Mr. Squire suggests that, apart from the ultimate achievement of any of these poets, the justification of our age lies in the wide diffusion of poetical merit. It is difficult to say. There are a number among those of his choice for whom I would anticipate no more than a dozen years of reputation. The style's the test, and that which has not that indefinable, continually elusive quality, however interesting, audacious or irreproachable in sentiment, is chaff to the winnower. Everybody knows that Edward Thomas has it and Mr. Davies and Mr. De la Mare, and though it is something different for each of these, it is essentially the same as that which raises Mr. Sturge Moore's contribution to its high position here. Those who are curious will find it more recently manifested in Wilfred Owen's 'Strange Meeting', in Mr. Graves's 'Christ in the Wilderness', in Mr. Turner's 'Soldiers in a Small Camp'. It springs up here and there with a cheering frequency. But when it is absent, the verse Mr. Squire has chosen has always some other quality which at any rate partly compensates us for our disappointment.

A FRAGMENTARY POEM

The Waste Land. By T. S. Eliot (The Hogarth Press)

Between the emotion from which a poem rises and the reader there is always a cultural layer of more or less density from which the images or characters in which it is expressed may be drawn. In the ballad 'I wish I were where Helen lies' this middle ground is but faintly indicated. The ballad, we say, is *simpler* than the 'Ode to the Nightingale'; it evokes very directly an emotional response. In Keats's ode the emotion gains resonance from the atmosphere of legendary association through which it passes before reaching us. It cannot be called better art, but it is certainly more sophisticated and to some minds less poignant. From time to time there appear poets and a poetic audience who prefer this refractory haze of allusion to be very dense; without it the meanings of the words strike them so rapidly as to be inappreciable, just as, without the air, we could not detect the vibration of light. We may remember with what elaboration Addison, among others, was obliged to undertake the defence of the old ballads before it was recognized that their bare style might be admired even by gentlemen familiar with the classics.

The poetic personality of Mr. Eliot is extremely sophisticated. His emotions hardly ever reach us without traversing a zig-zag of allusion. In the course of his four hundred lines he quotes from a score of authors and in three foreign languages, though his artistry has reached that point at which it knows the wisdom of sometimes concealing itself. There is in general in his work a disinclination to awake in us a direct emotional response. It is only, the reader feels, out of regard for some one else that he has been induced to mount the platform at all. From there he conducts a magic-lantern show; but being too reserved to expose in public the impressions stamped on his own soul by the journey through the Waste Land, he employs the slides made by others, indicating with a touch the difference between his reaction and theirs. So the familiar stanza of Goldsmith becomes

> When lovely woman stoops to folly and
> Paces about her room again, alone,
> She smoothes her hair with automatic hand,
> And puts a record on the gramophone.

To help us to elucidate the poem Mr. Eliot has provided some notes which will be of more interest to the pedantic than the poetic critic. Certainly they warn us to be prepared to recognize some references to vegetation ceremonies. This is the cultural or middle layer, which, whilst it helps us to perceive the underlying emotion, is of no poetic value in itself. We desire to touch the inspiration itself, and if the apparatus of reserve is too strongly constructed, it will defeat the poet's end. The theme is announced frankly enough in the title, 'The Waste Land'; and in the concluding confession,

These fragments I have shored against my ruins,

we receive a direct communication which throws light on much which had preceded it. From the opening part, 'The Burial of the Dead', to the final one we seem to see a world, or a mind, in disaster and mocking its despair. We are aware of the toppling of aspirations, the swift disintegration of accepted stability, the crash of an ideal. Set at a distance by a poetic method which is reticence itself, we can only judge of the strength of the emotion by the visible violence of the reaction. Here is Mr. Eliot, a dandy of the choicest phrase, permitting himself blatancies like 'the young man carbuncular'. Here is a poet capable of a style more refined than that of any of his generation parodying without taste or skill – and of this the example from Goldsmith is not the most astonishing. Here is a writer to whom originality is almost an inspiration, borrowing the greater number of his best lines, creating hardly any himself. It seems as if the 'The Waste Land' exists in its greater part in the state of notes. This quotation is a particularly obvious instance: –

> London Bridge is falling down falling down falling down
> *Poi s'ascose nel foco che gli affina*
> *Quando fiam uti chelidon* – O swallow swallow
> *Le Prince d'Aquitaine à la tour abolie.*

The method has a number of theoretical justifications. Mr. Eliot has himself employed it discreetly with delicious effect. It suits well the disillusioned smile which he has in common with Laforgue; but we do sometimes wish to hear the poet's full voice. Perhaps if the reader were sufficiently sophisticated he would find these echoes suggestive hints, as rich in significance as the sonorous amplifications of the romantic poets. None the less, we do not derive from this poem as a whole the satisfaction we ask from poetry. Numerous passages are finely written; there is an amusing monologue in the vernacular, and the fifth part is nearly wholly admirable. The section beginning

What is that sound high in the air . . .

has a nervous strength which perfectly suits the theme; but he declines to a mere notation, the result of an indolence of the imagination.

Mr. Eliot, always evasive of the grand manner, has reached a stage at which he can no longer refuse to recognize the limitations of his medium; he is sometimes walking very near the limits of coherency. But it is the finest horses which have the most tender mouths, and some unsympathetic tug has sent Mr. Eliot's gift awry. When he recovers control we shall expect his poetry to have gained in variety and strength from this ambitious experiment.

A POEM OF ENERGY

The Flaming Terrapin. By Roy Campbell (Cape)

Though it would seem natural for the young and vigorous life of the Colonies to express itself in poetry freed from the *clichés* and affectations of the Old World, the proportion of velleity is actually rather higher in their literary production than in that of an English garden suburb. But if environment is unimportant, race and personality are other determinants of poetic expression; and by their fusion in his work Mr. Campbell has achieved a poem which is at once new and traditional. *The Flaming Terrapin* idealizes in lyrical narrative the unsophisticated, exuberant joy in the struggle of life which we attribute to the Colonial character, but though the landscapes of the poem are those of the author's native South Africa it is as thoroughly English in idea as any which came from Kent or Essex. The terrapin of the title (a gigantic sea-turtle) symbolizes the instinctive life-power which drags the human ark out of the gloom of lassitude and disillusionment into a dawn of new and hopeful effort.

This conception has a primitive simplicity which enables the poet to evoke those broad emotional reactions which are denied to a more sophisticated intelligence. And this perception of a direct relation between impulse and action, which, if an illusion, is peculiarly fertile from the creative point of view, is matched by a similar directness of vision. Vision is the essential of poetic style, for without it imagery degenerates into rhetoric. Rhetoric which enables a poet to sustain his inspiration is not to be despised in itself, and without rhetorical power Mr. Campbell would not have been able to carry through his design on a scale remarkable for so young a poet. But the sincerity of the poetic impulse is attested throughout by the continuously concrete realization of the thought. One instance must suffice to define the characteristic directness of comparison which lies at the root of his imaginative power:

> Till the stream casting wide its forest sleeves
> Heaved out its broad blue chest against the sea.

A child must look at the world with eyes which in some such way grasp reality and extend its power by a bold bringing together of associates from which the adult, occupied in consolidation instead of acquisition, irrationally shrinks. This is a power which the poet retains in spite of the growth of the adult faculty; when neither usurps the whole mental energy he is in a state of creative maturity. This associative instinct may be applied not only to visualize the imagined by comparing it with a familiar natural object, but also by means of literary reminiscences, as in this simile of the waves defeated by the advancing ark:

> But like torn Hectors at the chariot wheel,
> She dragged their mangled ruins with her keel.

Except for a purely lyrical interlude the poem is written in five-foot rhymed iambics, the heroic measure, but the monotony which is almost inseparable from continuous couplets is avoided by the insertion of quatrains which vary the pattern without breaking it. One of the best of the sustained passages is that of about seventy lines which closes the Second Part and begins:

> Round the stark Horn with buckled masts she clove. . .

The impression it creates of an elemental struggle is dependent to a great extent on its development and climax; but a short passage may give an idea of the characteristic way in which imagery is used, both directly and indirectly, to rouse an emotional response:

Its four sad candles dripping from their wicks,
The Southern Cross disconsolately swung,
And canted low its splintered crucifix,
While all around the wolfish winds gave tongue,
And, in the silence of the nether shore,
With hateful patience by the hunted ship,
Their splitting fangs and feet that leave no spoor
Raced all night long in drear companionship,
Till, through the shadows of the Southern floe,
The awful ghost of Erebus at last
Flowered in the desolation of the snow.

Another passage, in which the creative power is displayed by the same means, though in quite a different mood, is that on pages 31–33, which evokes exotic landscape in very much the same way as the central stanzas of 'Bateau Ivre', and it is probably the first instance of the direct influence of Rimbaud on English verse.

As is inevitable in any early work, there are here and there images which have served their time and slip through the poet's guard by his very familiarity with them. I find, too, that when certain rhymes recur they sometimes bring with them images only partly made over. In construction the poem is confusing, for it reaches two or three apparent climaxes before it is half-way through, and the effect of the final spiritual victory is weakened by premature perorations. The cosmic theme demanded imagery on a mountainous scale, and for that reason perhaps a tendency to over-statement is rather prominent. These defects are not inherent but due to immaturity, and they are not pronounced enough to prevent this poem from being, in substance, in style, and in the vigorous gifts it reveals, as original and interesting a work as a young poet may produce.

AMERICAN POETRY AT QUARTER-CENTURY

American Poetry since 1900. By Louis Untermeyer (Grant Richards)
From Whitman to Sandburg in American Poetry. By Bruce Weirick (Macmillan)

When Poe was one of the reviewers of books he was forced to blunt his admirable critical faculty on verse which was below the level of achievement at which real criticism can begin. Even the best verse of the time was not distinctively American, and literary culture as a whole adopted a snobbish attitude to its environment. Mr. Untermeyer has rescued a few amusing lines from favourite poets of the period, such as

>My soul is far away today, sailing the Vesuvian Bay,

and

>Thou little girl of Astrakan, I join thee on the silk divan,

which show clearly enough that the dominant impulse of such verse was to escape from the rather raw home atmosphere to one more sensuously flattering. It is plain that a great nation's poetry could not be built on such a shallow foundation, and the finest work of the century was done in prose; it was only with the slow recognition of Whitman's genius that a healthy change of outlook was effected. Each of the present volumes, the first from the popular, the second from the academic, point of view, appears to reverence Whitman as the father of an independent national literature. Neither, however, attempts to criticize him aesthetically; from which we conclude that the function of his poetry as a revelation is still sufficiently active to defer the putting of that final test. It is enough to regard Whitman's work as a great prophecy which others will fulfil; his own voice was out of proportion to his expressive power. But his enthusiastic assertions wrought the necessary release from an exaggerated deference to the European sensibility; and though few modern poets show signs of having swallowed the particular medicine he prescribed, it was he who encouraged them to speak directly of their own experience.

Mr. Untermeyer has no philosophy of criticism, which, indeed, he thinks of as 'merely an annotated explanation of these (aesthetic) likes and dislikes'. Under this condition it is useless to expect an idea of general significance to emerge from his choppy flood of comment, in which his gift of epithet is too often lashed into mere foam. His particular observations, though, are frequently just and illuminating; and I do not know of another volume which describes so comprehensively that revival of the poetic impulse which has distinguished American literature during the last twenty years.

Some hints of the processes which helped to produce this promising crop will be found in Mr. Weirick's volume of reprinted lectures, as they bridge the gap between the appearance of Whitman and the early years of this century. He writes with a professorial decorum which carries rather more weight than Mr. Untermeyer's virtuosity; but his sensibility is restricted, and he flounders in his appreciation of the later moderns. The gap mentioned was, as he shows, empty of any poet of much importance, but a certain amount of good clearance work was done, and the spontaneous emotions began to shoot again. Hovey and Bliss Carman popularized poetic vagabondism. Lanier was a scenic poet with a small vein of verbal luxuriousness, and Moody had the power of straightforward emotional expression. The poets were beginning to discover America, and they were also recovering the sense of their language as a living tongue with loveable peculiarities, after it had been reduced for so long to the poetic idiom of a minor group. Whitman was the first to remind them that common speech is rich in poetic elements and superior, as the basis of a revival, to the more precious diction of any dominant contemporary school.

This is a truism which is monotonously evident in the history of each literary renaissance; and it is characteristic of the real American poetry of today. Colloquialism is, of course, a means and not an end in itself; it is a stage necessary to the realization of the poetry of fact, which must precede the ultimate poetry, that of idea. The distinction may be made clear by considering three poets each of whom has produced a substantial body of work, coherent in style, quite individual, and essentially American. In the regional classification which is sometimes applied by American critics, Edwin Arlington Robinson is labelled New York, Robert Frost belongs to rural New England, and Carl Sandburg to Chicago and the Middle West. These are also precise descriptions and show how closely the poets have lived to their environment, to the order of fact; for even when Mr. Robinson writes rural pieces he retains an urban sophistication and irony, and Mr. Sandburg by a moonlit lake thinks of the moon as a woman in a circus-rider's silver dress. This is a far cry, Mr. Untermeyer believes, from 'Poe's misty and moon-struck No Man's Land' and from the 'strange and soothing antiquity' to which Keats 'fled', thereby implicitly praising one of the poetic qualities at the expense of the highest excellence, which is to transcend the fact in the idea.

And the three poets named have in common this basic quality, that they live by the human heart. By their fidelity to the immediate reality, by their sympathetic perception of emotion in its meanest manifestations, they lift the poetry of fact to a pitch at which it expresses the deepest implications of its subject; but it is in the nature of their subject to inhibit the loftiest flight. With this reservation in mind it would be difficult to overestimate the value of their contributions towards the creation of a national tradition. They have taken their civilization as it is, and their language as it is, and simply under the impulse to create from it an object of aesthetic delight they have given it form, and so implicit meaning, each according to his own characteristic.

There are (Mr. Frost has said) two types of realist: the one who offers a good deal of dirt with his potato to show that it is a real one, and the one who is satisfied with the potato brushed clean. I'm inclined to be the second kind. To me, the thing that art does for life is to clean it, to strip it to form.

There is not much to add to that definition of style in regard to the verse of Mr. Robinson and Mr. Sandburg. Mr. Robinson uses the common traditional forms and a diction based on the movement and arrangement of familiar speech. Mr. Sandburg uses no regular metres or stanza forms, but he has such a gift of expression and sensitiveness to rhythmical patterns that his work nearly always has the form which is an essential attribute of poetic beauty. His language is full of slang and technical terms but it is always dominated by an artistic tact. He is the most powerful writer of these three poets, though he has not the tranquillity which assures the permanent charm of many of Mr. Frost's poems or the analytic subtlety which distinguishes Mr. Robinson's. A French writer has called Mr. Robinson a 'désenchanteur', a disillusionist, and the term is apt, for he works miracles of revelation instead of those metamorphoses into something rich and strange of which the great romantics are capable. The term might be generalized and applied with variations to all these poets, for they show the strangeness of the soul among its familiar surroundings, even among those so terribly familiar and in such common postures that too often it had been forgotten that man had a soul to be revealed.

I have considered these three poets at some length because they seem to have, apart from their individual achievements, certain qualities in common derived from the society in which they live, and so likely to determine the direction in which American poetry may fruitfully develop. It isn't possible to consider the rest of the poets in detail, or even mention by name all those who have produced some genuine work, but certain general considerations may be noted.

The doctrinal *intransigeants*, who believed that poetry could be written in any way but the old, have been unlucky in their followers, and little remains to prove the value of the manifestos and countermanifestos of the past decade. A few individual efforts stand out, detached from any group, such as that of Edgar Lee Masters, whose *Spoon River Anthology* showed that he had at least the power of provoking dramatic interest; and that of Vachel Lindsay, whose gift of recitative accounted for not a little of the popularity of his verses. Mr. T. S. Eliot is a European in all but the accident of birth; and Mr. Untermeyer, who would rather like to stage a literary Fourth of July, is in consequence unsympathetic to his emotional fastidiousness and does not appreciate the poetic irony that can be no less poignant than the direct cry.

The only group to cohere long enough to be recognizable as such is that of the Imagists. Their technical sensibility is narrow, but their example of sincere and uncontaminated expression stands out from a time of confusion and deliberate mystification. As a group, however, they suffered in including only one poet whose personality could flourish within the self-imposed limits. Apart from a few separate poems, only the work of H. D. remains to justify their theory of technique. The last few years have seen the traditional technique completely vindicated as the basis of expression, though the liberty of variation has rightly been reserved to the individual conscience. Conrad Aiken is a poet who does not venture far from the beaten track, and one would expect better work from him than he has yet done if he would shake himself free from an embarrassing regard for the literary and emotional associations of language. Three women poets are remarkable for the purity of their style – Sara Teasdale, Edna St. Vincent Millay, and Elinor Wylie – and all have produced work which calls for close consideration.

The 200 would-be poets of whom Poe complained had swollen to more than 2,000 even before the World War. Numbers do not count for very much in poetic values; but, within limits, poets produce poets, and no nation can express itself freely till a nucleus of good work has accumulated on its own soil. America has never been so well served by poets as it is today; poets who are native both in vision and in idiom. If one just man might save a city from destruction, half a dozen good poets should suffice for the salvation of a continent. It is remarkable that the three poets who are generally accepted as representative of the best effort of the present day are part and parcel of their environment to an extent which our own poets have rarely been, and to which the greatest poets perhaps can never be. But besides these native qualities and the community of language, their poetry speaks no less surely to us, and may serve to enrich our own tradition, besides doubling the opportunities, never too frequent, of poetic delight.

EARLY ENGLISH LITERATURE

The Cambridge Book of Prose and Verse. Edited by George Sampson (Cambridge University Press)

The present volume is an attempt, on the whole successful, to provide an anthology of the English literature before Chaucer, which is by no means so familiar to the general reader as it might be, for its immense interest as well as for its importance as an integral part of the living body of English literature. Though it is sometimes convenient to draw a line through a great cohesive effort like that of Chaucer and say that there modern literature begins, such a demarcation can never be absolute, and to attempt it too seriously is to lay ourselves open to the same reproach as did the Augustans. The literature of a civilized people – and the English had a civilization, a racial culture, long before the date of the first surviving written fragments – cannot possibly be called barbarous; though that reproach may be more exactly applied to the dregs of the writers of any age, who treat language, not as the habit of thought, but as a lifeless substance which can be built up into patterns independent of the rhythm of contemporary life. Examples of this may be seen in some of the translations of Early English poetry given in the present volume, where a sort of convention of sham archaic phrases is used with the same effect of unreality as the costumes in a patriotic pageant. This censure is general, so far as these renderings of often marvellously adroit verse-writers range from the merely inadequate to the clumsy and banal; the pieces of good work by certain individuals are too few to remove the air of shoddy inefficiency which hangs over these early pages. One must appreciate the difficulties which Professor Sampson set himself to overcome when he undertook to illustrate the period covered by the first volume of the *Cambridge History of English Literature*. Old English is, from the ordinary reader's point of view, a foreign language. The running gloss which the editor supplies successfully to poems of the Early Transition and onwards is obviously insufficient; but the immense increase in pleasure to be gained by struggling, even through a poem in the original is so much greater than in translation that we could have wished this method to have been stretched to the utmost. Both 'Pearl' and 'The Owl and the Nightingale' might have been treated in this way, since they are no more difficult than 'Sir Gawayne and the Grene Knight', which is followed only by the running gloss.

The whole question of the general reader in his relation to Early English literature is, of course, a matter for lengthy argument, but it can hardly be doubted that some three or four hundred years of our poetry are, though not now unread, at least unfamiliar. There seems to be no reason why narrative poems like 'Sir Orfeo', or collections of early lyrics, should not circulate as freely as Elizabethan tragedies and songs. Although this volume is a mine of delightful passages, it does not in itself give a complete view of the chronological period which it covers – up till the end of the fifteenth century. Langland and Gower have had to wait, and so have the Miracle Plays. But even without them the volume is a contradiction of the assumption, frequently implied, that civilized literature began in England only about four hundred years ago.

DEKKER'S JOURNALISM

The Seven Deadly Sinnes of London. By Thomas Dekker (Blackwell)

There is no one in whom one can feel quite the same confidence as in Dekker. It is not the conviction of ecstasy, which is reasonless, nor that of logic, which is often unreasonable, but a feeling of security, of certainty that he will not break his neck over any fantastic trapezes to gain us a laugh or a shudder. Not, perhaps the modern world will think, a good qualification for a journalist, but he was ready to grin through a hoop when necessary with the best of

them, though the good it did him the god of debtors alone can tell.
'Opus septem Dierum', says the title-page of the original edition,
and though it is a longish pamphlet rather than a small book, a
man must have had a stern creditor at his elbow to write it in a
week.

> You have another cruelty [he writes in the Seventh Day's triumph,
> which is that of Cruelty] in keeping men in prison so long, till sickness
> and death deal mildly with them, and (in despite of all tyranny) bail
> them out of all executions . . . I would that every miserable debtor that
> so dies might be buried at his Creditor's door, that when he strides
> over him he might think he still rises up (like the ghost in *Jeronimo*)
> crying *Revenge*.

We do not know if ever a flinty burgher heard his door-stone shriek
beneath him, but must hope that if any suffered such delusions it
were he who made Dekker 'acquainted with spunging-houses and
an inmate of the King's Bench prison'. For if ever generosity showed
itself in a man's work it does in his. Seizing the Seven Deadly Sins
of the medieval theologians, then most sickly and on their very
death-beds, he gives them a few deft touches of allegory and satire
and turns them sprightly once more, on to the London streets,
where they strut in immortal shapes of deceit and cruelty. Petti-
ness in any form is his target; he is not a satirist of morals so much
as of manners. Meanness he cannot tolerate, and his Sins are all of
that order – fraudulent bankruptcy, lying, apishness, cheating,
sloth, and, admirable title to the best of the seven, Candle-light:

> Let the world therefore understand, that this Tallow-faced Gentleman
> (called Candle-light) so soon as ever the Sun was gone out of sight, and
> that darkness like a thief out of a hedge crept upon the earth, sweat till
> he dropped again, with bustling to come into the city . . . He makes his
> entrance at *Aldersgate* of set purpose, for though the street be fair and
> spacious, yet few lights in misty evenings, using there to thrust out
> their golden heads, he thought that the aptest circle for him to be
> raised in, because there his *Glittering* would make greatest show.

There are passages here in which Dekker's imagination, moving
freely among the personifications of viciousness though never
passing London walls, takes on a delicacy which is not to be
matched even in his own 'Gulls' Horn-Book', though in that the
detail is richer, the satire more particular.

There are many virtues in Dekker, and not the least relevant to his merit as a writer is the continual blossoming of metaphor and simile out of the rank London thoroughfares. He is always true to his material and content with it as such, so that his plays contain no villains in the conventional sense. His characters are not chessmen, black and white according to the parts they have to play. If they had been, *The Honest Whore* would have been a mawkish affair, instead of marking, as it does, the only successful treatment of its theme in our modern literature. Life, for Dekker, was found so fully in his perceptions, so acute and so intriguing were they, he had neither time nor will to edit them in the way that has been the ruin of many writers.

Life, for him, was life in London. There is no poet so universal who is at the same time so local; he translates an incident from the trivial to the significant and robs it of none of its particularity. Leigh Hunt was a good journalist, and a good Londoner, but a page of his reads maidenly after any one of Dekker's.

> How then dares this nasty and loathsome sin of Sloth venture into a city amongst so many people? Who doth he hope will give him entertainment? What lodging (thinks he) can be taine up, where he and his heavy-headed company may take their afternoon's nap soundly? For in every street carts and coaches make such a thundering as if the world ran upon wheels.

And so on, in still more lively fashion till one is as much at home in the bustle of the Elizabethan city (or Jacobean, though we expect Dekker drew on his memory pretty freely) as round Ludgate Circus at midday. His prose is easy, but not in the too-much admired, the flowing style. It is constantly broken by similes; or metaphors, lurking beneath the surface, jar the bottom of the sense and awaken the languid reader to take a new conception of his meaning. These cross-references are always to things familiar, like that in his admonition to the reader:

> You stand sometimes at a Stationer's stall looking scurvily (like mules champing upon thistles) on the face of a new Book, be it never so worthy; and go (as ill-favouredly) mewing away.

One cannot help wondering what sort of a journalist Dekker would make today, when so much of the vitality of the wonderful language he was born to has been dissipated. One's deepest impression of Dekker is reinforced by this pamphlet. His sensibility is remarkable because it is more generous at least than most men's, and not, to a great extent, more delicate. He has not Webster's acute perception of horror and the horrid, nor Jonson's of the fantastic aberrations of intellect, but the humblest observation he met with in those streets, where too often he must have paced debt-distracted, was certain of Dekker's instant recognition, like that night-watchman with his legs 'lapt rounde about with peeces of Rugge, as if he had newe strucke off Shackles'.

THE CASE OF POE

Edgar A. Poe: A Psychopathic Study. By John W. Robertson (Putnam)

In the matter of posthumous fame Poe has had a strangely contradictory career. Whilst it is customary for the critics to purr at least in the obituary notices of a man of genius, the *New York Tribune* opened its two-column article with this astonishing piece of brutality: 'Edgar Allan Poe is dead. He died in Baltimore the day before yesterday. This announcement will startle many, but few will be grieved by it.' The defamatory memoir which followed was the basis for the longer study prefixed by Griswold to his 'Collected Edition'. This set the tone of criticism for some years by suggesting that Poe's genius was the result of a mental aberration intensified by the abuse of drugs and alcohol. Only gradually, as more friendly testimony circulated, the possibilities of a different interpretation became evident.

The latest of these is directed towards the proper understanding of those periods of irregularity caused by the morbid craving for alcohol which were the cause of much of his material suffering. They rendered him incapable of that routine work which by satisfying his moderate needs might have left him free of the incessant demand on his pen which he met so courageously in his intervals of normal health. Its influence on his creative power was more disastrous, for the work of his later years shows a falling off in both quantity and quality. The philosophic poem 'Eureka', though, is not so incomprehensible as Dr. Robertson finds it, and the professional alienist is exceeding his rights when he suggests that it is 'the pitiful exhibition of a decaying intellect no longer under the domination of a strong and directing intelligence'. For while Dr.

Robertson brings his long experience of abnormal intellects to the defence of Poe, releasing him to any unprejudiced reader's satisfaction from the moral responsibility of his lapses, he does not always show as keen an understanding of the poetic genius of his subject. 'Eureka' is more satisfying than most universal philosophies, but it reads in parts like clap-trap because Poe was unfortunate in his choice of a phraseology. His inability to forge a new implement adequate to the expression of his ideas is undoubtedly a symptom of disorganization in the mechanical part of the brain such as would correspond to the development of a disease like dipsomania. There is a good deal of evidence from intimate friends as to the involuntary nature of Poe's drinking excesses and to the disproportionate effects of a very small quantity of drink on his nervous temperament. Poe's own complaint – that his enemies referred his fits of insanity 'to the drink rather than the drink to the insanity' is amply justified by the establishing of these points in his family and personal history.

Having killed, or at any rate stunned, this moral dragon (and when all is said it is not one which seriously interferes with Poe's fame at this time of day), Dr. Robertson deals less than generously with his predecessors in the field. Ingram, Hannay and Woodberry were indisputably small men, but their effect was collective and cumulative. There is, however, one writer to whom Poe owes more than to all his native critics put together. Baudelaire's translation of the tales is of a rare excellence, and his study of the poet one of the oustanding essays in criticism of last century. Yet we are told, among other statements seriously at variance with the facts, that

> Baudelaire, who translated his work, and who set him up as a divinity, to be invoked and to be worshipped as a god, has seriously injured the standing of Poe among the greater French writers.

Dr. Robertson's adventures beyond the medical into regions of literary or philosophical criticism are so personal and expressed so ambiguously that his monograph would have gained in value by their suppression. He seems to say that Bishop Berkeley does not deserve a reputation as a philosopher, and that his name is honoured only because it was adopted by the University of California.

The appendices contain some interesting material which helps to explain the animosity Griswold felt for Poe, which he was able to satisfy when by some extraordinary misjudgement he was appointed Poe's literary executor. The actual memoir is here reprinted from the 'Complete Works' edited by Griswold, and its harshness is not so surprising (considering Griswold's lack of sympathy with the idealistic nature of Poe) as is the evidence he cites of deliberate falsification of the republished articles. It was all very long ago, and the more pathetic because the literary reputations Griswold sought to safeguard from Poe's destructive criticism have sunk of their own weight into the depths of oblivion. Poe was not a good-natured reviewer, and the amiable nullities of the New England coteries may have been justifiably offended at the tone of his attacks. Poe's article on Griswold's *Poets and Poetry of America* is given in full, and the personality of his attack is savage enough to hurt even at this distance. But it was America's first experience of a poet of genius, and it was an unfortunate accident that he should have been set to review contemporary verse.

A LITERARY MYSTIC

The Caerleon Edition of the Works of Arthur Machen. In Nine Volumes (Secker)

The sensation roused by 'The Great God Pan' on its appearance at the end of 1894, 'a storm in a tiny tot's teacup', as Mr. Machen describes it, was due to the *nouveau frisson* it evoked. This shudder, if no longer new, at least persists in the story, which is even today vaguely disquieting. Its quality has survived when the many stories which have imitated the trick of it are no longer readable, what became a trick to some was the expression of a very intimate part of Mr. Machen's character. He was once asked to write a series of 'horror stories', he tells us, but the effort was most painful to him and unsuccessful. He had no intention when he wrote 'The Great God Pan' of composing a horror story, but simply of communicating an experience which had moved him deeply and which seemed to him one of the most valuable of things to say; he has in some other place given the circumstances of this illumination. It is not, however, to that one form of the experience, the sense of the bestiality which might be re-awakened in man to which I referred as an intimate part of his character, but to the generalization of that conception. The sense of a mystery unfathomable to reason beneath the familiar surface of life, is the belief which animates quite the greater portion of Mr. Machen's writing, and explains his impatient and sometimes abusive treatment of the complacent materialist. If this is the first condition in the composition of a mystic, there is a second which confirms him in his calling: and that is the perception of the unity of things material and spiritual, with the usual corollary that the material world is the inadequate translation or symbol of a higher reality. Whether he remains solitary or assumes a prophetic utterance, the intrinsic value of his inspiration remains the same.

The mystic is not amenable to reason, but as soon as he descends to express or communicate the conditions of his ecstasy he comes within the region of the arts and is subject to the same canons as any other practitioner of poetry, painting, or music. The primary object of criticism must be to determine the limits within which communication is possible. In the case of 'The Great God Pan', our admitted thrill is evidence that the story has satisfied the first condition of literature, and that any further judgement passed upon it must be made under the name of the social or personal sensibility.

The stories in *The Three Impostors* spread from the same root as the preceding volume, but they enforce the idea without enriching it. Already the literary sensibility has played the mystic false by giving him only one string to play upon. Mr. Machen had 'a sort of recognition that I had squeezed this particular orange to death', and concludes that the agony with which he executed four more 'horror stories' in response to an invitation 'shows that I was a mere intruder, not a true craftsman'. From our objective point of view we have quite the contrary impression. One is amazed at the command of craft which serves up the same dish with so many different garnishings that it is necessary to bite deeply before tasting their real identity:

Although the mystic does not negotiate with the reasoning side of man (though he may be a subtle logician) he takes his stand on the faculty human nature has of being moved to ecstasy.

> O how soft shalt thou complain
> Of a sweet and subtle pain!
> Of intolerable joys...

In *Hieroglyphics* Mr. Machen sets out to bring his aesthetic

experience into line with his conception of life as I have outlined it.
He gives the palm of art to those works which convey beneath their
relation of external reality the consciousness of a vaster, universal
spiritual movement. With an audacity rare in literary criticism he
carries the war into the heart of the enemy's camp and seeks to
distinguish between ecstatic art, which he calls fine literature, and
the literature which is merely faithful to the surface of life, in works
of prose fiction. It is the old combat between poetry and prose
(irrespective of the verse form) which is reopened in his champion-
ship of *Pickwick* against *Vanity Fair*. The poet in Dickens perceived, in what was to the novelist's and to the novel-reader's
consciousness merely the intoxication of a middle-aged gentleman,
a symbol of the essential enthusiasm, or raising-above-self, of the
Dionysian rites. There is matter for eternal controversy in *Hieroglyphics*, but it does express, in this exaggerative way and with a
fine sensitiveness, the profundity of emotion in the heart of man.
It is, too, a humaner book than the two preceding ones; it shows a
greater readiness to accept the common things of life as being
themselves the terrestrial shadowings of ideal joys, a conviction
which is demonstrated in many pages of the later books. If the
materialist excludes the mystic, he himself is absorbed and his
extremest satisfaction redoubled in the all-embracing acceptance of
the latter.

A conviction, however, or a faith, whilst sufficient justification
for a solitary, demands a garment to show it off when it descends
from the mountain-top to the market-place. This garment must
be woven of sensuous experience, for how else shall the sensual
nature of man understand ecstasy? We have seen Mr. Machen at
work in the 'horror stories', and he has attempted again and again
to give bodily form to his inspiration, with most sincerity in 'A
Fragment of Life', but generally, the reader feels, falling short of
the original intention. He is not content, in 'The Secret Glory', for
instance, to allow the mood of sensuous exaltation to permeate the
reader with the sense of the deeper reality behind it. The sunset
and the cloud-countries are symbolized into parts of a superhuman
realm, in pages which destroy the illusion of extreme beauty they
first created. In the war-stories this tendency is even exaggerated.
The sense of supernatural assistance which may or may not have
sustained the rearguard of the British Army in its heroic stand is not
made real to us by the externalization of the idea in those hosts of

shadowy archaic bowmen; nor in the other short war-tales in which the invisible world arrays itself against the enemies of the Allies. These tales are not an important part of Mr. Machen's work, but they illustrate what seems to me an inherent defect in the imaginative part of it. The human soul is a mystery – without the slightest doubt; it is not even an exceedingly complex mechanism. But therefore the commonest experiences are just as mysterious as any other; there are, indeed, no common ones to the man who is properly alive. The search for the supreme revelation, the splendid vision, is one which may flatter the literary instincts of the mystic, but it is not one which is a necessary part of his endeavour. Wordsworth would have been a controlling influence, would perhaps have pruned Mr. Machen's exuberant Celticism, which De Quincey especially nourished by the example of his own austerity of vision.

The two volumes of autobiography which conclude this edition. *Far-off Things* and *Things Far and Near*, are those to which, I believe, readers will most frequently turn. The original inspiration of all the stories is contained there, free from the garment of fiction which never very well became them; and the first volume contains a continually charming account of the life of an imaginative boy in a wild corner of Wales when it was still in touch with the most ancient traditions. The later volume records the years of struggle in London and the hard literary apprenticeship, with a maturity of observation, a kindliness and sympathy, which make it unique of its kind. It is in these volumes, too, that the mystic communicates to us most surely his vision of wonder and beatitude, whether as a boy wandering along the wooded valley of the Usk or as a young man in the desert which is named the Caledonian Road, and the least pleasant districts of London. He never allowed the oppression of man's own works in bricks and mortar, or the more subtle oppressions which he records, to blind him to the vision of truth which was vouchsafed him on the threshold of life.

THE ENCHANTMENT OF A MIRROR

Jacob's Room. By Virginia Woolf (The Hogarth Press)

One might describe Mrs. Woolf's new novel as the opposite of *Night and Day*, her last, or say that it is rather like the method of

'Monday or Tuesday' applied to a continuous story. But this novel is limpid and definite. It would be truer to say that it is different from any other – Mrs. Woolf's or anyone else's – though the remark sounds both vague and sweeping. At first you may be drawn by resemblances. This bright and endless race of things and thoughts, small acts, incongruous sensations, impressions so brief and yet pervasive that you hardly separate the mental from the external, what is it but the new vision of life as practised by So-and-so or So-and-so? The vision may be as old, indeed, as Heraclitus; but could he, or Pater even, have guessed how far artists would carry the process of weaving and unweaving? Mrs. Woolf, you will say, is in this movement. Possibly; but her fabric is woven with threads so entirely of her own that it becomes quite different.

First, however, for its unlikeness to the normal. Jacob Flanders, absorbed with the half-savage, half-winning absorption of youth, and lovable since his friends and several women love him is, in the brief career which we follow by glimpses, the mutest of all heroes. He is a 'silent young man'; Mrs. Woolf's method increases his silence. But there is his room, his behaviour, his impressions; there are the scenes, the numerous people who float into the story for a moment or eddy round its centre. There is Mrs. Jarvis, for example:

Short, dark, with kindling eyes, a pheasant's feather in her hat, Mrs. Jarvis was just the sort of woman to lose her faith upon the moors – to confound her God with the universal, that is – but she did not lose her faith, did not leave her husband, never read her poem through, and went on walking the moors, looking at the moon behind the elm trees, and feeling as she sat on the grass high above Scarborough ... Yes, yes, when the lark soars; when the sheep, moving a step or two onwards, crop the turf, and at the same time set their bells tinkling; when the breeze first blows, then dies down, leaving the cheek kissed; when the ships on the sea below seem to cross each other and pass on as if drawn by an invisible hand; when there are distant concussions in the air and phantom horsemen galloping, ceasing; when the horizon swims blue, green, emotional – then Mrs. Jarvis, heaving a sigh, thinks to herself, 'If only some one could give me ... if I could give some one ...' But she does not know what she wants to give, nor who could give it her.

Is Mrs. Jarvis, then, a vivid little excrescence? When we ask what she and others are doing to the story, and find possible but not very obvious answers, we are getting nearer to the real interest of Mrs. Woolf's novel. It is not Jacob's history simply, nor anyone else's, but the queer simultaneousness of life, with all those incongruous threads which now run parallel, now intersect, and then part as unaccountably. Jacob is in the middle like a waif or a little marching soldier. And these odd conjunctions and sequences of life, which are much too delicate to be called slices, have been brought to a focus in Mrs. Woolf's mirror.

It is an amusingly clear and yet enchanted glass which she holds up to things; that is her quality. This stream of incidents, persons, and their momentary thoughts and feelings, which would be intolerable if it were just allowed to flow, is arrested and decanted, as it were, into little phials of crystal vividness. Mrs. Woolf has the art of dividing the continuous and yet making one feel that the stream flows remorselessly. The definite Mrs. Durrant, the romantic little light-of-love Florinda, shy and charming Clara, the people in the street, the moors and the sea, London and Athens – they all rise into delicious moments of reality and light before they melt back into the shadow. And each of those moments has caught a gleam of wit from the surface of the mirror, or a musing thought from the reflective depths in it. Ought we to complain, then, because Mrs. Woolf can make beauty and significance out of what we generally find insignificant, or because her own musings tinge those of her personages sometimes? We know the stream of life at first-hand already; what this novel adds, with the lightest strokes, and all the coolness of restraint, is a knowledge of the vision of the author.

And it is much to be taken as far as we are here, into that subtle, slyly mocking, and yet poignant vision; for Mrs. Woolf has seldom expressed it more beguilingly than she does in this novel. It will even make us forget to treat the novel as a story. If, however, we come back to that, we should have to say that it does not create persons and characters as we secretly desire to know them. We do not know Jacob as an individual, though we promptly seize his type; perhaps we do not know anyone in the book otherwise than as a really intuitive person knows his acquaintances, filling in the blanks, if he is imaginative, by his imagination. And that, Mrs. Woolf might say, is all we can know in life, or need to know in a book, if we forgo the psychology which she spares us. But it might still be questioned whether her beings, while they intersect, really act upon each other, or whether her method does not condemn them to be external. It is an ungrateful suspicion to have about a book which has embodied their passing thoughts so vividly. But what she has undoubtedly done is to give a quickened sense of the promise and pity in a single destiny, seen against those wilful, intersecting lines of chance and nature. And, with the pity of it, there is the delicious humour which infects every page, the charm of writing that seems as simple as talking but is always exquisite. It is a great deal to have brought back from an adventure; yet, after all, what we relish as much as anything in Mrs. Woolf's method is its adventurousness.

RICEYMAN STEPS

Riceyman Steps. By Arnold Bennett (Cassell)

The love and marriage of a middle-aged second-hand bookseller is the substance of Mr. Arnold Bennett's *Riceyman Steps* (Cassell). Such a theme might have been made to yield the specious gold of sentimentality in abundance, but only by an evasion of the realities which Mr. Bennett's artistic code does not permit. He might without undue compromise have set these amours in a pleasant suburb or given to the bride the charm of youth or of distress. He scorns to meet the reader half-way, but with a fine boldness chooses that unlovely district of Clerkenwell and leaves it only to describe the honeymoon trip to Madame Tussaud's and a Corner House. The woman who inspires this forgotten passion in the ageing bookseller is a widow comfortably provided for; and yet, for we have insisted on these details to give a measure of the achievement, Mr. Bennett succeeds in extracting from this base material a glint of a fugitive human beauty. There are even depths of baseness which we have not indicated, such as the miserliness of Mr. Earlforward, which led him to buy his wife's wedding ring out of the proceeds of the sale of her previous one, and to inquire of the men with the vacuum-cleaner whether they sold the dirt they sucked out of his house and shop. It was the short-sightedness of this economy in the matter of food which brought to an early and disastrous end his marital enterprise.

It is in the setting rather than in the story, which has about it something of the *tour de force*, that Mr. Bennett's remarkable instinct for reality is most surely displayed. He is a master of detail, but always of living detail; and though the mind sometimes flinches from the conclusion his unflagging observation implies, it can never be said that he darkens the colours of life in the limits he sets himself. One Sunday morning the courting couple take a walk through Riceyman Square, a decayed square off the Farringdon Road, and the horror of the scene is conveyed with the freshness which comes from seeing again things which had become so familiar as to be neglected:

> Newspapers, fresh as newly gathered fruit, waited folded on door-steps for students of crime and passion to awake from their beds in darkened and stifling rooms. Also little milk-cans with tarnished brass handles had been suspended in clusters on the railings.

It is these small things, which might mean nothing, which to Mr. Bennett mean so much. Life depends on the materials of life, he seems to say, and then leads us like Dante to a yet lower circle – to the interior of one of the houses composing that square, an over-crowded, inconvenient house shared between several families. It was typical that he should write these two sentences in succession, and say of the square, 'Evolution had swirled round it, missed it, and left it. Neither electricity nor telephones had ever invaded it, and scores of windows still had venetian blinds.' Mr. Bennett the novelist here joins hands with the common-sense sociologist. Both are aware of the connexion between comfort and happiness, and that gives the zest of curiosity to his study of this couple who sacrifice their comfort and yet enjoy a sort of happiness. And because he does not quite understand such perversity he has rather overdrawn his characters, and the catastrophe looks more like the revenge of the author than the judgement of natural law.

PIPERS AND A DANCER

Pipers and a Dancer. By Stella Benson (Macmillan)

Miss Stella Benson likes to cut her story to the bone, and in *Pipers and a Dancer* (Macmillan) she is as ruthless as heretofore. Two hundred and forty small pages are enough for her; in these she can find room for all that she can bear to say about the dancer and the pipers. She writes as though she grudged them every word they cost her. She does not stay to contemplate her characters, to give them time and to draw them out; she jumps on them and riddles them with a phrase. She is so quick and so sharp that she gets her phrase home nearly always; it is nearly always the right stroke, hitting the right point. But her method, with its air of constant exasperation, seems bound to fail in one quarter, and that the most important. Her lightning touches may serve for the pipers, the objective figures surrounding the girl through whose eyes they are seen; but for the girl herself, explored from within, the strokes are far too summary – the girl never gets her chance. Miss Benson, perhaps, has felt the difficulty; for she shifts her point of view more than once, rather awkwardly, as though to give the girl her turn to be seen from without. But this only confuses the design of the story, which is much too short to disguise such makeshift; and it comes to this, that a highly ingenious little piece of work is damaged by the inadequacy of the figure in the midst. The scene is excellent, the seer is not really rendered at all.

The scene is laid in China, and cleverly laid. Why China? There is always the suspicion, in such a case, that it may only be China because the author is acquainted with China, not because the story needs it. But the story does need it here, or profits by it; for the half-dozen men and women of the story require the isolation of strangeness to make their effect. The tangle of attraction and re-pulsion in which they are caught might equally have caught them in Pimlico; but in Pimlico it would have spread too far, it would not have been cut off by a surrounding void as it is in Yunnan. It tells in Yunnan more sharply. So here we see the girl, and the heavy young man to whom she is engaged, and his sister, and the other man, the young American who understands the girl as she would rather wish to be understood.

The small drama works out as it may, but the point of it is not in the issue, such as it is: the point of it is in the nature and temper of the girl, one of those teased and teasing creatures, bewilderingly mixed of unreality and genuineness, whom Miss Benson takes her formidable pleasure in dissecting. These girls (not that they are always girls) are distracted between that which they wish to be, that which they are, that which they think they are, that which the presence of other people makes them; and each of these parts is in turn distracted by its own multiplicity, it is all good and true, and Miss Benson's slickness is kept on the stretch by the girl's confusion within; but there is not room enough, nor time enough allowed, for the girl to bring her scattered selves together and be seen for what she is, one young woman. Miss Benson is far too short and abrupt with her: the girl is dismissed before she has taken shape. It is quite different with the rest, for they are seized from without and need only to be seen as they affect the girl. The heavy young man with his grievances, the protective and predatory sister (the best and most dreadful bit of observation in the book), and also, though with less sureness, the attentive-eyed young American – these are very shrewdly understood and held. And the Chinese background, discreetly kept in its place, is touched with the lightest and neatest of hands.

PSYCHOLOGY AND LITERATURE

L'Evolution Psychologique et la Littérature en Angleterre, 1660–1914. By Louis Cazamian (Paris: Alcan)

There are, M. Cazamian points out, two tendencies or groups of tendencies which alternately dominate literature. It is a phenomenon which has been frequently observed; and his book, consisting of a course of lectures on the history of English literature delivered at the Sorbonne, is the first coherent essay we have seen to attach this alternance to a psychological reality.

Taine long ago laboured to demonstrate that events play the pipe, to which the poets must dance. But events are only one of many methods of expression the spirit uses; literature is another, and if the art of words runs a parallel course to the art of action it may be because the movement of each is determined by the same underlying necessity. The historian would not be too fantastic who termed certain of his happenings classic and others romantic. The invitation to William of Orange, a reasonable, polite, and formal action, might be distinguished by the former term, while the outburst that was the French Revolution is more easily conceived as romantic. But the difference between the impulse behind each of these events will not be made entirely clear by this terminology – may, indeed, be obscured by the associations aroused; and there is the same objection to its use in literary criticism.

We may assume, with M. Cazamian, that men are urged by a simple force, called what you will, and that the energy so supplied to us must be used in two ways, to satisfy our two main desires – that to feel and that to know. Here is a distinction which, if not fundamental, at least corresponds to a certain reality. It is the inequality in the urgency of these two desires which sets in motion the psychological rhythm (as he phrases it) to which history in all its branches must vibrate. This primal energy, working in one of these directions through an organism, either individual or social, which is known to be limited in endurance, will in time exhaust the faculties connected with that particular desire.

On these assumptions, the desire for knowledge, for instance, the endeavour of the intellect to arrange experience in a logical relation, would make no demand on the emotional part of the organism, and thus would become dominant as soon after the exhaustion of its opposite as external circumstances permitted. To follow M. Cazamian, then, the Elizabethans exhausted the national sensibility for emotion (and with emotion he includes imagination among the romantic qualities). In the subsequent period, which is dominated by the Metaphysical poets, there is an effort, generally desperate, to stimulate the tired nerves by means of novelty in technique and imagery, and by the exploration of byways of emotion the first enthusiasm had overlooked. But here, too, there must finally be an end, and with the attainment of political equilibrium, with the Revolution of 1688, the neglected reasonable faculties established a society on common sense. This date is only an approximation, for even before it, as Dryden shows, the desire for order and the creation of a standard of literary decorum had led that age to consider its predecessors as barbarous and much of their work personal aberration not worthy the respect of cultivated men.

It is undeniable that this attitude was favoured to perfection by the constitution of the society in which it evolved – a society numerically small, in a condition of material independence for the most part, and having a very strong tradition of culture common among its members, based on the compact foundation the literatures of Greece and Rome, at that distance in time, presented. The restricted audience such conditions entailed reacted on the nature of the literature produced, and M. Cazamian's careful enumeration of this development is detailed evidence in support of Drydens' own concise description of it:

Gentlemen will now be entertained with the follies of each other; and, though they allow Cobb and Sib to speak properly, yet they are not much pleased with their tankard or with their rags. And surely their conversation can be no jest to them in the theatre, when they would avoid it in the street.

For a good many years to come the tradition in culture of this small, semi-aristocratic society was strong enough to absorb the foreign elements which were forced into it by the dissemination of wealth and influence among the higher *bourgeoisie*. But what gentlemen were not pleased with, the burghers were; and they could not long maintain towards the problems of religion, philosophy, and literature the cold, reasonable scepticism of the Augustan circle. The revival of sentiment came with the novels of Richardson, with Steele, Addison and Goldsmith. Fervour was brought back, into religion first, by Wesley, and here the masses, too, were touched. When the sentiment of nature was reintroduced from the continent through German and French originals, all was prepared for the Romantic Revival. This would be about the sixth decade of the eighteenth century, and yet the revival made no indisputable appearance for another thirty years.

This delay is attributable to the fact that the now rejuvenated faculties of emotion had as yet no channels through which to employ their energy. The rapid onset of the Industrial Revolution, and political enthusiasm, particularly that coming from France, stimulated the mind with the promise of unimagined possibilities. Thus at the end of the century the ascendancy of emotion over thought was completed, and though from a literary point of view we may date it there, psychologically the revival had come much earlier. As M. Cazamian observes:

> In this explanatory scheme, the earliest plays of sentiment – sentimental comedies – innocent though they be of the slightest artistic innovation, are more deeply at the source of romanticism than is, for example, Percy's collection of old ballads, *Reliques of Ancient English Poetry*. The plays belong to a primary order of phenomena. The ancient poems, models for and direct encouragement of a new poetry, belong to the order of derivative things.

This dating back to the first half of the eighteenth century is important, as it weakens the objection one might make – when M. Cazamian fixes the beginning of the counter-romantic movement at

1830 – that romanticism had run an exceptionally short course for so strong an impulse. But even the removal of this objection does not prevent his treatment of the nineteenth century from entering the controversial, which hitherto had been avoided. Briefly, he postulates a transition period from about 1830 to 1850; then, with the establishment of the Victorian compromise and a considerable material prosperity, a neo-classicism till about 1880; thereafter, till the World War, a recrudesence of romanticism.

It is impossible here to examine this arrangement in detail, and it must be stated that M. Cazamian admits the mingling of both tendencies to an almost baffling degree. We are still too near the century to judge it dispassionately; and here M. Cazamian, by the detachment of his nationality, has the advantage of us. But even Arnold, Herbert Spencer, Butler, Hardy and Meredith seem to be feeble champions for the revival of classicism, especially when one remembers their Pre-Raphaelite contemporaries. We should be inclined to say that what M. Cazamian observes is the formation of the classicism of romance. We have spoken of one of the principal peculiarities of the Augustan period being the possession of a strong traditional culture. Of the two traditions discernible all through the nineteenth century by far the most widespread was the romantic, which was founded on the myths of 'primitive' peoples, on the legends of the half-civilized Middle Ages; and, so far as it went back to the Greeks, it was concerned with their myths rather than with the intellectual achievements of the Athenians. The other, tradition was much younger, and may be called that of experimental science, but it was in a condition much too indeterminate to provide that common standard of reference which is essential to classicism.

The Augustans never differed about ultimate values. When their satire held an object up to ridicule, every gentleman knew why that object was ridiculous. Erewhon, Butler's satire, however, is based on a personal standard, to which he refers even when he strikes at the generalization of science. It is possible that the twentieth century will widely accept his values, in which case he will assume the appearance of a classic; but up till the present his dissatisfaction with the very laws of nature, such as they were, prohibits us from regarding him as such.

It would be more precise, perhaps, to say that a nation can have only one classic period, when it has built up behind it such a body of work that the minds of that period have not enough energy to dispute its values, or, what is the real test, to carry its conclusions farther. Then it can only settle down to imitation and refinement, and the achievement of decorum becomes its ideal. Our own Augustan age was only pseudo-classic, and due to our inheritance, from the Renaissance, of the classical texts. That this is the case is rather borne out by what we know of literatures which have completed their cycle. That M. Cazamian is in error respecting a vibration between two poles cannot yet be determined. That his distinction between a classic and two romantic periods is a true one we have admitted; but we cannot see that this distinction is sufficiently at the root of things not to be accounted for merely by the action and reaction of the surface sensibility. Besides, intellect, emotion, and imagination are not definite psychological entities. Their separation is purely arbitrary and cannot even be based on critical experience, for it is impossible to regard an aesthetic sensation as simply emotional or intellectual. Imagination, too, has a more general importance than as a mere associate of emotion; and though the discussion would lead us too far into metaphysics, this faculty seems to constitute our sole means of perception and the other two merely to be the servants who deal, in their several ways, with the material so acquired.

These are controversial matters; but a more generally acceptable objection to M. Cazamian's theory of vibration lies in the fact that his observations are made over such a small sector of literary history. The shorter the range over which recordings are made, every practical scientist knows, the greater is the liability to error; and the obtrusions which, in the 300 years under survey, seem to constitute the configuration of the system may, as time unfolds, shrink into place as barely perceptible deviations from the norm. The value of M. Cazamian's interpretation of our literary variations does not rise or fall with the fate of its main premises. His achievement, and it is a considerable one, is by his method to have clarified the course of literature, thus bringing the work of art into a more precise relation with the age which produced it. Though he does not attempt judgements of particular writers, he has many excellent remarks on such as he finds necessary to introduce: and all through the book there are delightful passages of an acute common sense which illuminate that most obscure and bewildering corporation, the collective spirit of a period.

PSYCHOLOGY AND POETRY

Psychoanalysis and Aesthetics. By Charles Baudouin (Allen and Unwin)

The title chosen by Professor Baudouin for this work is unnecessarily general. By far the greater part of the book consists of a psychoanalysis of Verhaeren's poetic production, and aesthetic problems are rather cursorily dismissed. There is no attempt to institute comparisons between Verhaeren and other poets, such as might lead to the 'judgement of value', which the author renounces as beyond the prerogative of the scientist. None the less he lets it be clearly seen that he considers Verhaeren's symbolistic style the most direct method of expression, and that this corresponds to his standard of aesthetic excellence. His analysis is illustrated by a great number of quotations from the poet in question, which the translators give in good renderings beside the original, and it is an extremely skilful piece of work. It is in the main an application of the principles evolved by Freud from his study of the Œdipus complex and of the extension derived from it by Jung and others to cover the phenomena of introversion and extroversion. If these hypotheses are accepted, the rest follows automatically; but there is a point at which some of the observations may be checked without entering the controversial field of psychoanalysis. His identification of the non-reasonable element in poetic creation and appreciation with the activity shown in dreams and hypnotic trances was a subject of discussion among critics long before the new psychology was heard of.

From the earliest times there has existed in the popular judgement, a great reservoir of wisdom, a distinction between ordinary speech and the manner of expression connected with transcendental experiences. The prophet was supposed to have been entered into by the god, as the bard by the spirit of the race, and in this explanation the people showed their sense of the superior intensity of feeling to which these originals of poetic utterance moved them. We cannot but be equally struck by the hesitation with which even cultured races distinguish between their poets and the mentally afflicted, at least those kinds which, like the paranoic, display an astonishing fertility of invention. Even at the end of the last century this scepticism came to the surface in the works of certain alienists, of a paradoxical turn of mind, who tried to identify artistic activity with that of some types of mental degeneration.

In this instance, again, popular instinct might have been a guide, for such locutions as 'poetic frenzy', 'mad with love', and numerous others reveal a tendency to group beneath a common denomination the madman, the lover, and the poet. More widespread still is the association, which needs no illustration, of the poet and the dreamer, or of poetry, and a dreamy character or a state of dreaminess.

The confusion of thought would be less evident it it were not that the types so brought together are those most revered and those most despised by humanity. It seems as if society had determined to take its revenge on those who, if they were charlatans, would most richly impose on it, by making degraded figures of them the most common objects of their ridicule. The frequency, in our comedy and farce, with which the traditional fool is represented by would-be poets, absent-minded men and unlucky lovers, even the popularity of the comic curate, points to such a motive. All these people are, as the Elizabethans would have justly phrased it, fantastic. They have ambitions or longings which we spectators recognize as unreasonable in them; and by going their way as if their wishes were capable of fulfilment they trip over the realities of this world, to the great amusement of us all. Evidently cause and effect are not, in their minds, linked by physical laws but by those of phantasy, or dream, which know no obstacle to fulfilment. The difference between the real and the sham poet must arise at the point at which the unreasonableness becomes disagreeable to the audience – at which, that is, it becomes noticeable. If it could be said that the audience were hypnotized (as to a slight extent it is, no doubt), then the laws of aesthetic propriety would simply correspond with those of the association of images as observed in dreams and morbid mental states. But though this is partly the case, and almost wholly in that of Verhaeren, had Professor Baudouin cast his net more widely he would have caught some fish which did not so readily answer his description. We have only to examine our own aesthetic sensations in order to discover that nothing could very well be more different from the experience of a dream than that of a poem or a play. Evidently there is in art an important element whose presence differentiates the poet from the mentally afflicted, in spite of those which he has undeniably in common with them. This factor, which must be correctly estimated before there can be any pretension to aesthetic criticism, is Realism, in a wider sense than that in which it is attached to a certain school of novelists.

Professor Baudouin, however, is a champion of the pre-eminence of symbolist art, and of the school of poetry known by that name he says:

> Psychology completely justifies it – justifies even the vagueness with which these poets have been so irrelevantly reproached. Of course, there may be other forms of art, but this form is peculiarly true and is admirably consonant with the nature of the psyche.

It would have been enlightening if he had mentioned some examples of these non-symbolic arts, for I find it hard to name any literary work of eminence which was not symbolic in its significance. This is not the same thing, however, as being symbolist in execution. We can believe that Othello, Desdemona, and Iago are symbolic of a deep-lying, emotional reality without believing that the handkerchief is a symbol of anything. It is an element introduced from reality, and gives an exquisite naturalness to the drama beside which many of the inventions of poetic fantasy seem extremely childish. This element of reality will surely be found predominant, after the symbolic theme, in all classic art. It is difficult to see how, under a symbolist definition, our Restoration dramatists would be acknowledged at all. But even the great poets are comparatively sparing of fantasy, much more sparing than Verhaeren, because it is actually an infantile trait. The subconscious from which the psychoanalysts say we draw our symbols, is the mental life of the past; and the non-reasonable, illogical way of associating images which we meet with in dreams and morbid states is the survival of an archaic way of thinking. We can understand now the popular suspicion of the man who exhibits this faculty.

None the less, as it is in this past that the roots of our emotional life are fixed, it is to this region ultimately that the poet must appeal. Classical art brings about the subordination of these non-reasonable elements in mind to the highest degree of sophistication which the intelligence has reached. We might agree with M. Baudouin that classical art can never be so emotionally stirring as that which makes use of the symbolist method – just as Negro music is very much more exciting than that of the average concert hall. A musically educated person would not, however, argue that, though there are other forms of music, the Negro, being consonant with our subconscious sense of rhythm, was peculiarly true. Symbolist art is true to the past, and to the present so far as the past lives in it, but we have to some extent developed another method of thought during the ages. Poetry cannot but continue to approximate more and more closely to the reasonable and the real, sacrificing some of its primitive effects for others in keeping with the faculty which mankind has nourished so jealously. This necessitates that the solution of the aesthetic problem should embrace a synthesis of elements much more complex than the statement presented in this volume.

EARTHLY PARADISE

Tahiti. By Tihoti (George Calderon) (Grant Richards)

When Captain Wallis of the *Dolphin* came across the place his acquisitive instinct marred his sense of fitness, and he named it 'King George IV's Island'. A few months later de Bougainville dropped anchor there on his way round the world, and with the allusive grace of an elegant period remedied his predecessor's incivility by calling the island La Nouvelle Cythère. Such it then was, for he found the people 'decorated with pearls and flowers ... singing and dancing to the music of the tom-tom and nose-flute'.

It was not a guise of jollity put on to attract tourists, but an everyday happiness which led them to such delights. True, their enjoyment may have been stimulated by the novel appearance of these sailors. Those jabbering fellows with little pigtails, their bodies swathed in coarse cloth, must have seemed curious to the graceful islanders. Probably some of the sailors were tattooed, and that may have given the savages a reassurance of kinship.

These people of Tahiti were a noble and beautiful race. Life was not to them the painful industry Europe knows, but a happy flowering of the senses in a garden hospitable to all manner of kindly growths. Gauguin in his diary has captured the original spirit of their heyday, when the West first discovered them:

La vie s'éveille au matin, dans la belle humeur de la terre et du soleil, comme elle s'était endormie en riant. Le plaisir est la seule affaire, et le travail lui-même se fait plaisir d'exercer sa force, de montrer son adresse, d'obliger un ami. La sagesse aussi doit être un jeu, jeu de vieillards au veillées et, la fantasie sans doute aussi d'avoir peur, de rien, jeu de femmes.

Their religion must have been very different from any evolved under the harsh necessities of domineering civilization, for they needed not to pray for the fulfilment of any of their desires. The early travellers found them praying at the rising and setting of the sun, and this would have been a gesture of thanksgiving; to the mysterious powers of the past or coming night for,

> Quant à des classements en chrétiens et païens,
> Ni le climat ni les moyens.

Such were the child-gods who swam out to the first white man's vessel and attacked it. But when they met with no retaliation, they admitted their over-hastiness (which was, after all, justified) and received the sailors as guests. Doubtless the maidens wove garlands of flowers for their heads, and placed a gardenia behind the ear of each, as they did to George Calderon and his friend but a few years since. They gave of their best, for they feared, not men but only the spirits that gleam phosphorescent in the night. They gave everything that they had, and received in return, as the first-fruits of civilization, ague, dysentery and syphilis, which in a few years removed more than three-fourths of their number. Fortunately, for the missionaries of all denominations who flocked to reap the new harvest of souls, a few thousands survived. These were taught hymns and the use of firearms, among other things, and, later, they were introduced to the habit of tinned salmon and other benefits of a French administration.

It is about this residue that George Calderon wrote his charming and distinguished book. It is a deep misfortune that he did not live to put the finishing touches to the whole of it, for the parts which have had this care can hardly be surpassed for the ease and brightness of the descriptions, alert humour and keen intelligence illuminating everything.

But there is a bitterness beneath his graceful fluency; the shame of an honourable man for the havoc done by his own race. He had a more than passing love for the Tahitians, and he admired and comprehended their particular type of civilization. But their native hospitality and yielding courtesy rendered it peculiarly vulnerable, first of all to insouciant adventurers, and later to the 'mission civilatrice de l'Europe'.

The islanders now enjoy the inestimable benefit of a choice between a secular and a religious education. The following incident was observed on a visit to one of these schools during the hour when the daughters of a ruined race of poets were being 'taught poetry' by a French mistress with a 'cold, grey Protestant face':

> Another girl recited a touching poem about an old sergeant hearing a bugle-call as he hobbles along on two sticks, pushing his great-grand-children in a perambulator before him. After the recitation Madame X. put questions like this on the meaning of the poem:
> Quel sentiment éprouvait le vieux sergeant en entendant le bruit de la trompette? Qu'est-ce que signifiaient les larmes chaudes que laissa tomber le pauvre vieillard sur les têtes innocentes de ses arrière-petits-enfants? . . .

Calderon feared Pape-ete, the capital, was a 'show-place'. Incredibly charming as the natives were in that town, they were on show to some extent, and he was determined to penetrate beneath the superficial romance, or at least to see if it corresponded to anything in the spirit of these people. He himself was that valuable anomaly, a romantic with a passion to see clearly. Artist enough to make a beautiful book, he was not so intensely an artist as Pierre Loti, who wrung his stories from the mere fringe of the island life. Calderon's artistry was mingled with a curiosity and an intellectual integrity which gave him a horror of being duped by the garlands of a few sophisticated dancing girls. But, looking back from the villages to Pape-ete, he could see, as Gauguin did, that the reality survived even in the tourists' town:

> Ces yeux-là et cette bouche ne pouvaient mentir. Chez toutes ces tahitiennes l'amour est tellement dans le sang, qu'intéressé ou désintéressé, c'est toujours de l'amour.

Calderon seconds the painter's conclusions, though the girls he met remained for him charming companions or mocking, mischievous sisters. There are these differences between the three artists mentioned; something of the Parisian remains in Loti, and something of the Londoner in Calderon; Gauguin alone of the three became really absorbed into the native life. Calderon went on foot from village to village, from hut to hut. He travelled like an islander, and in every way submitted himself to the conditions, with the only reservation – and this is extremely important – that he remained consciously an observer. His journey is as incredible as Marco Polo's. Is there really anywhere such abundant hospitality, such a delicious freedom of come and go . . .? All day long voices hailed him from the shadows of huts – 'Viens mancher' (come and eat); and in the evening:

> 'Haereo e hia?' ('Where are you going?') a soft voice asked out of the darkness, and from among the bushes by the wayside started two figures of girls, dimly discerned, with bare limbs and their frocks tucked up into waist-cloths.
> I replied that I was bound for Vaapuru.
> 'It is a long distance. Come and sleep here.'
> This was charming, but I refused, and continued along my path, which led me past a house. In the door-way sat a man, who called out:
> 'Haere moi toto!' ('Come and sleep!') . . .

So Calderon spent the night there, and found the girls who had spoken to him in the darkness; and of one of them, Marae, he made one of the delightful drawings which illustrate his character studies. Amaru, another of his hosts, became his friend. Through him he became more closely in touch with the nature of the people and their ways. He finds a correspondence between them and the people and ways in the *Odyssey*, where the poet is careful to describe the management of the most trivial artifices:

> Amaru's life is one long poem of this kind. Everything he does he does from the beginning, and so do all his unsophisticated countrymen. This is, indeed, the greatest difference between the child of nature and the 'civilised man', however near the civilised man may seem to come to nature. You cannot be a child of nature and a lover of art or anything else; a cultured person; there is no time. It is an exclusive occupation to be a child of nature.

It takes most of the morning to make the coffee for breakfast; wood has to be gathered, for the wood-pile has not yet been invented in Tahiti:

> Life would lose its savour for Amaru if he had a wood-pile. It is a real pleasure to him to find the wood for the fire each time; he grins good-humouredly as he returns trailing a long, crooked, dead branch after him; the children look pleased; his wife comes out and grins at the door . . . All look pleased. There is no pleasure in getting a log off a pile.

It is in such a little thing that the secret of the island is revealed; the way they live from day to day, rather, from hour to hour. The inefficiency of the method is, of course, appalling; it irritates some people into writing books and making lectures on 'The Backward Races', in order to get them to manufacture something, no matter what; for a nation without exports cannot be considered civilized. It is only too easy to be sentimental about the 'noble savage', and on the other hand, most people despise the white man who yields to the seductions of the islands.

Here, as in many other matters, Calderon sees the essential clearly enough, 'Work is the gospel of northern climates ... Our energy is called out by hard conditions.' The typical beauty of northern vegetation, he says, is patience. 'The twisted thorn is green and flowering, the stunted furze-bush is crowned with gold ... The beauty of the other is luxuriance, unfitted to meet with hardships, unresisting and prolific. So likewise the nature of the people: they blossom. Then we come with our winter-crabbed, tough natures and they fall an easy prey ... *We try to stimulate the northern struggle in places where it is impossible.*' Like a man walking with a lantern, the Northerner dispels the obscurity in which happiness may flourish; it wilts at his approach. He is suspicious of the lotus-scented dusk, fearing that anything so pleasurable must conceal a snare. It is too late to embark for Cytherea. It was always too late.

THE NEW BEDLAM

The Experiences of an Asylum Patient. Introduction and Notes by Montague Lomax, M.R.C.S. (Allen and Unwin)

The subject of these experiences voluntarily entered an asylum, as a paying patient, in 1900, because her brother, a medical man, had told her that this would be just the place in which to recover her nervous equilibrium, lately upset by her husband's death in tragic circumstances. A few weeks later, without her knowledge, she was certified insane by a magistrate who had never seen her, on the written evidence of two doctors who had conversed with her in the grounds of the asylum for less than half-an-hour. This so-called medical evidence is not only inconclusive but frivolous, and would not have served to convict in a case of petty theft, yet on the strength of it she was confined in mad-houses for twelve years, and would have been there now except for her extraordinary importunity in demanding an examination by an independent mental specialist. The evidence of the two examining doctors is frivolous as it stands because there is no check on it, even the questions which elicited from her the most salient of the remarks which, in this expert opinion, indicated insanity, are not recorded, nor are her replies given verbatim, and when this is not the case it is so easy and natural unconsciously to twist their significance. Even then it is obvious that the interview was farcical, for what is a lady, admittedly unwell, to say when she is accosted by two strange men who question her as to her desire to live? 'As the doctors continued to press me on the subject, I said I had sometimes thought there was not much use in my living.' One sees at once the procedure by which a person can be proved insane. The test gives the appearance of validity to a judgement which has already been passed. The alleged lunatic was not examined personally by the magistrate (as everyone by this time was convinced that she was insane her evidence would not have appeared trustworthy), nor was the doctor's evidence given on oath. There is no doubt that the lady could have explained away all that evidence against her had she been allowed the opportunity. But an alleged drunkard has only to stumble over a stone to condemn himself for ever, and all his remonstrances will only involve him more deeply in the spectator's certainty. It is worse to be called an idiot; the more one attempts to convince people to the contrary, the more pitiful they become: 'The poor thing doesn't even *know* he's mad,' they say.

There is, then, an obvious flaw in the Lunacy Act, since it does not prohibit a person from being confined for twelve years on the strength of a twenty minutes' conversation with two doctors, and this flaw is the section which provides for summary certification if the evidence of the person's insanity is beyond doubt. *In all other cases* there is to be a sort of trial, where evidence must be taken on oath and where the alleged lunatic may be present, or represented, in order to defend his mental integrity. The summary treatment permitted in certain circumstances is bound to lead to abuse so long as the ordinary man retains his uncritical belief in the infallibility of professional opinion; the only real safeguard is to abolish it altogether.

The Lunacy Act is a well-intentioned piece of work, and provides that, in case any person has been unreasonably confined, patients may send a petition in a sealed cover to the Lord Chancellor stating their grievances, and notices to this effect are to be exhibited in each ward. Consequently, the Lord Chancellor's office is flooded by protestations from lunatics who are convinced that they are sane, or it would be if a certain amount of censoring of these 'sealed' petitions did not take place in the institution itself. In any case, how discriminate between the genuine and the specious complaint? Theoretically, by an exhaustive examination of the allegations; actually, since the petitioner is a patient in a lunatic asylum, by an elastic theory of delusions. The other safeguard, that of Visiting Commissioners, presents the same vicious circle of argument, the doctor says the poor thing is mad and all this protestation must emanate from the overheated brain.

If the patient, whose carefully circumstantial evidence throws discrepancies into relief, had kept her mouth shut about the brutal treatment she received and saw inflicted on others, there is no doubt that she would have regained her liberty much sooner. It was only when she was removed to a kindlier asylum, where the authorities were not so interested in her silence, that she was allowed to be examined by the late Sir George Savage and another specialist, who testified to her sanity and secured her release. Yet these 'delusions' as to her brutal treatment persisted, which is contrary to the symptoms of temporary insanity, so unless she is still insane, she must be lying or speaking the truth, or part of the truth. The first hypothesis is disposed of pretty thoroughly, not only by the specialist's testimony, but by every word of her narrative and by her subsequent life, in which she has managed her own business affairs and taken certificates in nursing and midwifery. She has names and dates for many of the acts of brutality, and has done her best to force a public inquiry into the truth of her allegations – 'too horrible to be believed'. This seems an inadequate excuse for withholding an inquiry, especially as anyone who has penetrated further into an asylum than its pretty, cheerful visitor's rooms will recognize in her statements certain plausibilities.

It is always dangerous to relegate personal responsibility to a system, and the modern man has done it more completely with regard to his mentally defectives than to any other type, not excepting the criminal. The criminal comes out, sooner or later, and his statements are as suspect as the returned lunatic's. The only solution, so far as we can see, would be to combat the tendency towards stricter isolation of the insane. A week in an asylum ward might suffice to drive some people mad. The great number of lunatics makes it difficult to provide the skilled, detailed treatment which should be given to each one, till the present combination of prison and workhouse can be replaced by a mental hospital. And as a step towards this, personal responsibility should not be too easily put aside. It is, at any rate, better to be a little sentimental than to be lazier than a savage and flatter ourselves that a clumsy way of losing sight of the afflicted is a credit to civilization.

WAR AND PEACE

The Fighting Instinct. By Pierre Bovet (Allen and Unwin)

The wonder is that this book was not written long ago. Organized warfare, if not the most important, is at any rate the most obvious phenomenon of social evolution; and if, as the story goes, the proper study of mankind is man, it is strange that at this late date we should still be without conclusions that can claim general acceptance. The anomaly of war among civilized societies has been debated for more than twenty centuries, and in the end there is nothing to show for it all but that gallant yet pathetic piece of empiricism, the Leage of Nations. The whole trouble, of course, is that war has almost invariably been treated as an ethical problem, the psychological basis of which was so simple that it could be taken for granted. Both pacifists and apologists for war start upon the assumption that war is simply a manifestation of the primitive fighting instinct and join issue only on the question whether it is a phase in social evolution or an integral part of human activity. When conclusions are in dispute it is usually advisable to inquire into the premisses, and that is what M. Bovet does with notable results. He finds reason to believe that the relation of organized war to the fighting instinct is much less direct and far more complex than is generally supposed. It would, perhaps, be correct to say that he regards modern warfare as not so much a manifestation but a derivative of the primitive fighting instinct, and rather a remote derivative.

M. Bovet, as director of the Jean-Jacques Rousseau Institute of

Geneva, examines the problem from the standpoint of an educational psychologist. As fighting is one of the principal occupations of childhood it is possible to study the instinct in its most primitive manifestations. Now the most prominent feature of fighting among children, as among the lower animals, is its immediate and strictly personal quality. It is an explosive activity of the 'psyche' that finds its natural satisfaction in relation to another individual. As the child grows older the instinct does not weaken – rather it grows in strength – but under social influences it is gradually diverted into socially useful channels. In the team games, like cricket and football, the boy learns, not to suppress his instinct for aggression, but to socialize it. Whether this process is continued in adult life is open to question. In some careers, such as the Services and certain of the professions, it is; but in others, where the ideal of 'success' rules, there would seem to be a regress towards a manifestation of the fighting instinct that is not far removed from primitive pugnacity.

When we turn to modern warfare we are confronted with a paradox. In the Great War what irked the citizen-soldier most? Undoubtedly the military discipline which forbade him to pit himself against the men with whom he was placed in personal contact. The team spirit is inculcated to the last degree, and at the same time the conditions of modern warfare reduce the adversary to complete impersonality. Consider the work of a battery of heavy artillery monotonously firing round after round at an enemy that is not a live reality in front of them, but a mere direction so many degrees from a point in their rear. It would be hard to imagine a less bellicose exercise. It is quite true that war affords many opportunities for displays of pugnacity on the part of individuals, but they are isolated and exceptional.

Broadly speaking, it is only at G.H.Q. that war is experienced as a continuous contest with a human adversary. The enemies that the ordinary soldier has to contend with are death, danger, difficulty, and privation – formidable certainly, but not at all peculiar to war. They demand courage, endurance, self-sacrifice, and resource, which are derivatives of the fighting instinct, but not pugnacity, which is the fighting instinct in its most primitive manifestation. Against impersonal forces mere pugnacity is simply irrelevant, as it is in the case of Ajax, the perfect type of the purely pugnacious soldier.

But Ajax is the exception. One of M. Bovet's most illuminating chapters is that in which he shows that it is the least pugnacious type of man who is most attracted by the profession of arms. To him the Army is as the cloister to the monk, a refuge from the dangers, the uncertainties, the responsibilities, the incessant strivings of man against man, that are the lot of the civilian. He reads the aphorism *Si via pacem para bellum* in a special sense.

The influence of the professional soldier in bringing about wars may therefore be discounted. It is the community in whose hands he is merely a weapon that must bear the responsibility. Here lies the problem. Civilization means that society has reached a state in which the fighting instinct is deflected, canalized, sublimated towards peaceful ends, and individuals are strictly subject to the rule of law. Why, then, should societies composed of peaceable individuals break out into periodic orgies of collective bloodshed and destruction? One theory is that societies, like even the best regulated individual, occasionally 'see red', but to this there is, among others, the objection that it assumes in the fullest sense the hypothesis of the 'group mind'. The explanation of collective pugnacity must be sought elsewhere. M. Bovet apparently does not feel himself in a position to give one, though he gives some useful pointers. For example, he emphasizes William James's observation that war is a mere episode in international conflict – 'that the intensely sharp competitive *preparation* for war by the nations *is the real war*, permanent, unceasing, and that the battles are only a sort of public verification of the mastery gained during the "peace" interval'. One might describe international rivalries as cases of 'imperfectly deflected' pugnacity. There is no desire for bloodshed in the conflict, but bloodshed is a necessary incident, however regrettable. German *Realpolitik* had a glimmering of James's notion when it formulated the doctrine that war is but a continuation of peace policy by different means.

M. Bovet's conclusion is that a scientific study of the fighting instinct gives no warrant for the view that war must be a permanent phenomenon of human history. Private war has disappeared among civilized peoples, and there is no reason to suppose that public war also may not in time be eliminated. But, though he reviews the question sympathetically, he thinks 'pacifist' education of individuals is of little account. He suggests instead 'a programme of political education rendering effective the control of the anti-social tendencies of the governing classes by the democratic masses' – which is, surely, self-contradictory?

THE REAL CYRANO

Voyages to the Moon and the Sun. By Cyrano de Bergerac. Translated by Richard Aldington (Routledge)

We are glad to meet Cyrano at last, even though he be shorn of most of the trappings with which Rostand endeared him to the romantic multitude. But when his nose has been reduced to credible proportions, the privileges of nobility withdrawn, and the real cause of his quixotic courtship and abstemious living made apparent, a something remains which is still very far from trite; a personality whose career was picturesque and whose intelligence exalted. These Voyages, though it cannot be said that they are as fresh as when they were first written, are still very much alive and likely to retain their interest for an indefinable period. This perennial attraction is due not so much to his fantastic invention, nor to his anticipation of modern mechanical devices, like the gramophone, or of vegetarianism, as to the freedom of his intellect from the prejudices which in one form or another are a continual menace to the cultivation of a reasonable life. This emancipation is evidently a thing of the personality and has nothing whatever to do with literary achievement. We are as likely to find it in a farm labourer's cottage as in a university common room. It is something which cannot be taught nor acquired with the most assiduous practice, and those who learn a few parrot-cries of revolt, in a few years appear merely ridiculous.

'The Comical History of the States and Empires of the Worlds of the Moon and Sun' (so runs the title page of the incomplete translation of 1687) was not intended as a romance of Utopia. Mr. Aldington points this out in his entertaining and informative Preface, and it was important to do so, for nearly all the point of the recitals is lost if their satiric purpose is ignored. The parallel is not between the 'Voyages' and 'News from Nowhere', but with 'Gulliver's Travels'; Swift, in fact, did Cyrano the honour of borrowing from him. In the middle of the seventeenth century, when these tales were written, the Church exercised a very stringent censorship on printed literature, and all kinds of powerful and non-religious interests were vested in it. Even a hundred years later, it will be remembered, Helvétius's *De l'Esprit* was condemned to the stake, and in Cyrano's time the philosopher might quite well have been consumed along with his book.

Cyrano had gained a reputation for impiety with his play, *The Death of Agrippina*, but the 'Voyages' contain much more dangerous attacks on established religion. Neither was printed until after the author's death, and even then a considerable proportion of the most daring satire was omitted. Mr. Aldington has taken advantage of recently discovered manuscripts of 'Voyage to the Moon', with the result that his translation is the most complete in this language, and contains material lacking in the two most widely circulated French editions.

The signs of wear and tear are most apparent in Cyrano's chemistry and physics; he was obsessed with these sciences, but his ingenious speculations are too distant from the well-organized knowledge of the present day to be of interest. In general ideas, unfortunately, we cannot claim the same undoubted progress. In 'Voyage to the Moon' he gets his satiric effect by making the inhabitants of our satellite treat their visitor as an animal and shut him up in a cage with a Spaniard who had left the earth because he could find no country where even the imagination was free. This, no doubt, was Cyrano's own reason for evading the earth, but even when in the moon he does not indulge in any poetic fancies; he is fighting all the time his terrestrial opponents. Religion was only one of his foes. There are some remarks on the royal and ancient sport of war which yield nothing to more recent invective. He had some insight too into herd psychology. During Cyrano's trial in the moon the Great Pontiff spoke against him:

> in declaiming he made use of an instrument whose noise deafened me; it was a trumpet which he had chosen on purpose so that the violence of its martial tone should heat up their minds for my death, and by this emotion prevent reason from performing its office; as in our own armies, where the clamour of trumpets and drums prevents the soldier from reflecting on the importance of his life.

Cyrano belongs to a type of writer who forms what Mr. Aldington very well calls the 'heterodox tradition' in French literature. They are the men who have built up and propagated the great impulse of scepticism. They are all, from Montaigne and Rabelais to Voltaire and Anatole France, moved by the desire to 'live freely', a phrase which Cyrano himself uses somewhere. At its best it expresses in satire and criticism its distrust of institutions and the relativity of dogmas. At its worst it ends in a positivism as bigoted as any superstition. The desire for assurance, for measurements, and explanations is seen in Cyrano's elaborate physical reasonings, which undoubtedly helped to pave the way to the rationality of modern science. He delights in tremendous discussions, and if they are preposterous he likes it the better. Yet even in so wild an argument as that of the submission of parents to their children he never quite forgets that he is a Frenchman; and if it were not the most certain thing in the world that we shall ourselves be old one day, it would be easier to appreciate the justice of his attack on the present convention of waiting for dead men's shoes.

His denial of the spirituality of the soul is accomplished neatly and its consequences received with mock horror: 'They maintain that this soul, which can only act imperfectly when it has lost one of its tools in the course of life, can work perfectly when it has lost them all after our death.' It is the moon-dweller, of course, who says this, and when Cyrano talks to him of the resurrection he cries: 'Hey! Faith! who has deluded you with that fairy-tale? What! You? What! I? What! My maid-servant be resurrected?' Cyrano assumes the features of strictest orthodoxy: 'This is not an amusing tale, it is an indubitable truth which I will prove to you.' 'And I,' the moon-dweller replied, 'will prove to you the contrary. To begin with, suppose you ate a Mohammedan' – and so on through those dialectical ingenuities which are tedious to read now, but expressions of some courageousness when they were written.

The 'Voyage to the Sun' is more elaborately divided than that to the moon, and, though it has passages of admirable force and clarity, like the 'Pleading made in the Parliament of Birds against an Animal accused of being a Man', it is not so wholly effective as its predecessor. In the later work, however, Cyrano permits his luxuriant fancy to function more freely, so that this voyage is the more picturesque: it contains some quite poetical descriptions. The style of Cyrano is virile, but not in general bizarre, and the problem before the translator was how to keep it alive in the transference. In this Mr. Aldington has succeeded admirably, and if the interest flags in certain places it is not from any fault of his. He has given us a volume which should hold a place by right among our translations, for we have no writer to replace Cyrano. Even Swift, though he is so much the greater man, does not include him. Henceforward the reader of Swift will be compelled to look into Cyrano, and then he will find beneath the fantastic exterior a reasonable and generous soul.

BAUDELAIRE: A REAPPRAISAL

Baudelaire: L'Homme et le Poète. By Pierre Flottes (Paris: Perrin)

If the French Academy were to encourage posthumous canonization, as tacitly it must when contemporary judgement has been glaringly at fault, there can be little doubt that Baudelaire would now honour the fauteuil he tentatively solicited in his lifetime. Yet, only thirty years ago, when certain men of letters were about to raise a monument to the poet, Ferdinand Brunetière, then the doyen of orthodox critics, 'spread himself in imprecations'. Since then university opinion has evolved till it has achieved the expression of what M. Flottes describes as a 'courteous neutrality'. The poets themselves, of course, never denied Baudelaire warm appreciation, but the larger public has not greatly modified its first shocked reaction to *Les Fleurs du Mal.* In 1861 the Academy (with a few exceptions of which Alfred de Vigny is the most notable) regarded his candidature to the vacant seat of Lacordaire both as an impertinence and an outrage to its honourable body. The supreme achievement of *Les Fleurs du Mal* has, however, been vindicated at the expense of a score of forgotten Academicians; and M. Flotte's study of man and poet, inscribed to the present Head of the Ecole Normale, Professor Lanson, himself a keen critic of Baudelaire, seems to indicate that in time even official approbation may erase the legendary stain which obscures a finer understanding of the poet's work.

Research has shown that the poet suffered from gross misrepresentation even in his lifetime. With ill-simulated aloofness he relates that a woman once said to him: '*C'est singulier, vous êtes fort convenable. Je croyais que vous étiez toujours ivre et que vous sentiez mauvais!* Elle parlait d'après la légende.' The legend was a loan drawn on fame during his early years of dandyism in Paris; but the above extraordinary inversion of it betrays scurrilous

gossipers, unless we can attribute it to an almost incredible mis-
understanding of his 'déshabillé le plus habillé du monde'. This
advance of notoriety exacted, like his money debts, a cruel and, in
most cases, dishonest interest throughout his life. Long after he had
ceased to manipulate his bogey-self in the desire to horrify the
bourgeois, it continued its gesticulations. It assumed a life beyond
his control and became an intolerable monster dragging its begetter
along its miry passage through the imaginations of his friends:

> . . . c'est Galatée aveuglant Pygmalion!
> Impossible de modifier cette situation.

Even, indeed, he complicated his position towards the world, in
exasperation bespattering the vile back, playing hysterical jokes with
his own reputation:—

> J'ai passé ici [in Belgium] pour *agent de police*, . . . ensuite, j'ai passé
> pour un *correcteur d'épreuves*, envoyé de Paris pour corriger les épreuves
> d'ouvrages infâmes. *Exaspéré d'être toujours cru* j'ai répandu le bruit
> que j'avais *tué* mon père et que je l'avais mangé; . . . ET ON M'A CRU . . .
> Je nage dans le déshonneur, comme un poisson dans l'eau.

M. Flottes guards against the present tendency to base criticism
of the poetical work on the revelations of the intimate diaries and
letters. The discovery of a philosophical Baudelaire who elevated
the conception of the dandy to that of a hero of modern civilization opened such amazing prospects that it is not surprising the
poet has been for a moment submerged by the thinker – more
especially since criticism of the poet as pure artist has become
stereotyped, and most critics in this country have been content with
minor variations on Swinburne's eulogies.

Though the deductions drawn from the *Journaux Intimes*, which
were composed some years after the greater number of the poems,
will give a true result when applied to this earlier work because of
the remarkable homogeneity of Baudelaire's production – which
formed the basis of an article in the *Literary Supplement* dated
April 7, 1921 – it is a correspondence which does not elucidate the
fundamental problem of the poetry. The later notebooks are the
translation into ethical terms of the temperament which had already
created *Les Fleurs du Mal*, and, as is usual in translations, the
aesthetic quality of the original is only intermittently conveyed.

Baudelaire's tragedy was that of a man who begins life with many rich and brilliant acquaintances, whom he welcomes proudly, though with their continued visits he begins to long for less exacting guests. When his health became bankrupt he could not receive these flocking sensations worthily, and a feeling of shame embittered his still unbroken pride. In sober terms, his nervous energy gained in excess of his functional capacity, and so the seduction of his poetry is not principally sensuous but nostalgic. He continually sought an ideal condition in which, without abnegating his sensations, he might be freed from his torment of continual aloofness from them. 'The beauty to which he aspires is an object not solely of enjoyment,' M. Flottes writes, 'but of a recondite aesthetic meditation in which the intellect has regained its dominion over the senses.' His sense of the importunity of sensual excitement when the mind is in the more exalted state is expressed symbolically here as in many other poems:

> Et son ventre et ses seins, ces grappes de ma vigne,
> S'avançaient plus câlins que les anges du mal,
> Pour troubler le repos où mon âme était mise,
> Et pour la déranger du rocher du cristal,
> Où calme et solitaire elle s'était assise.

It is one of the marks of his greatness that the sensation with him never remained a mere irritation of the epidermis, and M. Flottes does not, unfortunately, expose the difference between Baudelaire's

> Et le ver rongera ta peau, comme un remords

and Gautier's line, which is said to have suggested it:

> Oui, mais le ver un jour rongera ton œil creux.

That is one of the crudest examples of the difference on which the superiority of Baudelaire's aesthetic is based. His finest effects are not imitations of the plastic arts, as Gautier's preface to *Les Fleurs du Mal* rather persuades the unwary reader.

> De longs corbillards sans tambours ni musique

can only be fully appreciated as a symbol, one in a series which evokes a complex sense of the absence of desire, or, in other instances, of the loss of that which was desired, such as only the literary arts can express in such lines as:

> Les cocotiers absents de la superbe Afrique.

and

> Je pense aux matelots oubliés dans une île.

which no plastic art can represent.

It is in his immense power of absorption, which only the greatest artists have had in his degree, that his strength lies. 'Sa limite est dans les bornes même de sa personnalité, qu'il n'a osé jamais franchir', concludes M. Flottes, naming as a shortcoming that which we recognize as the distinctive virtue no less of Shakespeare than of Herrick. To be able to absorb in the products of one's own senses the extra-sensual emotions with which, as human beings, we are both burdened and endowed, is the peculiar function of the artist, and it is on the complications of the personality that the richness and variety of the achievement depend. 'His art', says M. Flottes, 'is one which only Victor Hugo and Leconte de Lisle can equal, without surpassing.' It is almost morbid to cavil at such a magnificent testimony, yet it is one which may still be subjected to revision.

HUYSMANS

Saint Lydwine of Schiedam. By J. K. Huysmans (Kegan Paul)

Though not one of the more important of Huysmans' books *Saint Lydwine* holds an interesting position. In it the primary Naturalist and the imposed Catholic have come full circle and realism and mysticism join hands in a common abnegation of reason. 'Huysmans is an eye,' said Rémy de Gourmont, and might have added the four other senses in varying degrees. It is, in effect, the impression of a sensual alertness one receives from his books, of a sensitiveness oppressed and exacerbated by the world of gross vulgarity. His progress as a writer and as a moral being was determined by the search for a form which would more clearly allow the expression of his personality.

There is little resemblance to the novel in his mature works. They are the record of the passage through certain states of sensibility and only objectified so far as to make a presentable whole. His development consists in the rejection, first of the naturalist formula, which confined him to the normal and the impersonal, and later, of the philosophical parent of naturalism, positive science, which reduced him to a phenomenon of infinite banality. The only way in which he could regain the very necessary sense of an individual significance was by rehabilitating the theological ethic and metaphysic. It was also, no doubt, an effective way of putting out his tongue at the respectable infidelity of his century. There need be no question of his sincerity; but the old Adam was hard to kill, and it is the brusque reappearance of this harsh and arrogant but finely perceptive egoist which make the later works of edification readable from no such pietistic point of view. It is a very old friend who says in *Saint Lydwine*, 'Faith seemed expiring, and was destined, after dragging on for two centuries, to perish in that sewer disinterred by Paganism, and known as the Renaissance.'

At the conclusion of the saint's incredible biography, he says, that it will 'no doubt rejoice the pious and distress the numerous Catholics who, in weakness of faith or in ignorance, would relegate the mystic to the lunatic asylum, and the miracles to the region of superstition and legend. For these the expurgated biographies of the Jansenites [sic] would suffice, if they had not at the present time a whole school of hagiographers ready to satisfy their hatred of the supernatural by fabricating histories of Saints confined to this earth and forbidden to escape from it; of Saints who are not Saints.' The same voice speaks, through des Esseintes, of the Church which 'is suspicious of men of talent, like Veuillot or Hello, because they don't seem subservient enough, or dull enough'. Huysmans was to be, in his turn, an equally embarrassing champion of the Faith.

His own early books were like those expurgated biographies of which he speaks; the supernatural (or abnormal) was strictly excluded and the *roman type* of this period, *A Vau l'Eau*, recounts the embarrassments of a little bureaucrat in assuring himself a tolerable dinner; only the distinctive tang which clings to anything Huysmans wrote makes it tolerable. At the same time he suffered ferociously from being 'confined to this earth and forbidden to escape from it'. The little jumps he had attempted in his prose poems did not carry him very far, and it was not till *A Rebours* that he spread his wings and soared out of the clutch of Zola. In that precious and fantastic volume he attempts to escape through the refinement of the sensibility, but des Esseintes, shut up on the outskirts of Paris with his Moreau's and Redon's, his scent-organ and unique poets, naturally overtaxes his nerves and is obliged to return to the miserable deceptions of ordinary life. In *Là-Bas*, the

successor, Huysmans, now and henceforward identified as the
character Durtal, plunges into the unnatural, and the book is a
skilfully woven tissue, which recounts the atrocities of Gilles de
Rais, a type of Bluebeard, and the author's adventure with a woman,
who is a religious pervert, and introduces him to a celebration of the
Black Mass. This is the ripest of his books, the plumpest fruit of
his inquisitive and greedy palate, and contains some most delicate
renderings of those moods of absolute boredom peculiar to the
condition of stagnation his mind had then reached. If some depravity of his mistress or curious acquisition of knowledge seems to
tear its velvet surface, it is only to reveal for a moment the black
hopelessness beneath.

En Route records the reaction set up by his disgust at his experience of anti-Christianity; as the title implies, he is moving
towards a return to the Catholic Church. The exquisite analysis of
his sensations is carried here to its finest degree because there is
little external action to interrupt the mental development, which is
its entire interest. In *La Cathédrale* the sensibility is petrified into
a magnificent but inanimate form. His culinary fastidiousness is
still active and his curiosity delights in the religious symbolism of
flowers and gems, and his gross Flemish sensuality in the odours
of sanctity and of the malevolent one; but he is a servant of the
Church and that is not without its effect.

Barbey d'Aurevilly, reviewing *A Rebours*, said that the author
must choose between the mouth of a pistol and the foot of the
cross. He had previously offered Baudelaire the alternative of
blowing out his brains or becoming a Christian. The poet did not
accept the limitation, Huysmans did. *Saint Lydwine* shows the
supreme humiliation of his reason and the triumph of faith.

Lydwine, a Flemish girl of poor parents, who lived in the fourteenth century, was ordained to be a receptacle of pain, what is
known technically as a 'saint of reparation', suffering the torments
of those too weak to bear their own. At the age of fifteen she was
courted for her charming appearance, but she already knew that
she must vow her virginity to Christ. Her fear of her beautiful
body ('which was destined to become, before burial, something
monstrous and without form') is typical of the mediaeval theology,
which still sends out blanched and subterranean shoots. She was
glad when she became ugly 'and implored God to help her to love
Him alone'. Here follows a typical passage:

Then He began to cultivate her, to root out all thoughts that could displease Him, to hoe her soul, to rake it till the blood flowed. And He did more; for as if to attest the justice of the saying of St. Hildegarde, at once so terrible and consoling: 'God dwells not in bodies that are whole,' He attacked her health. This young and charming body with which He had clothed her seemed suddenly irksome to Him, and He cut it in all directions, that He might better seize and mould the soul it contained.

The fascination of Huysmans' style is in its fecundity of metaphor; though he is an adept of the art of pure plastic representation, he is most distinctively himself in this squeezing out of the juice of words. He pounds them in the mortar of his rich memory with hungry sensationism, and he is not content till, crushed between the two terms of the comparison, the pungent aroma of his meaning is disengaged.

A limited number of themes are continually cropping up, elaborated or reduced, in his successive works, and *Saint Lydwine* is in a sense a development and sublimation of the charming chapter on flowers in *A Rebours*. Here he assembled the most outrageous productions of nature, imitating, in their foliage and blossoms, flesh gnawed by disease, speckled with the rash of an hereditary taint. The body of Lydwine is such a flower, the real climax to that chapter. She was afflicted with every conceivable disease, except leprosy, as that would have entailed her segregation, and for thirty years lived in a condition of such unequalled misery that her mere existence proved the divine origin of her torments. Her spiritual exultations were of corresponding intensity and she was on several occasions rapt into Paradise and on others her Heavenly Spouse communicated with her in person. 'The sum of her maladies continued to overwhelm her and she was attacked by a furious recrudescence of disease. Her stomach finally burst like a ripe fruit, and they had to apply a woollen cushion to press back her entrails and prevent them from leaving her body.' But she still lived.

Huysmans is not a tepid hagiographer; once he believed he stopped at nothing and delighted to drag into the light evidence of the Divine Justice, which more responsible spokesmen might prefer, in concession to modern criticism, to leave in obscurity. Huysmans despised modern criticism, and his books are the debris of his hatred. *Saint Lydwine* is only less interesting than some of them because the subject is not the man himself. When he has himself for subject he is superb and in some degree anticipates Proust, especially in his analysis of ill-defined states of emotion. It is curious, too, that in spite, perhaps because of, his intense revulsion from the modern, he is through Baudelaire and Guys the authentic 'peintre de la vie moderne'. He would have been shocked by the younger generation's excessive veneration of modernity, and he might not have quite appreciated their cosmopolitanism, but it was he who encouraged them to exploit the fantastic brutality of *fin de siècle* Paris.

JULES LAFORGUE 1860–1887

The accidental resemblances between Laforgue and Keats, each of whom behind the public back gave poetry a wrench from the prevailing rhetoric, are as remarkable as their profounder differences. The same consuming fever burnt in their veins so that neither reached his twenty-seventh birthday, though Laforgue died within two days of it. Both were minions of the moon, and Keats, moved by the desire of her 'argent luxuries' came nearer than he could consciously have thought to the later poet's:

O pilule des léthargies finales . . .

but the telescope and sixty years of science lie between them. A comparison of the two poets ought not to be based on such a distinction, to which aesthetic standards are indifferent, but in passing, it may be suggested that the superior mastery of Keats is due to his use of legendary or absorbed material as the vehicle of his emotion; his currency is easily acceptable, but Laforgue pays us in the coin of a daring, not-yet-established, speculator.

Everybody will remember Keats's affectionate letters to his sister away at boarding-school. The young Laforgue, poor and alone in Paris, had a sister in the provinces to whom he recounted the events and petty incidents of his life. Affection sweeps away his reserve, and his sentimentality is unabashed by its own excess – that sentimentality which is a clue to the labyrinth of his monstrous philosophy. 'My father was hard from timidity,' he said, and the son was hard on life for the same reason. He was maidenly sensitive at heart, 'un bon, loyal, et délicat garçon'. He stood apart

from his contemporaries by the characteristic restraint of his cos-
tume and sobriety of manner; his correctness was even 'un peu
clergyman', as a friend has remarked. Something of a Hamlet
perhaps, dragging his indecision through all the foggy coasts of the
modern intelligence. A Hamlet dismayed by the spectre his curiosity has raised, which lays on him the awful charge of preaching
the new gospel, 'the book of prophecies which will empty all
cities' – for that is what one comes to who has understood the
Madrepore and in whose head floats the moon, magic mirror in
which earth may scan her future face.

But he shrank from the predicatory manner, which at that time
could only have seemed an absurd travesty of the apocalyptic Hugo,
whose spirit still swayed the crowds from its island pulpit . . . The
King and Queen, the modern audience, he must slink around and
catch their conscience at its secret play. His message, the certainty
of ultimate desolation, has had its prophets stoned before now; it
was a pill to be gilded with fictions; a tragedy played by a clown.
Besides, the ghost may be simply an emanation from his own
brain and in any case '*Let us console one another*' cries the incor-
rigible sentimentalist. He clutches at every trivial bough on his
precipitous journey, for the trivial, the snatch of song that rises to
the lips is perhaps the only sign that he is not fettered by that
ghostly injunction, that the pathway to the Ideal is not after all a
cul-de-sac with the Moon's dead pierrot-face leering at the bottom.
Since love is the most trivial and the most mysterious of journeys
he serenades (with brief and sometimes disconcerting analyses) the
Ophelia of the eighties, devout and sentimental, practising her tinkling piano-pieces in the hush of cosmic melodrama. He knows that
only the trick perfected, the sincere gesture become a habit, weaves
the osier-cage for the mind; and he imitates the acrobat, who seems
to bungle a turn that inferior skill, dominated by reflexes, could not
avoid carrying through. That is as far as his verse technique goes,
but it is a good distance. Mallarmé, after speaking of M. de Rég-
nier's discreet tinkering with the alexandrine, says:

> Autre chose, ou simplement le contraire, se décéle une mutinerie
> exprès, en la vacance du vieux moule fatigué, quand Jules Laforgue,
> pour le début, nous initia au charme certain du vers faux.

Even if the mind does not imprison itself, the chances are that it is
already a captive, the caged lion in the circus procession of the

Unconscious, roaring imperial threats as it is drawn to a servile destiny; ignorant even of the next town at which it must perform.

> Je m'agite aussi! mais l'Inconscient me mène;
> Or, il sait ce qu'il fait, je n'ai rien à y voir.

It was fitting, though hardly to be expected in our exigent democracies, that Hamlet, poor amateur of letters, should go to Court. By a rare jest of the sullen Fates (who withheld their laughter for five years) he was saved from his penurious existence in Paris by a friend who secured him the post of Reader to the Empress Augusta of Germany, grandmother of the last Kaiser. He was scarcely happy there; the loneliness of exile was harsh to the man (boy, rather) for whom every paving-stone he trod was saturated with sentiment – and this with no mawkishness. But the position meant comfort, leisure and access to books; and broadened him besides. He was compelled to cast wider nets, to overhaul his previous catches for mediocre specimens, provincialisms and the like. The rich food at first choked him, but for consolation he wrote whimsical letters to his sister. There is something heroic in the way he faced the unknown horrors of a Court – as though Kipps had sauntered on to the stage during Grand Opera, but horrors none the less real, to a nervous man, for being operatic. 'Do watch me,' he laughed to his sister, 'mounting the broad white staircases.' Actually he met with nothing but kindness in an atmosphere of rather Victorian domesticity. An evening he describes in the Empress's apartments – the first time he exercised his functions as Reader – there were, round a table, the Empress, her lady-in-waiting, two princes and four young princesses. The princes were turning over some picture books, the girls doing embroidery, the Empress painting in water-colour. Laforgue, who confesses his nervousness, began to read and regained that self-possession and exquisite urbanity which struck M. Bourget, for almost immediately he came to a passage a little indelicate, and skipped it without turning a hair.

The next five years, almost the whole of his adult life, were passed in a state of tremendous intellectual activity, in which his sensibility was continually getting the better of his reason, strive against it as he might. The debris of this combat, is gathered in the 'Mélanges Posthumes'; exquisite fragments of an adolescent philosophy quite invalid as they stand, but by some miracle of art moulded into perfect symmetry in the 'Moralités Légendaires'.

Among his aphorisms we find:

Nous supportons tout le travail de la planète depuis l'histoire. Ce travail nécessairement est stupide et boite, *parce que la femme n'y prend pas part*. Avec la Femme nous avons jusqu'ici joué à la poupée. Voilà trop longtemps que ça dure!...

O jeunes filles, quand serez-vous nos frères, nos frères intimes sans arrière-pensée d'exploitation! Quand nous donnerons-nous la vraie poignée de main!...

Nothing could be more revealing of the delicacy of his character than the spontaneous loyalty of the last phrase.

His philosophical efforts made him an admirable gymnast, but it must have been as a writer of social comedy that he would have excelled; a comedy more purely subjective, more nearly lyrical, though lacking nothing in wit, than we have ever had.

The reign of the philosopher was brief; his overthrow, by an English governess, a Miss Leah Lee, (from whom Laforgue was taking lessons in English pronunciation) swift and final. At a bound he broke clear of the seductive thicket of generalizations and abandoned himself to the path of simple feeling, tormented by this affection which his fastidious propriety obliged him to conceal. 'I know that many women do not disdain sudden declarations, but for the world,' he told his sister, 'I would not have said a word, nor even looked her in the face but after months and months of loyal and delicate devotion.'

When, at last, they were engaged he wrote to his sister (telling her everything with the shamelessness of the very innocent): 'I have not yet embraced her but last evening we were riding together in a carriage and the idea came to me that I might caress her hair – and it made me giddy, and I have not yet gone so far – far from that.' And again, 'Since the day before yesterday [the date of his engagement] my life has no longer belonged to me alone and I feel all the grandeur of that idea.'

But these two consumptives (for Miss Lee was so, too) were not even to share their lives for long. It was necessary to leave the foggy German capital, so Laforgue resigned his post and followed his fiancée to London, where they were married (in a West Kensington church), on the last day of 1886. They returned to Paris, and lived there for eight months in that brave companionship the poet could hardly have expected to realize.

'It needs a thousand francs a month to be decently comfortable,' he writes, 'we spend 15 a day. Heureusement, le petit personnage que j'ai épousé est d'une vraie santé de maigre, toujours gaie et fantaisiste . . . Je porte des articles çà et là.'

But those articles here and there would have been quite in-effectual without the devotion of a few friends, among whom may be mentioned M. Paul Bourget, Laforgue's senior, if only to give the perspective to our loss. At last he found it impossible even to write and breathing became torture; it was arranged that he should leave Paris for some more suitable climate before the winter. But one night, in the middle of August, his young wife found him dead at her side. She survived him hardly a year.

In the letter before his last, when he rallied sufficient strength to write to his sister, he said, 'It is a long time since you heard any-thing of my literary affairs. It would take too long to go into details but, in a word, I have the right to be proud; there is not a writer of my generation who is promised such a future.'

TRISTAN CORBIÈRE 1845-1875

Corbière is a naked man among his carefully-tailored contem-poraries. Rimbaud and Verlaine do not soften this contrast, for in the clang of metal and tapping of chisels which the Parnassians set up on the eve of their downfall, those two were almost unheard, and more than theirs Corbière's verse lacks the outer garments of sonority and plastic imagery at that time the only wear. In 1873 the critics were no keener than usual to appreciate essentials, and *Les Amours Jaunes* was born in silence and seemed to die in the same silence, not of hostility but of incomprehension.

Ten years later it might have seemed that the thaw had de-finitely set in. The group that gathered round the review *Lutèce*, amorphous though it was, had at least in common among its mem-bers a sort of reverence for other gods than those of ivory and of gold. It was then that the editor of that insurgent review brought a copy of Corbière's neglected volume to Verlaine, who at once appre-ciated the excellence of the poetry that was half-hidden by pieces of 'disjointed rhythm and excessive dandyism'. For all practical pur-poses Verlaine's enthusiastic notice in *Les Poètes Maudits* (1884) marks the birth-date of Corbière's unique volume.

There are a few features of Corbière's life which had an important influence on his work. Some of the best of it is based on his intimate knowledge of the Breton coast and of its people, where he spent the more impressionable years of his short life – he died in his thirtieth year. His reaction to his surroundings was complicated by his sense of a personal repulsiveness – more apparent, probably, to his extreme sensitiveness than to the casual observation of his neighbours. However that may be, it is said to have led him to seek solitude and even death on reckless expeditions in his cutter in the worst weather.

Yet it seems that this period may have been a comparatively happy one; he was not without friends among the sailors and with them his leper's pride (he was crippled by arthritis as well as ugly) is likely to have suffered less humiliation than in the city where he spent the last three or four years of his life.

In Brittany he first became a poet. The group of poems called *Armor* (Armorica being the Latin name of the region) and *Gens de Mer* proclaim the inspiration of his earliest poetry. Brittany, that unassimilated province with its deep Celtic inheritance and long wild coasts where he first achieved his cherished independence, provides all the matter of his earliest known poems. And indeed one of them 'La Rhapsode Foraine et Le Pardon de Sainte-Anne' is the poem most closely associated with his fame.

In its opening stanzas, 'Paysage Mauvais', he sets the scene at once and unforgettably in this country where 'the sand is dust of old bones and the waves fall like the passing bell'. It was a wise economy. Everything hereafter moves in that scenery and there is no need for subsequent description. It is a country whose people are peasants, beggars, wreckers, sailors, and excisemen, and Corbière depicts them swiftly but vividly. Religion is interwoven with their lives, a very immediate religion which salts their daily bread and colours their slang (*grippe-Jésus* stands for gendarme), in which all their hopes and fears are centred.

The Pardon is a popular religious festival which provides him with the material for his most sustained poem. Superficially, 'La Rhapsode Foraine' is a description of the annual pilgrimage to the chapel of Sainte-Anne-de-la-Palud. Actually, it is a realization of the entire lives of these people suspended at the moment of their mystic ecstasy when they drag themselves on their knees three times around the chapel of Saint Anne, and for three days and three

nights implore consolation of her. It is a succession of pictures which
unrolls, and as the last are exposed the unity of the design absorbs
the separate components. To quote is to insist on one aspect of a
many-sided poem (kindly irreverence is not absent), but two stanzas
will illustrate a tenderness which is predominant:

> Fais venir et conserve en joie
>   Ceux à naître et ceux qui sont nés.
> Et verse, sans que Dieu te voie,
>   L'eau de tes yeux sur les damnés!

> Reprends dans leur chemise blanche,
>   Les petits qui sont en langeur.
> Rapelle à l'éternel Dimanche
>   Les vieux qui traînent en longeur.

The impression received most insistently from the various stanzas
of this poem is that of a pitiful understanding, or not to impose
one's own interpretation, a sympathetic understanding of the
meaning of life for those rough Bretons. It enables him to translate
their inarticulate prayers, all the hidden aspirations that wring them
as they bow beneath the wooden image of the divine aunt who is
their only refuge from a hostile or incomprehensible universe, into
a prayer which must remain valid wherever, and so long as, death,
love, birth and hunger retain their brutal significance:

> Prends pitié de la fille-mère,
> Du petit au bord du chemin . . .
> Si quelqu'un leur jette la pierre,
> Que la pierre se change en pain!

> . . . Ton remède de bonne-femme
> Pour les bêtes-à-corne aussi!

> Montre à nos femmes et servantes
> L'ouvrage et la fécondité . . .

Curiously enough, considering the current notion of the poet as a
fanciful creature dwelling in his own world of pleasant hallucinations, it is only those poets who have such a precise sense of the
actual emotional range in the hole and corner which they occupy
who produce work to transcend time and circumstance. All that is
lacking in the fruitless acreage of Millet's 'Angelus' is filled in by
Corbière in the few poems which he writes about the peasantry. He
does the same service to the sailors so unscrupulously employed by
the buccaneering romantics.

This is part of a conversation between a sailor on shore and his sweetheart:

> – Votre navire est-il bon pour la mer lointaine?
> – Ah! pour ça je ne sais pas trop,
> Mademoiselle; c'est l'affaire au capitaine,
> Pas à vous, ni moi matelot.

The whole poem is composed in that tone of quiet, almost prosaic simplicity, but there are others in which the reckless, devil-may-care seaman makes his expected appearance. He would have been false to his subject had he ignored that side of it, but here again his intimate and detailed knowledge produces the necessary illusion of reality. It was this knowledge which brought him a violent contempt for Hugo ('garde-national épique'), to whose 'Oceano Nox', a typically sentimental poem on the fate of those lost at sea, he makes an ungracious but magnificent retort:

> ... Qu'ils roulent infinis dans les espaces vierges! ...
> Qu'ils roulent verts et nus,
> Sans clous et sans sapin, sans couvercle, sans cierges! ...
> – Laissez les donc rouler, *terriens* parvenus!

'Un Riche en Bretagne' and 'Le Bossu Bitor' are companion pieces. Each is swiftly etched, a type of the outcast, localized, yet individual. The 'rich man of Brittany' is a tramp of the *landes*, living on such hand-outs as come his way, yet out of his destitution conveying charities of a kind among his neighbours. He has no bed to die in and his body rots in a ditch.

Bitor the crookback is similarly alone among his mates, the matelots who work the boat; within, yet not of, their community. His end is an orgy of self-assertion, a frenetic binge in a whorehouse, flaring up into a knife-brawl. Days later a bloated corpse is dredged up on the quay-side. The laughing children beat sticks on the sodden hump as if it were a muffled drum.

What sombre passion drove a now-forgotten nobleman to bring his elegant mistress into the bleak desolation of this part of Brittany is a far conjecture, but there she and Corbière met, and he conceived for her a distorted affection which drew him after her to Paris. He calls her Marcelle in the poems dedicated to her.

In Paris he must have suffered. His poems of that time have no tranquillity. He is scornful of himself and cynical towards woman in the abstract, though not without tenderness when there is the suggestion of an individual behind the poem. But the mirage of a mutual passion mocks him from far-off:

> Ah si j'étais un peu compris! Si par pitié
> Une femme pouvait me sourire à moitié,
> Je lui dirais: oh viens, ange qui me consoles!...
>
> .   .   .   .
>
> Et je la conduirais à l'hospice des folles.

The last line embodies a quality very characteristic of Corbière, which we call wit for want of a better name. Its artistic value is not that it makes one laugh – most often it does not – but in the sudden shifting of the angle of vision. As the intersection of two lines determines a point, so the conjunction of these two aspects concentrates what else were nebulous emotion. It provides that fantastic but necessary contact with reality which one misses in poems of sustained sublimity.

There is in this side of his work much unshrinking analysis and (surface) cynicism which arouse one's interest, as the exposure of a brave and tormented spirit. Yet though there are failures of communication in this part of his work – those poems in which slang jostles literary allusions and the most elliptical phrases sandwich those of penetrating directness – out of the darkest corners of obscurity, of reminiscences of his vagabondage, gleams now and then a ray which illumines his sympathetic understanding of the process of living as it affects those whose existence wavers on the fringes of polite society. Here is the fate of Zulma, *vierge-folle*, with whom he spent some time and some money:

> – Puis après: la chasse aux passants,
> Aux vingt sols, et plus aux vingt francs...
> Puis après: la fosse commune,
> Nuit gratuite sans trou de lune.

Obviously, its theme associates it with the 'Regrets de la Belle Heaulmière', where Villon concentrates its whole intensity, but this is a variation with merits of its own – the swiftness with which the essentials are seized; the impression, forced home without any wasteful description, of continual futile effort and final peace in annihilation.

These pieces of an urban inspiration are jerky and loose-limbed in rhythm, but there is one poem amongst them, which reverts perhaps to his first meetings with Marcelle on the coast of Brittany, and makes a momentary calm in the turbulence. It is a song a young sailor sings as the ship carries him away from the girl-passenger with whom he had fallen in love:

> Déjà le soleil se fait sombre
> Qui ne balance plus ton ombre,
> Et la houle a fait un grand pli...
> – Comme l'oubli! –
>
> Ainsi déchantait sa fortune,
> En vigie, au sec, dans la hune
> Par un soir frais, vers le matin,
> Un pilotin.

It is clear how much Corbière gains once he is outside the city. Paris killed him, or at least silenced him before his time, though it is improbable that he would have advanced much further. To the end he remained an amateur succeeding by strokes of genius.

Too much has been omitted already to justify the exclusion of yet another aspect, that by which he is seen to have anticipated the manner and method of the most characteristic symbolist poetry. Significantly, these are placed in a group (of six short poems only) after *Les Amours Jaunes*; perhaps signifying a transcending of those tormented loves:

> Il fait noir, enfant, voleur d'étincelles!
> Il n'est plus de nuits, il n'est plus de jours,
> Dors... en attendant venir toutes celles
> Qui disaient: Jamais! Qui disaient toujours!

There are no previous examples of this delicate versification in French poetry, so far as we know it. It is the poetry of rhythmic agitation of the subconscious. Verlaine is nearly contemporary (*Romances sans paroles*, 1874) but there can be no question of his influence. In fact, it is beyond our power to talk conclusively of debts and influences. It is possible that certain tendencies in later French poetry may be traced to an origin in *Les Amours Jaunes*, as the last quotation suggests; and Laforgue's sorrowful jesting from time to time is reminiscent.

Corbière had the first qualification for the poet – a mind of his own. Because he paid no more attention than suited him for the moment to conventional notions of a poetic style he is interesting even at his least successful, and never serves up a hash of elegant sentiments acquired at second-hand. Such is his naturalness, his spontaneity, that *Les Amours Jaunes* is as varied in mood as the days of one's life; but the general tone is sombre; his wit is powerfully destructive; the flourish, last vestige of romantic ancestry, is reduced to a shrug. The intense realism of his best poems perhaps accounts for his lacking the enthusiastic following which crowds on the heels of a more flamboyant genius. His studied self-depreciation, his *blague*, his brutal audacity and ridiculous foolery, do not for long obscure the impatient compassion of which his sarcasms and tangled ironies are the reflex.

IN CADS' COUNTRY

Laurent Tailhade: Son Œuvre. By Fernand Kolney (Paris: Edition du Carnet-Critique)

Satire is awkwardly placed between two stools. It must, like the rest of poetry, express itself through the particular, but it has not so great a reservoir of common emotion to draw from as the lyric. The danger of degenerating into a family joke, a reference to weaknesses of which the public is unaware and in which it is not interested, awaits it on the one hand; on the other, the gulf of abstraction, where social failings, magnified out of all proportion, become shadowy vices, fleeing the bell, book and candle of theological lore, but too tenuous for the poet's net. At each extreme it passes beyond the range of the literary observer into that of the moralist or the historian. Though not a polite art, satire has flourished only in polite periods, when it has been possible to impose a number of conventions on otherwise intractable details, such as those of personal offensiveness, so that the lash may cut other backs than that of the immediate victim.

A good deal of the satiric verse of Laurent Tailhade is restricted to an audience conversant with the personalities, the enmities and conflicting ideals associated in the mind of the young symbolist generation. It was a time when popularity and the obvious were equally despised, when the Odéon and the Academy represented like the Albert Memorial for our contemporary generation, a tyrannical and ridiculous past. But when one finds Tailhade driving such writers as Barrès, Moréas and Bourget into his slaughterhouse, as well as many others whom even the decadents were content to admire, it becomes necessary to recognize that he stands apart from the movement with which he was, in many ways, closely associated.

He was not a propagandist of new theories; and he ridiculed not only academicians and the heroes of the big papers, but the charlatans of the 'intelligentsia' as well. He has in the *Poèmes aristophanesques* a 'Ballade pour assainir la chose littéraire'; and that is the beginning and end of his intention. He loved good writing, old or new, but what he saw round him infected with vulgarity immediately roused the pugnacity in his nature. However strongly entrenched in popular esteem, those who vulgarized the art he held sacred must answer to him, since he was prepared to stand by the consequences of his intolerable goadings, of which the 'Lettres familières' to Jean Lorrain and Jean Richepin are among the most merciless. This was no light responsibility; and private honour more than once demanded satisfaction, whilst the State felt itself obliged to condemn him to a year's imprisonment for his unpolitic article on the occasion of the Tsar's morganatic marriage. But his nature was not jealous or bilious; for, though the opportunities to exercise it were rarer, he was a graceful exponent of the art of praise; his satiric foam only marks the strong current of his enthusiasm for rightmindedness breaking against the snags of pretension and stupidity.

Stupidity in its most powerful and eternal form he did not hesitate to attack. His literary campaigns are matter for the student or the curious, they have the particularity of which we spoke – these family failings hardly excite us on this side of the Channel, where we have sufficient to our own needs. But there is another, a general form of stupidity, which affects a people's manner of living, from which no modern civilization, in whatever country, is exempt, and in which the vast masses of the population begin and end their days. The grossness and vulgarity, the utter lack of grace and appreciation of fineness in literature and manners which characterizes the busy citizens of the everyday world, exasperated a sensibility naturally refined, by familiar contact with the classic elegance and with that of the lingering remnants of aristocracy rendered almost morbidly acute.

The absence of delicacy, the satisfaction of an appetite with the object nearest at hand, the evident intention, so naïvely disguised, of serving both God and Mammon – these are the common habits of those who populate the 'land of sots' which he described (or created out of his spleen) in the verses collected under the title *Au Pays du Mufle*. They are the expression of an intense nausea with life as it is at present lived. His revulsion is fundamentally a sensual one, and only intellectual at a remove; the manners of the bourgeois repel him before their ideas do. Many of his bitterest sarcasms are directed against little gastronomic weaknesses, like that of the excursion-makers who, in the train,

Soignent le melon qu'ils portent à la campagne.

The fastidious senses find much to disgust them in populous thoroughfares, and Tailhade has revenged himself on his unhygienic contemporary by embalming him with his malodorousness, in verse the sharper for its apparent unconcern.

Yet one cannot be sure that the satirist does not enjoy a delusive contentment and that however matchless his art, it may not be barren of fruit. It is very entertaining to write, and to read, 'Dix-huit Ballades familières pour exaspérer le Mufle,' but whom do the darts pierce? Who is the victim M. Kolney so enthusiastically depicts in anguish?

It is not, certainly, the sot, wrapped in the impenetrable cloak of his sottishness. In the last resort it must be the satirist who is exasperated when his thunderbolts, rebounding from the shoulders of the damned, are passed from hand to hand among the saved as specimens of exquisite workmanship.

Tailhade would not have been discontent, to know that his satiric work had failed in what seems its immediate purpose. His real purpose, in the satires as elsewhere, was the aesthetic creation with which he was passionately occupied, and on which his achievement rests. On that, too, the hostile critic may found the case for the prosecution. Tailhade was not a creator of myths nor fertile in metaphors, like the great poets and stylists. His art depends entirely on arrangement, on balance and design, and his strength is in the abundance of his material, the exquisite choice he makes from his great reserves of erudition. His weakness, consequently, the overcrowding of accessories. He seemed able to absorb only nourishment which had been predigested; his culture is so purely literary that a great deal of his work consists of variations on ancient themes in highly conventional forms. He resuscitated the ballade, both as a lyric and a satiric form, and mastered it as no other modern has done. Though the *Poèmes aristophanesques* contains his most original work, there is a plaintive charm in many of the elegiac pieces, such as 'Ballade surannée de la consolation automnale', which is unsuspected in the author:

> Le temps déjà, furieuse Lamie,
> Des cœurs aimants ruine le trésor,
> Sans épargner beauté, ni preud'homie.
> Cassandre vient qui remplace Lindor.
> Adieux les jours fervents de Thermidor!
> Adieux Lignons, Cythères et Formoses!
> Vendange est faite aux ceps délicieux.
> Le souvenir bourgonne quelques gloses
> Et peint d'azur ses frêles camaïeux.
> La Belle a dit: 'Ne pleurez pas les roses.'

Though no single ingredient can be claimed as the poet's own, the material is so fused by a personal alchemy that it forms a pure gem.

It was rather disdain of bourgeois statesmanship than love for the proletariat which inclined him for a time to the political left, one would surmise on the evidence of M. Kolney, whose sketch lacks nothing of vividness but nearly everything of real intimacy. He draws us an admirable figure (for, though the text of his quotations is not impeccable, he has an enthusiasm for his subject), but one which shines rather than lives. Tailhade was not a humanitarian, but a humanist; and in classical literature he found the types of a noble life for whose sake he attacked the baseness of the present. 'From Xenophon to Rabelais,' he said, 'the question of the rearing of men has occupied the noblest minds.' He saw the slavery of modern life 'où nous répétons à satiété le même geste, où nous prenons le pli d'un seul état,' sharply contrasted with the Hellenic ideal of a body and mind harmoniously tuned; and this, consciously or not, gives the sting to his satire. The seduction of pagan art, above all its clarity of colour and outline is the marrow and flesh of his work. Beyond it his resources are few, and he has no reliable safeguard against an elaborate but unconvincing rhetoric.

His impulsion is always sensual first and finally aesthetic, of a kind which is rarely encountered in so pure a state. Little occupied with the exact sciences, with the subtleties of philosophy, nor with religion except as a harmonious cult, his work might seem based on a single line of his 'Hymne Antique,' an invocation of Aphrodite: –

Avant tout, garde-moi de l'infâme laideur.

As time passed the range of his satire lengthened, and at the very end of his life the upheaval of war raised him an antagonist to try the final temper of his steel. The ordeal of a nation in arms threw into sharper contrast the ignominy of the opportunist and the self-seeker. Tailhade scarcely survived the war; but the second series of *Lettres familières* shows that he retained in that catastrophe his fine sense of justice when that of many around him was overwhelmed by the necessity of collective emotion. The cruel irony of half a dozen of these small masterpieces is still too pungent to be widely appreciated; but when or where the personal element has evaporated the amateur of satire will affectionately finger the smooth metal of the shaft which tapers guilefully to the sudden point, so bitterly envenomed.

M. VALÉRY'S POEMS

Charmes ou Poèmes. By Paul Valéry (Paris: Nouvelle Revue Française)

The latest of M. Valéry's infrequent collections of poems contains work of which it seems possible to say that in it lyricism is driven to the limit of its endurance; crammed with more significance the mould must scatter into rhapsodical fragments.

The sensuous refinement of his early verses, which already seemed sometimes to tremble on the verge of revelation, has quite naturally, in the course of years of intellectual discipline, developed an additional subtlety which it would be misleading to call abstract, but which none the less can only be expressed by some such word indicating his escape from the sensual illusion. If the first poems are described as being in two dimensions, then the later must be considered as if in three. The matter of an early poem, 'La Fileuse', which begins:

> Assise, la fileuse au bleu de la croisée
> Où le jardin mélodieux se dodeline,
> Le rouet ancien qui ronfle l'a grisée...

seems to have become reanimated in his later consciousness, giving rise to the sonnet 'Dormeuse':

Quels secrets dans son cœur brûle ma jeune amie,
Ame par le doux masque aspirant une fleur?
De quels vains aliments sa naïve chaleur
Fait ce rayonnement d'une femme endormie?

The first version is a charming study of surface effects, but the second has the intangible solidity such as is given to a picture by the use of perspective. To render this sense of depth a relation must be established and the poet has based this on the discrepancy between the appearance and the reality. This discrepancy is the fact of existence, and, as the legend of Narcissus may be thought to symbolize, the two can only be confounded at the cost of annihilation. The 'Fragment du Narcisse' included in this volume is not in M. Valéry's later manner, but bears more resemblance to the 'Hérodiade' of Mallarmé. It points the direction in which his thought was bearing, and, though missing the perfect limpidity of the elder poet, it has a number of eloquent passages. A poem short enough to quote in full may help to re-cast the legend in modern terms. There is no untroubled mirror for the contemporary Narcissus, but he must build up the adored image, behind the representations of the senses, on the scaffolding of pure intelligence. 'Intérieur' is the confession of a man to whom abstractions are already as real as the common matter of sensation:

Une esclave aux longs yeux chargés de molles chaînes
Change l'eau de mes fleurs, plonge aux glaces prochaines,
Au lit mystérieux prodigue ses doigts purs;
Elle met une femme au milieu de ces murs,
Qui dans ma rêverie errant avec décence,
Passe entre mes regards sans briser leur absence,
Comme passe le verre au travers du soleil,
Et de la raison pure épargne l'appareil.

When as much as this has been said, and as little, the poet of the 'Odes' and 'Le Cimetière marin', the deepest parts of his work, still remains undiscovered. Yet even here the legend of Narcissus may be of some use. We ventured an interpretation of it, but said nothing of the manner in which the poet's sensibility reacted to such an interpretation. Personified as Narcissus, he reviles the impassable gulf which separates the imagined form from the mind which imagines. The same exasperation is expressed in the poem 'Ébauche d'un Serpent'. The old arch-enemy, the Snake of Eden, speaks and invokes the sun as the 'dazzling error' which, with a mask of sky and flowers, conceals from the hearts of men that the universe is only a flaw in the purity of Nothingness. Yet this error is the root of existence, and pleases the Serpent's sense of irony. There is no attempt to evade reality, to crave absorption into Nirvana. Rather, the maligned Tempter hymns with a reverence which subdues his derision, the God whose vanity dissipated the image of His own perfection:

> En conséquences, son Principe,
> En étoiles, son Unité.

He offers to His glory the triumph of his despair, satisfied that the hope of bitter joys impassions the sons of dust – the thirst for the fruits of knowledge which exalts the strange omnipotence of Nothingness into Being.

It is obvious that, moving in these regions, poetry must carry its own nourishment, like the camel, or perish in a desert of ratiocination. It is not to be wondered at if the poet sometimes (but so rarely) falters; the marvel is that he animates the barren scene as he passes. His intellectual scaffolding is not a dead trellis, but a tree in espalier, hung with the fruit of ripe perceptions and the cool foliage of reflection. For pure lyricism it would be hard to equal the ode 'Aurore'. The poet, waking, assembles his mental world and fears that in the night his ideas, 'courtisanes par ennui', may not have betrayed him. But they reply that they have always been faithful to him:

> Nous étions non éloignées,
> Mais secrètes araignées
> Dans les ténèbres de toi!
>
> Ne seras-tu pas de joie
> Ivre! à voir de l'ombre issus
> Cent mille soleils de soie
> Sur tes énigmes tissus? ...

It is a long poem, but as fresh as dew, and the verse flows with the same limpidity throughout. Sometimes it passes through dark places, as though under trees, but there are always stars to spangle it. Only shallow streams are perfectly transparent. The metaphysical poet breathes an atmosphere too rare for ordinary lungs; he is the most solitary of the poets. But when he does succeed in his tremendous task, to

Donner un sens plus pur aux mots de la tribu

the words he purifies are those ordinarily the most obscure, on which the structure of reason most delicately depends.

THE RIDDLE OF RIMBAUD

Rimbaud: L'Artiste et l'Etre Moral. By Ernest Delahaye (Paris: Messein)
Le Problème de Rimbaud: Poète Maudit. By Marcel Coulon (Nimes: A. Gomès)

The best-known biography of Rimbaud is that by his brother-in-law, the late Paterne Berrichon. The memoir which M. Delahaye published in 1906 and which was given, unfortunately, a rather limited circulation, is a more intimate study of the poet by one who was his school friend. In the present volume, after a summary biography, he turns to criticism of the 'artist' and the 'moral being', but before considering his views it is necessary to measure the angle at which he approaches his subject. No one has suffered more than Rimbaud from the bias of his critics; he has been extolled as a saint and condemned as an inhuman monster. He was not a fixed star. His passage through the literary world was meteoric, and baneful to the ignorant. Whatever their other differences, both the books before us finally agree that he was a presage of good. M. Delahaye traces the poet's trajectory as though it were wholly passed in the heavens. M. Coulon insists that this heavenly body had a terrestrial path which led through some of the earth's lowest and darkest places. Whilst M. Coulon's abusive references to certain 'hagiographers' are at times justified, particularly in reference to Berrichon's pious interpretations of awkward facts, his own treatment of critical problems is not all that we might expect from an exponent of the scientific method. In the most fully documented Life there are so many gaps that it is rash to lay down any hard-and-fast reconstruction of the subject's mental or moral processes. In these circumstances, it is possible that M. Delahaye's Rimbaud corresponds more nearly to the real man, based as it is on a personal friendship, than M. Coulon's, for which the material has been gathered less directly. M. Coulon recognizes the sincerity of M. Delahaye's version, while checking it at certain points, and reserves his wrath for Berrichon and M. Paul Claudel.

The problem of Rimbaud, who, though gifted as no other poet has ever been, renounced his achievement and his ambition before he was nineteen, has already employed many pens and is likely to occupy critics for many years to come. It was even made the subject of an enquiry by the poet himself. He sums up the results of three and a half years' intense creative effort, the years from his fifteenth birthday, which were occupied not only by an immense literary effort but by a political idealism of equal intensity. He says:–

> J'ai crée toutes les fêtes, tous les triomphes, tous les drames. J'ai essayé d'inventer de nouvelles fleurs, de nouveaux astres, de nouvelles chairs, de nouvelles langues. J'ai cru acquérir des pouvoirs surnaturels. Eh bien! je dois enterrer mon imagination et mes souvenirs! Une belle gloire d'artiste et de conteur emportée!

Strangest thing of all is the fact (a platitude by this time) that his claims are substantial and his renunciation was absolute. No one has come nearer to complete originality than he did, yet his work is often more serenely classic than that of any other modern. 'Une page des plus attirantes et durables de l'anthologie' M. Coulon reserves for him, and on this, we suppose, would be printed the 'Bateau Ivre', 'Patience' – from which Dr. Bridges quoted in *The Spirit of Man* – it is hardly easier to name the exclusions, for Rimbaud never repeated himself and every poem, if not perfect, has something in it distinct and unforgettable. Then there are the poems in prose, among which, for all our distrust of that hybrid form, we must recognize a score of pieces of an unequalled purity of line. And lastly, in his valediction *Une Saison en Enfer* we come across those phrases which are truly fragments of what Verlaine called 'une prose de diamant':

> Ne voici-t-il pas [writes M. Coulon indignantly in his Preface] un nouveau volume d'Ernest Delahaye, préoccupé surtout d'établir que l'auteur de 'Soleil et Chair' et de 'Premières Communions' a fait une fin chrétienne, et que son caractère et son œuvre l'y prédisposaient?

That is a fair description of the first book under review, but it is one which is not so obviously ridiculous as he seems to think it. The greatest sinners are often ripe to become saints such as the cautious would never make. But, apart from his sister's account of his dying confession and desire for the sacraments, we have no evidence that Rimbaud ever regarded the established form of religion with anything more friendly than disdain. Yet he does not strike one as an irreligious man; his blasphemies are always intensely sincere. The 'hagiographers' build for the most part on *Une Saison en Enfer*, their opponents on the earlier work. On the last page of his strange autobiography Rimbaud writes:

> Le combat spirituel est aussi brutal que la bataille des hommes, mais la vision de la justice est le plaisir de Dieu seul.

The second half of the sentence is perhaps intended ironically; it is the first half which strikes us as most significant. M. Coulon's book does not account for the severity of Rimbaud's spiritual struggle; that of M. Delahaye, rightly or wrongly, does do so. In the latter's version the sincerely Christian childhood of Rimbaud, his Rousseauesque humanitarianism and the basic tenderness and good will of his nature, are arrayed against the pagan culture, the materialism he learnt from the eighteenth-century philosophers, and the pride and anger which were admitted blemishes in his character. In the interpretation of M. Coulon we find the poet's revolt directed principally outwards; it is that of an extreme egoist directed against the institutions and prejudices which irritate him:

> Je suis celui qui souffre et qui s'est révolté.

But if there were not a foundation of generosity, of disinterested affection, Rimbaud's cries and perplexities lose half their meaning. It is not likely that a mind of his quality would refer in phrases such as 'L'amour est à réinventer' and 'J'ai trouvé quelque chose comme la clef de l'amour' to mere physical abnormality, and, if not, then criticism should not deal too harshly with the commentators who have attempted to define the significance to Rimbaud of that word 'amour' which he constantly employs. In this matter the positivist critic may go as wide of the mark as the pietist.

M. Delahaye's study is most suggestive in outlining the part played by Rousseau and Helvétius in the poet's mental development. The idea of 'human equality', which, in spite of his pride, was an ineradicable part of his sensibility, was confirmed in him by the former. From the latter he learnt that intellectual materialism which led him (since 'rien dans l'esprit qui n'ait d'abord été dans les sens, aucun mouvement d'esprit qui ne vienne pas de la sensibilité physique') to excite his sensory system by all manner

of stimulants and mortifications. In the biography of Verlaine, published by M. Delahaye a year or two ago, he made an heroic attempt
to clear that poet's personality of the slurs and slights so plentifully
bestowed on it. He knew Verlaine well, so we may yield again to the
personal impression, but it is not at all certain that Rimbaud saw
Verlaine with such uncritical eyes. The older poet's weaknesses
were only too obvious to him towards the end of their friendship,
and in the *Saison en Enfer*, under the heading 'Délires I', he gives
a cruel but quite objective analysis of Verlaine's character – the
'Vierge folle' he calls him. M. Delahaye believes that this section
refers to an affair of sentiment with a girl Rimbaud *once* talked to
him about. None of the other biographers even mention this affair,
and we should require more evidence to dissuade us from the
identification of the 'Vierge folle' with 'Pauvre Lelian'.

RIMBAUD
The Boy and the Poet

I thought of Chatterton, the marvellous Boy,
The sleepless Soul that perished in his pride
– Wordsworth

EXTRACTS

First edition, London, Wm. Heinemann Ltd., 1924
Second edition (revised), Daimon Press Ltd., 1963

Introductory

At first as a legend and afterwards in real terms, the character of Arthur Rimbaud has not ceased to excite enthusiasm and abuse. The originality of his work, though, attracted perhaps less attention than his absolute abandonment of literature at the moment when anything appeared possible to his genius. For this boy, whose verse brought into French poetry a responsiveness it had rarely known, wrote his last poems in verse before he was eighteen and his last line of prose when he was barely twenty. Then he burnt all the manuscripts he could lay hands on and for the eighteen years of life left to him wandered about Europe, and latterly became an intrepid merchant in North-East Africa. He only returned to France because of an accident to his leg, of which he died. He lived to be thirty-seven, but after his twentieth birthday he referred only twice to the work by which his name will live, and then with disdain. He printed only one book, *Une Saison en Enfer*, a brief autobiography of his mind, just before he renounced literature. His poems and the poems in prose called *Les Illuminations* were found and printed without his knowledge. When he heard of this he had been in Africa for some years, and at the news that his fame was spreading among the young men of the Latin Quarter he became furiously angry.

There is a pretty puzzle here which would be insoluble if we considered Rimbaud at any moment of his creative power to have been a man of letters. He lost all respect for literature as a profession, though he had a familiarity with classical and modern poets remarkable for his years. He wrote always as a poet, to satisfy a secret impulse. When this impulse no longer found satisfaction in literature, he had no motive to go on writing. He is said to have called his early work absurd, ridiculous, and disgusting, which shows that, as literature, it meant nothing to him. He took no pleasure in the perfection of its art, since it was to him an inefficient tool.

The impulse which Marlowe translated so superbly in the dramatic symbolism of *Dr. Faustus* was the same as that which tormented Rimbaud in a metaphysical hell. The desire for more power, more joy, for entire perfection, for the absolutes of duration and sensation which inhere in Helen's fabled beauty, is enough to damn a man to suffering in this life with no need for the metaphor of Hell. And so universally true is the Faustus myth that Rimbaud, hypnotized by the idea of the absolute, rebelled against the gods of order and tradition and sought in unlawful means, in nihilism and destruction, the power which the normal faculties denied. The role of pride in such a drama must obviously be a major one.

Because of the precocity of his genius and the compression of his work into scarcely five years, and also because this work was almost always a direct transcription of a state of mind, the study of his life is of more importance than in criticism of most poets. He did not, after the first exercises of his pen, write a line of impersonal literature; *his poetry was his life*. So it is really necessary to know that the most remarkable poems since the death of Baudelaire were written by a schoolboy in a small industrial town in the Ardennes, and to trace with as much precision as possible the inner and outer circumstances of his life.

CHILDHOOD

Jean-Nicolas-Arthur Rimbaud was born at Charleville, 20th October 1854. His father, an infantry officer, was often away in garrison and finally, when Arthur was six years old, separated from his wife, since each was of a proud intractable nature. The father was irritated by domesticity and the presence of children, but Madame Rimbaud determined to rear and educate her family with her own hands, according to her own precise notions of propriety. In these circumstances Arthur's childhood came almost entirely under the governance of his mother, her law was the first he knew and the first against which he revolted. The family included another son, a year older than Arthur, and sisters four and six years younger of whom only the elder, Isabelle, is at all intimately concerned in his emotional life.

His mother brought up her children in the purest tradition of petit-bourgeois ethics, which is, in essential, the subordination of pleasure to duty; of everybody's pleasure, if necessary, to one's own duty. This stern religious woman, a pious Catholic, to whom sentiment was unknown, impressed her character most deeply on Arthur, (his elder brother fled the family for the Army) and the stamp of it was never effaced.

His birth was portentous, it has been said, and his infancy prodigious, but we have no reliable testimony till his ninth year when
he certainly displays a precocious assertion of independence. For as
soon as he began to go to school, and was faced with the immense
ascent to be climbed, he protested and rebelled.

Why, he asked himself in his earliest essay, why should he trouble
to learn Latin? Even if it means a degree and if a degree is the only
means of getting a good position – well, he doesn't want one. He
will be a *rentier*. 'As for Greek, the vile language is not spoken by
anyone, anyone in the world. *Ah saperlipote de saperlipopette!
sapristi!* I will be a capitalist. To become a shoeblack one must
pass an examination. The positions they give you if you pass,' he
sneers, 'are either those of a shoeblack or a pig driver, or a herds-
man.' It must have been a formidable child who, at the age of nine,
could write such a vigorous and witty condemnation of a classical
education and the system of competitive examination. 'I will be
a capitalist' he repeats again and again, and this, his first ambition,
was also the dominating one in the later part of his life. After his
school-time, when he had been an exceptionally good classical
scholar, he became more and more contemptuous of the humanistic
ideal, but turned with energy to the modern languages and applied
sciences – to all that would help him to earn an independence.
Meanwhile, after his entering school, his mother kept his nose to the
scholastic grindstone.

Under the rigorous conditions of his home life, it is natural that
his happiest moments should have been out of doors, on the pleasant
banks of the Meuse, and when he writes joyously it is always about
the open country. He used to delight to get into one of the boats
moored to the bank and dabble his hands in the clear water, or at
other times to lose himself in the contemplation of its depths. On
other days he paddled about on the bank and filled up holes with
water, to which he would carry the little fishes and other creatures
he could catch in the shallows. As he grew older his need of movement increased; he climbed out of the valley and explored the wooded heights above the town. In his quest of tobacco he would go
even as far as the Belgian frontier, where he made friends with
the smugglers. On all these excursions, for he was extremely
susceptible, he absorbed a multitude of impressions which he trans-
mitted to his verse and his prose, where they are often recognizable.

At the edge of the wood, where the flowers tinkle and shine, he sees the spirit of the country as a girl with orange lips, her knees crossed under the clear flood of sunlight, shadowed by the rainbows which traverse it, the sea and the vegetation which clothe it. The sea, though he has never seen it, is always present in his imagination as in that of all children, from books and stories. He sees ladies on terraces near the sea, superb black children and giantesses, the flowers are jewels standing up in the fat soil of thickets and back-gardens after the thaw. There are young mothers and big sisters with their eyes filled with pilgrimages – sultanas, princesses with a tyrannical dress and bearing, little foreign girls and people quietly unhappy.

From this world, which he arranges at will, from these splendid toys, his mother's voice recalls him to hours of wearisome solicitude.

Or he walks out along the Flanders road. It is autumn and the gold leaves swirl round the house of General Noiset, who has gone to the South. Along the red road they come to the empty inn (this continual use of the definite article shows that it is a child's itinerary). The château is for sale, the shutters are coming off. The priest will have taken away the key of the church. Round the park the gamekeepers' cottages are empty. The palings are so high that one can only see the rustling tree-tops.

Magic flowers buzz in the hedges. Creatures of a fabulous elegance move round. A bird's song stops you and makes you flush. There is a bog with a nest of white beasts, a little carriage abandoned in the coppice, or which runs down the path, enribboned. On the road, through the edge of the wood, one can see a troupe of little players in their costumes . . . In the end, when one is hungry and thirsty, he says, there is someone who drives you away.

There was, it is to be feared, always someone to drive him away from the unhampered enjoyment of his thoughts, and it was in the home that this discipline was most severe. There he was subjected to a concentration unnatural for any child, which made him irritable and drove him to revolt against all that his mother represented. Her religion and social ambition threatened to beat all joy and disinterested activity out of his life. When we think of the immense energy which must have been pent up in Rimbaud and the suffering that these years of restriction caused him, it is not difficult to understand the restlessness that grew upon him. A country walk meant, originally, a temporary freedom from his mother and all that she implied, and this association of liberty and movement, once formed, did not cease to develop, and its influence will be strong on all that follows. The only other way of escape was within himself, in the cultivation of his sensations and their application to an imaginary evasion. Both go to create the freshness of *Sensation*, one of his earliest poems, which reveals the sensitive and idealistic child whose nature underwent such strange transmutations in the course of a few years . . .

THE REBEL

The spring and summer of 1871 were filled with intense intellectual activity. He devoted himself to that destruction of prejudices which more than a year before, he had conceived to be his duty and expressed to Ernest Delahaye in his remarks about the child of nature. The ideas of pleasure and pain were the first to be examined, and he undertook the revaluation of values as the poet's first task. Pleasures, particularly the delights most highly prized by the people he knew and despised, were naturally suspect.

He no longer knew the gaiety of his first freedom, and the frank enjoyment of dewy nights on the roads, and coarse meals eaten hungry in strange inns, and mischievous, big-breasted servant girls. He was no longer the amorous libertine of *Première Soirée*;

> She was almost undressed
> and tall indiscreet trees
> flung their leaves at the window,
> saucily, close, quite close.

or the youthful *flâneur* of *Roman*, lounging with his bock or lemonade in the cafés of the promenade. In March he would not write:

> One is not serious when one is seventeen
> And the lime-trees are green along the promenade.

He was only sixteen, but he was immensely serious. He knew now no frivolous dissipations. He turned with fury on the sweethearts who had, by bringing him to desire them, reduced him to the level of the abominated Musset:

> Oh! my pretty sweethearts,
> How I loathe you! . . .
> I could smash your hips for you
> For having loved you!

He increased his reading with a savage and unfastidious appetite – books on magic, eighteenth-century librettos, Eastern legends, science, and philosophy jostled one another in his head. The aged librarian did not supply his needs with sufficient alacrity, was indeed disgruntled by this display of unexampled curiosity which obliged him to search remote shelves for the satisfaction of a young ruffian. In Rimbaud's acquisitive frenzy the least delay roused his fury and if, as it is said, the librarian sometimes hid himself to avoid giving books to Rimbaud, the invective of *Les Assis* is not too severe.

To Rimbaud, of course, a lazy librarian would be a great enemy. Many months afterwards (years in a normal life), he complains of 'the terrible amount of strength and knowledge fate has always kept out of my reach'.

The esoteric vocabulary and grotesquely erotic symbolism of *Les Assis* have a poetic vigour recalling the sixteenth century, before Malherbe came. But these few lines are simple enough, picturesque and deadly satire:

> Oh! never make them get up! That's disaster . . .
> They start up, grouching like beaten cats . . .
> And you can hear them, thumping their bald heads
> Against the drab walls, clumping and clumping their twisted feet,
> And their coat-buttons are wild-beast's eyeballs
> Which transfix your own from the other end of the corridors.

The laureate of the *Concours académique* was by this time a despised lout. Once admired by those whose opinion he disdained, his pride commanded that he should be able to ignore their disgust. He disciplined himself to do without the approbation of those around him and to withstand their hostility. He pursued in isolation the mental exercises which culminated in his theory of the development of the poet into the seer.

Among the many influences which went into this theory (primarily that of the poet as *vates*, which was current among the first generation of Romantics, Lamartine and Hugo especially), was that of the eighteenth-century materialist philosophers. It may well have been in the weeks between his return from Paris (disillusioned, as his poem *Le Cœur Volé* or *Supplicié* reveals) about 10th March and the drafting of his poetical Manifestos on 13th and 15th May, that he read Helvétius. That philosopher's theory of the mind as the product of the senses and of the memory (a reservoir of past sensations, weakened) was the necessary basis for the belief that the derangement of the senses would make possible the creation or discovery of a new reality, or of hitherto concealed aspects of reality.

Helvétius's exposure of self-interest as the paramount motive behind the façade of ethical systems was a powerful impulse in deepening Rimbaud's cynicism. When Delahaye asked Rimbaud to try and get him the works of Helvétius, he answered, 'Better for you that you don't read them!'

When Rimbaud had been home about a week, the Government set up by the ultra-Conservative National Assembly, under Thiers, attempted a coup to disarm the politically advanced battalions of the National Guard, as a first step in the subjugation of working-class Paris. Their aim was frustrated by the vigilance of the Guard and the mass turn-out of the populace. The Government accepted its defeat for the moment and fled to Versailles to concoct a better plan.

Power in Paris then lay with the Central Council which had during the siege been elected by the National Guard. This body decreed that immediate elections should be held in the muni-cipalities to form a Central Government for the city which, follow-ing precedent, would be known as the Commune. Whilst the Commune thus ensured itself the letter of legality, the regular army was withdrawing unmolested from Paris, an army largely peasant in origin, docile to the powers of Church and State, without any understanding of the aspirations of the people of Paris, of their immense altruism.

Even in the midst of his introspective labours, the news must have aroused Rimbaud's latent passion for action and we can believe that he wished to return to Paris. But he had twice been beaten by lack of money and this time he waited. His mother, of course, did not give him a penny, and as he had stubbornly refused to return to school, preferring to go and live in a cave in a disused quarry, she had pestered him to 'get something to do'. For a few days in April he was employed as correspondence-clerk to a local paper, the *Progrès des Ardennes*, but on the 17th it was suspended by the Thiers Government. It has been said that then, hearing that recruits for the National Guard received thirty sous a day, which would this time give him a foothold in the city, he set off again by road and reached Paris in the short space of six days. There are many improbabilities in this and I can no longer think the story plausible. Of the intensity of Rimbaud's feelings there can be no doubt. In his letter to Izambard on May 13th he writes of the 'wild rages that urge me towards the battle of Paris where so many workers are dying still, even whilst I am writing to you'. But he gives precedence to his own 'work', the torment of making himself a *voyant*, a seer, first mentioned on this occasion. A week later *La Semaine Sanglante* raged in Paris.

The four poems which are definitely inspired by the events of the Commune are poems of hatred for the bourgeoisie; a tremendous force of rhetoric falls upon and lashes the bestial in human nature. Admiration of the Communard *mitrailleuses* there is, and a wonderful rhetoric of faith in the re-birth of the Sacred City of the Revolution, but there is nothing specific to show that he could not have written the poems at Charleville on the basis of newspaper reports, and his own hyper-aesthetized imagination.

SPLEEN AND THE VISIONARY

The young man, faced with the hideousness of the world,
Shudders in his heart, profoundly disturbed.

The war was over, the Commune cruelly dispersed, and the bourgeois re-established in his complacency. It will be easy then to account for the irritation which has to be constantly in mind when describing Rimbaud's emotional state during the summer of 1871. The tendency of education has been to create in the young mind the illusion that Nature is kind and Man benevolent, but there comes a time when youth bounds to the opposite conclusion. Rimbaud's experiences had been exceptionally bitter. It has been shown with what confidence of generosity he twice threw himself on the hospitality of Paris, only to be rebuffed in the first place with insult and the second with moral injury. His disentanglement from political endeavour must have been hastened when he found that his ideas left his political allies as far in the rear as he had left his conventional school friends when he became a revolutionary. Henceforward he is a solitary, and his references to fraternal aspirations are made with an air of doubt, regret, or wonderment; always as from a distance, as a measure to be taken for others.

It is easy to account for his political disillusionment, but there is a mystery about his sentimental life, which had begun to break up before the Commune. In a number of his early poems, in *Roman* and *A la Musique*, he displays the usual adolescent interest in girls, though with a maturity and a detachment quite his own. But not even the accusations in *Soleil et Chair*, or the attack in *Vénus Anadyomène* prepare us for the personal rancour he suddenly expresses. Certainly from this moment, Rimbaud became convinced of the insufficiency of women to bear the share which is assigned to them in the emotion of love, and we shall see him treating the theme with gravity in *Les Sœurs de Charité*. He had desired affection and understanding, and received neither. Even his friendship with Izambard was ruptured when he sent him the letter containing his profession of faith – 'profession de foi littératuricide,' in which all the poets from Homer to Hugo are ranged together as one body which 'absolutely disgusts' him; he had passed the point to which his schoolmaster could follow him.

His mother did not give him a penny, and when, exhausted by long hours of mental concentration he desired a relaxation, the boredom of life in the little provincial town closed remorselessly round him. He might go to a café and sit and listen silently to a radical journalist and a republican, anticlerical tax-collector, figures of public note, till the banality of their conversation drove him to some outrageous paradox. Such men, good fellows though they may have been, drew out rather his instincts of revolt, the anti-religious and the anti-social; in his aspirations he was alone, and it was for this reason that he still looked eagerly to Paris, expecting to find there, in spite of the deceptions he had suffered, a companion who would respond with an equal disinterestedness to the fervour of his ambition.

His altruism had been transmuted or shorn of much of the wool which hid its core of egotism, by his successive disappointments, and now he sought in the sheer intensification of personality the means to lead men to their redemption. Through the discoveries made in his own torments he promised to bring them power, as Prometheus brought them fire – the poet is truly the Fire-Stealer – 'he has accepted responsibility for man, for the *animals* even.' On 15th May, whilst the tragedy of the Commune was reaching its climax, he outlined (in a letter to his friend Paul Demeny) the method by which the poet, already the most richly gifted of men and endowed with the finest powers of expression, might transform himself into a Voyant or Seer and excel them all in *feeling*, in perception, as much as he had previously excelled them in expression:

'The poet makes himself a *visionary* by a long immense and reasoned *derangement* of *all the senses*. He seeks in himself every kind of love, of suffering, of madness, he exhausts all the poisons in himself in order to keep only their quintessences. Unspeakable torment, in which he has need of all faith, all super-human power, in which he becomes among all the great Sick Men, the great Criminal, the great Damned – the supreme Scholar! – For he comes to the *unknown*! Since he has cultivated his soul, already more rich than anyone else's! He comes to the visions, he has seen them! Though he collapses in his leaping among things unheard-of and nameless, other horrific labourers will come; they will begin at the horizons where the other sank.'

This was the fire fed with the self-deification of Hugo, the Romantic's satanism and the new scientists' evolutionism which was burning behind those 'beaux yeux d'azur noyés dans l'extase' while he strolled with hypnotized steps through the streets of his dull town, or remained sunk in contemplation among the chatter of his mother and sisters. There is no need to relate to any mystical or pathological condition this strange detachment from his surroundings, he was simply out of place as Shelley would have been on the Stock Exchange. The reality of his defiance, perhaps seeming obscured by rhetoric in the passage quoted, appears in the sincerity of a phrase, 'Imagine a man cultivating the warts which he has himself made grow on his face!' Thus was the POET of the Romantics transfigured! But beneath all the extravagance of expression there are flashes of intuitive reason.

In the early summer he continued actively to excite disapproval by his appearance and his manners. He allowed his hair to grow till it flowed in glossy chestnut waves down his back, and smoked an offensive-looking pipe with, to emphasize his bad taste, the bowl upside down. One day a clerk, lounging with a group of others at a street corner during the luncheon hour, called him and said, 'Here youngster, here is twopence to go and get your hair cut.' It was not in Rimbaud's programme to be ruffled by such things, and Delahaye met him directly afterwards highly pleased with the stroke of luck which enabled him, in those days, to buy a considerable quantity of tobacco. He accosted the priests he met on his walks with impolite gestures, and though they generally ignored him, if one asked him what he meant he would turn away with a sneer. At the same time he used to scrawl 'MERDE A DIEU' on the public seats or on the walls where the people coming from church might see it, and what most amused him was the fact that no one had the initiative or a strong enough conviction to rub it out.

He continued to extend his scepticism with all manner of reading, and under the strain of these acquisitions the scaffolding of his official education began to collapse. After the philosophers of the Enlightenment it was probably Renan and Darwin, or their forgotten popularizers who put in his hands the pick and crowbar with which to rifle the tawdry virtues of the conventional mind. But his scepticism was innate. There is something in him which makes him so much tenser and sharper than anyone else, and was the cause of his failure in society. He complains of it himself as of a disease. 'It's just what I've always had; no belief in history, neglect of principles.' This trust, which he lacked, in generalizations is the basis of society and civilization, and also, if carried far enough, mental death.

In August Rimbaud was so oppressed by his surroundings that his antagonism lost the vigorous invective of his early letters. Charleville is not an attractive town. Bound in its parched and stony streets, its squalid, lack-lustre cafés, deprived even of the relief of pocket money, even of the price of a postage-stamp with which to frank the poems he sent to a friend, with a mother so vigilant that he has his letters addressed elsewhere, he searches desperately for any means that may enable him to live in Paris. Even his friend Demeny to whom he wrote the famous letter on Voyancy, as well as his local friends, deterred him on account of his youth. The former had told him casually that manual labour might be in demand at fifteen sous a day, but finally advises him to wait. To reply to this letter Rimbaud summoned all his self-control: 'You force me to begin my petition over again; very well. Here is the whole complaint. I try to find calm words, but I am not well versed in that science . . .' He sums up the unhappy position to which his secret ambition has brought him: 'For more than a year I have quitted ordinary life for the one you know of. Endlessly confined in this indescribable countryside, not mixing with anyone, absorbed in a shameful labour, awkward, obstinate, mystifying, responding

to questions only by silence, as to coarse and ill-natured remarks . . .'
How well that characterizes his attitude, who all his life refrained
from the mutual panderings of confidences. The fury with which
he heard, when in Africa, of the publication of some of his early
work was shame at the thought of those poems in which he had put
his naked feelings, passing through the hands of people he despised.

By his self-restraint, he says, he would show himself worthy of
his extra-legal position, but his mother was equally firm – a situation
in Charleville by such and such a day, or the door, he accuses her
of saying. He refused that sort of life 'without giving my reasons;
that would have been pitiful.' He asks nothing, nothing but a piece
of information. He wishes to work voluntarily, in Paris, which he
loves, but he adds: 'I beg you to tell me of jobs which are not
too engrossing, *because thought demands long stretches of time.*'

Nothing could better indicate the seriousness and the religious
fervour with which he pursued his mental revolt than the spontaneous confession I have italicized.

In the meantime another means of departure was discussed. It
was suggested that an entry might be made into the literary world
through the introduction of an established poet. Rimbaud indeed
had already written to Théodore de Banville but with no result. It
was decided otherwise because his friend Bretagne had previously
been employed in connection with a sugar refinery at Fampoux,
near Arras, owned by Verlaine's cousin, and had become well
acquainted with the poet during his frequent visits there. We
have seen that, a year ago, Rimbaud was attracted by Verlaine's
poetry, which showed a freedom from prejudice and a delicate
insouciance so different from the prosaism of his contemporaries. It
was Bretagne, then, who provided the introduction which had
such tremendous consequences on the lives of both poets, and
enabled Rimbaud to write to Verlaine, who relates: 'On my return
to Paris at the end of the summer holidays, 1871, I found a letter,
signed Arthur Rimbaud, which contained *Les Effarés* and *Les
Premières Communions.*' Rimbaud had not misjudged his man, for
those poems woke a response in the older poet, not yet the pious
Christian who found the spirit of the second poem so detestable. In
reply to another letter containing more poems, and in which the
urgent question of coming to live in Paris was put before him,
Verlaine replied with more praises and the advice to come. 'You

are prodigiously well equipped for the struggle', he unwisely concluded. Then, after Rimbaud had insistently reminded him of his youth, his inexperience, and lack of social polish ('a filthy kid', he described himself), and his complete lack of material resources, Verlaine consulted a number of his literary friends, Charles Cros, Valade, and Mérat among them. Assured of their assistance he offered Rimbaud the hospitality of his home (he was living with his father-in-law) and exhorted him to come 'Venez, chère grande âme, on vous appelle, on vous attend.'

It was the end of September before these arrangements had been completed, and whilst he was waiting in anticipation of his freedom, Rimbaud gathered himself together for an effort which should surpass everything that he had yet written. In *Bateau Ivre* he expresses the intoxication of the last months, of his mad voyage over the ocean – need it be said – of imaginative experience, for he had never seen a wider stretch of water than the flooded meadows of the Meuse.

On a warm and sunny afternoon of early autumn Rimbaud told his friend Delahaye that he would like to take a last walk in the country round Charleville. 'It was just such a day as induces hope,' Delahaye relates, to whom we are indebted for almost all the personal reminiscences we have given, 'and everything added to the delight of this hard-won freedom. We sat down at the edge of a wood and Rimbaud said, "This is what I have done to show *them* when I arrive." And he read me *Bateau Ivre*.'

'Rimbaud, who had hardly been to the theatre at all nor received any teaching in elocution, read his lines without emphasis and with no vocal flourishes, rather convulsively, like a child telling of some great grief and in a kind of hurry; hungry, hastening to re-live it all. His sensitive voice, still childish, rendered naturally the vibration and the power of the words. He spoke as he felt, as it had come, as if in a precipitous flow of violent sensations.'

He had asserted his mental independence more than a year before, but except in his brief periods of gipsy wandering he had never been free. Now that his entry into the real world was at hand, free of the restraints of his home life, he looked back over the great distances travelled since he had first slipped the cables of priest and tutor. Those are the seascapes of *Bateau Ivre*, and in the opening movement he recaptures the sigh of relief with which he had then glided out of the placid reaches of ordinary life.

It was, strangely, a declaration of failure that he took to show them in Paris, a premonition of the failure of his superhuman effort, in face of the merchants and the pride of force and riches. It is a confession, too, that though he will struggle now without love, as a pure egoist, he is haunted by the eyes of the Communards he has deserted, imprisoned in the hulks.

'After the fleeting emotion this reading had caused him,' continues Delahaye, 'he remained sad and downcast. "Ah, yes," he replied to his friend's enthusiastic praise, "no one has written anything like it, I know that well . . . And yet . . . this world of writers and artists . . . salons, fashion . . . I do not know how to behave, I am clumsy, nervous, I do not know how to talk . . . Oh, as for Thought, I am not afraid of anyone . . . but . . . what am I going to do down there?" '

What, indeed, was he to do after *Bateau Ivre*? It was his fate to exhaust the art he touched, like a sailor who whittles his block of wood till it is a disembodied image. To produce a second poem like it would be to deny its sincerity, just as a repetition of *Le Voyage* would have been a factitious pastiche. But Baudelaire wrote that valediction near the end of his life, Rimbaud was not yet seventeen. It is here that the problem of his renunciation first appears acutely. He had truly burnt his boats when he wrote *Bateau Ivre*, and henceforward his poems became more and more delicate till they are only an air, or suggestion of unhuman ecstasy. When he denied his full strength of love the possibility of sympathy went with it, and he had engaged himself in a path which grew ever narrower and narrower. This was a blow at the base of art and the first version of his vow of silence. Arthur Symons well remarked that the things Rimbaud had to say were 'each an action with consequences'.

The consequences of *Bateau Ivre* will presently be apparent.

HALLUCINATION: FAILURE: ESCAPE

The manner in which Verlaine introduced his guest to his literary friends, as one who was going to outdo them all, was not the most tactful he could have chosen. For himself, he was without jealousy, and all his life maintained the genius of Rimbaud to be something sacred and supernatural. Less intimate friends, without the benefit of the experience of that vigorous spirit which Rimbaud had, but which his nature prevented him from disclosing except to a few in real sympathy with him, saw in Verlaine's infatuation only a physical aberration. There was, none the less, an intellectual attraction, which is understood if we can see Verlaine as the child he morally was, irked to desperation by the discipline of the nursery, by his father-in-law's disapproval, his domestic tyranny, the lack of employment, and anxiety as to the future. A man of so fine and delicate a temperament, the very type of instability, cannot cope with evil circumstances; he is capable of a brief, not of a prolonged, effort of that kind. To such a nature evasion always presents itself as the most attractive course, and the arrival of Rimbaud corresponded to the culmination of such a desire. We have seen to what a pitch of scepticism Rimbaud's mental exertions had already risen. When the first shock caused by his boyish appearance had subsided, Verlaine relished with avidity the extraordinary fascination of the young poet. 'He is intellectuality itself, he has all its powers and seductions to an unprecedented degree.' Delahaye reports Verlaine as saying, 'his speech is the diamond-like prose of *Les Illuminations* and *Une Saison en Enfer* . . . The extraordinary moral maceration which he willed himself to submit to, freed him from every weakness, from every prejudice.'

To Verlaine, living as he was among people of inferior sensitiveness, whom he met only too willingly on the common ground that drinking made them, this pure and lucid mind in which he found admiration and sympathy for himself, appeared like an angel from heaven armed with a sword which would cut all the ties of wearisome obligations. He need not for this reason have been insensible to the physical beauty of one who had at this time an indefinable, but unmistakable, charm, the beauty of personality rather than of flesh and bone. A photograph dated 1872 shows a great difference from the sulky guttersnipe of the year before. The marks of repression have gone, and if the mouth is repressed it is in determination. The nose is tilted mockingly and the eyes, of a large and luminous blue, are sleepy in their pride. He knew that he was a master.

All the controversy as to the good and evil of Rimbaud's character springs from the use of a system of evaluation to which he will not be reduced. Only Verlaine was, at that time, able to discern beneath the pride, anger, and crapulous life the others saw, the nobility of the mission Rimbaud had set himself to accomplish before he would absent himself for ever after an illustrious epiphany. The confusion of the ancient notions of good and evil in a single vital impulse, was, like an unchecked inflation of a currency, the first step necessary to the realization of his ideal. In *Crimen Amoris* Verlaine has given in terms characteristic of the author of *Sagesse* an interpretation of the moral crusade which inspires Rimbaud's early *Illuminations*, which we imagine to have followed his detachment from ideas of social reform and to have occupied him during the last months of his stay in Paris:

> Now the most lovely of all these wicked angels, was a sixteen-year-old youth, garlanded with flowers...
> What is it he says in his deep and tender voice which mingles with the sharp crackling of the flames, and to which the moon listens ecstatically!
> 'Oh! I will be he who becomes God!'

The whole of this beautiful poem condenses Verlaine's vision of Rimbaud as he had seemed to him in the summer of 1872, enmeshed as he was himself in the chagrin and disappointment of his domestic life. An aroma of the intoxication of Rimbaud's conversation lingers in those verses: in the tone of the line

> 'Oh! je serai celui-là qui sera Dieu!'

his very voice seems to ring.

But his message was one which Verlaine was too weak to follow alone, one of freedom from human obligations, from love, duty, affection, citizenship, parenthood, and all the daily facts which irked them both. It was a message which demanded, too, the renunciation of human joys, as Rimbaud knew, and of which he paid the price. But Verlaine, poor Verlaine, was all his life trying to get his money back, not ignobly in spite of the indignities of his last years, but as one who realizes that this freedom is too austere for him. In some of the phrases of *Génie* Rimbaud has fixed for his part the vision of Messiahship with whose specious promises he had seduced Verlaine:

> Away with these superstitions and these ancient bodies, these households and these ages, it is this very epoch which has foundered!

How Verlaine admired the eagle-like or angelic soaring of this youngster's mind which swept off his own simple aspirations to an unpremeditated heaven! It is impossible to estimate the proportions of their mutual influence, for at this moment the genius of the one was complementary to that of the other. They have part of their creation in common. Rimbaud, as the swifter and more astonishing of the two may claim the suffrage of the picturesque, but there was a brooding fecundity in Verlaine. Rimbaud's passage was that of the fertilizing male. Verlaine, though unreasonable and grossly sensual, was filled with secret creative desires which were called forth by the mysterious delicacies of the younger poet. Rimbaud had dogged his reason to the borders of nightmare and subdued his needs to the exclusion even of imagination.

Rimbaud's influence was certainly a psychological one. He broke down inhibitions of emotion and of style and enabled Verlaine to express himself. This forcible freeing of our true selves was, as Jacques Rivière has well pointed out, the meaning of Rimbaud's reiterated 'love' and 'charity' – 'The help he brings us is to make our existence here unbearable', he writes . . .

I fell into slumbers of several days and, awakened,
continued the saddest dreams.

One of the principal causes of Rimbaud's failure to cope adequately with the problem of sociability was his absorption in the system of intense introspection which he had outlined in his theory of the *Voyant*. It has been recorded that Verlaine used to find him basking on the pavement; his habit of sleeping or drowsing on café seats originated in the same desire for concentration. When he was roused he would sit up rubbing his eyes with the backs of his hands. He had now the opportunity of experimenting with many forms of poison, and he moved among these men of letters like a drunkard or a visionary. He intoxicated himself, systematically, with alcohol, hashish, and tobacco. He relished the impressions of insomnia, and lived like a somnambulist, at the mercy of his visions. The strange condition of his existence, though it did not mitigate the offensiveness of his behaviour, renders it at least explicable. There is an account of a dinner to which Lepelletier, to please Verlaine, had invited him, which reads much more naturally if we imagine Rimbaud to have been half sunken in a trance.

He did not open his mouth during the first part of the meal, except to ask for bread or wine, as if he were in a restaurant; then, towards the end, under the influence of a heavy burgundy to which Verlaine freely helped him, he became aggressive. 'He uttered provocative paradoxes and apothegms intended' (so Lepelletier interprets it) 'to provoke contradiction. He particularly made fun of me by calling me "salueur de morts", as he had seen me raise my hat to a passing funeral procession. As I had lost my mother two months before I imposed silence on him on this subject' (the fact that such an immediate example of superstition and conventionality might have irritated Rimbaud, or that he had his own sensibility which might be wounded by current notions occurred neither to Lepelletier nor to anyone but Verlaine, it seems) 'and I looked at him in a certain way which he took in bad part, for he rose and advanced, threateningly, towards me. He had taken nervously and stupidly a knife from the table, as a weapon no doubt.'

Lepelletier forced him to sit down and began a grandiloquent harangue intended to impress his guest. 'I told him that I had just come from the war, and that as I had not been afraid of the Prussians it was not a little blackguard like him who would frighten me. I added, not really in anger but rather jokingly, that if he had not had enough, and if he persisted in worrying us, I would show him to the door with a number of good kicks on his backside.' For the rest of the evening Rimbaud remained silent, drinking heavily and covering himself in a cloud of smoke whilst Verlaine recited some poems. This anecdote tells us more of Lepelletier than of Rimbaud. It is obvious that this pompous republican journalist, a brave man probably and a generous one, at least a good friend to Verlaine, was the last person in the world to observe accurately the reactions of a poet like Rimbaud. Lepelletier asserts his disinterestedness and that need not be questioned, but the conclusion of these reminiscences is too comic not to be quoted: 'Afterwards I saw Rimbaud only once or twice, but I know that he had not any friendly feelings for me. He affected, *ironically*, always to refer to me by such titles as "Saluter of the dead", "old troubadour", "pisser of copy". It was very inoffensive.'

Those epithets, in their accuracy more than anything else, make us understand why Rimbaud was not popular. He was freed for the moment from anxiety about a livelihood, as a pensioner on Verlaine and his circle, and able to indulge in thoughts for those large tracts of time he had said they demanded. But he cannot have had enough money to gain a wide experience of drugs, and it is easy to exaggerate his submission to their influence. The hallucinations on which certain of his poems are admittedly based, to which he frequently refers, were noticeable whilst he still lived in Charleville (cf. *Les Déserts de l'Amour*), and if their origin was pathological it is most likely that it was induced in the first place by the rigours of his early escapes from home. Not the least powerful of intoxicants, one which may have borne the weirdest fruits of hallucination and which is, at the same time, so innocent that the puritan might regard it with approbation, was the empty stomach in which he had so often to indulge. In this state a little alcohol would have a tempestuous effect, or fatigue alone would be sufficient to disintegrate the normal system of perception. From some or all of these causes the products of his senses and of his memory, light and sound, colours, forms, and sensations swept in a vertiginous procession through his brain, and marched to the weakening beat of the classic discipline.

The technical innovation which he had prophesied, though its character was predetermined by his conception of it as a language immediate and all-embracing, was not constructed theoretically. Its origin was physiological, which gives it its absolute superiority over that abandonment of metre which has been a reasoned literary reaction. It is not until he had in Paris immensely deepened his consciousness of his own sensations and ideas (the words here become synonymous) to such a degree that he could not fix them with sufficient rapidity in the conventional forms, that we find him using a liberated technique. That this technique was actually as rigorous as the old will appear when examined in detail.

The momentary lifting of restraint which the life of Paris effected did not continue very long. His capacity for irritation was infinite, because his desire was for absolute freedom. Like a morsel of gas which will fill a vessel no matter how tremendous, Rimbaud, free of cities and countries, battered at the walls of life itself.

Still, at present he was completing his destruction of institutions, though by the time he came to Paris little of this remained to be done. We can, in the smashing consonants of an untitled poem which begins *Qu'est-ce pour nous, mon cœur, que les nappes de sang*, measure the extent of his emancipation:

> What does it mean to us, my heart, the pools of blood
> and the embers, the thousand murders and the long howls

of fury, sobs from every sort of hell overthrowing
all order; and the Northwind on the ruins still;

and all vengeance? Nothing! But still, nonetheless,
we will it! Industrialists, princes, senates:
perish! Power, justice, history; Out!
It's our right. Blood! blood! the golden flame!

Everything to war, to vengeance, to terror,
my spirit! Bite deeper: Ah, pass away
Republics of this world! Of emperors,
regiments, colonists, nations, long enough!

The poem culminates in a frenzied vision of the dissolution of
the earth and ocean.

The company of literary men and artists was at first a stimulus;
at least he had more sophisticated targets for his sarcasm than at
Charleville. But with the speed which characterized his development, the novelty was soon exhausted. He had acknowledged
Hugo's paternal greeting, 'It is the child Shakespeare!' with an
obscene phrase. His first remark to Théodore de Banville was, 'Is
it not about time we got rid of the alexandrine.' In almost anyone
else this would have been posing, in Rimbaud it is quite unself-
conscious, a reaction from a touch on a raw spot.

But after some months of this mental exercise he found Paris
intolerable and in May 1872 fled to his refuge-prison, Charleville.
It was the first of the series of impulsive flights towards the solitude
finally achieved, as that journey to Paris had been his last movement towards the society of men. That voluntary flight *home*, a
direction strange for Rimbaud, indicates that he had reached a
definite stage in his ascent; he had, one must believe, reached the
culminating point of his ambition, where he lost consciousness of
his visions, and he was afraid. He says as much in the narrative of
his magical attempt, *L'Alchimie du Verbe*. Of the poems there reprinted, which he chose to illustrate the stages of his progress, the
latest we know to be dated 1872, and that enables us to fix the limit
of time to this adventure. The journey to Charleville was not far
enough; there, perhaps, he compiled the manuscript describing his
visions (left behind and never since discovered, *La Chasse Spirituelle*)
and judged it an incomplete revelation. Then, too, in the monotonous hell of his little town, where the sneers now meant nothing
to him, he could think without prejudice. Perhaps he discovered
that he had fled from the very completion of his task, that he had

shrunk from the last note of his atrocious fanfare. No doubt he had been tempted, as he confesses in *Une Saison*, by the return of 'noble ambitions'; like a Satanic St. Anthony before whose eyes the forms of all moral and intellectual ideals of loveliness revolved. These ideals which he had slurred with all manner of disdain, returned in the terrible moment in which he doubted himself. He was angry with himself and pitiful too, doubting whether, after all his efforts and sufferings, his magic sophisms might not hide in their angelic phrases only the ordure he had scorned in others. He would not now turn back, he who had promised his created soul a universe built solely from the products of his memory and his senses, he would not offer it the music of the ancients, the phrases sanctified by time.

A letter of this period, June, shows him acquiring that monstrosity of soul at which he had aimed. It was written in Paris after his brief return to Charleville, and he misses the rivers and caverns of the Ardennes. The restricted life of the city, particularly oppressive in the summer, exasperates his rawness. He finds a furious satisfaction in deforming words: he would not, if he could help, use the same language as the human pigs – thus Paris, June, and Absinthe become Parmerde, Juinphe, Absomphe. He delights to hover on the brink of incoherence, and afterwards to plunge into a brute sleep.

'It is the most delicate and quivering of any way of getting drunk, by virtue of that sage of the glaciers, absomphe! Only, afterwards, to go to sleep in the muck.'

He would defile even his own most exquisite vision, and sacrifices that delicious poem, *Les Corbeaux*, soon to be published in Blémont's *Renaissance*, to the basest usage. It is obviously to himself he refers as the child in *Honte*, who will not cease 'like a Rocky Mountain cat, to fling his stench over everything'.

'The serious thing is', he tells his friend, 'that you must really torment yourself.' Yet, in the midst of this implacable disgust, self-disgust, and brutification, he wrote some of the loveliest of his poems. To the preceding weeks spent in Charleville belong some of the most delicate and original of his verse poems, those which he grouped under the title *Fêtes de la Patience*, that is, *Bannières de Mai*, *Chanson de la Plus Haute Tour*, *L'Eternité*, *Age d'Or*. He had already begun to search for 'new forms' and no later than his return to Paris in May, he must have begun to write the earliest of the prose poems now known as *Les Illuminations*.

In the same letter to Delahaye, he describes very vividly his method of working. Whatever he meant by 'brutification', it did not deaden but intensified his nervous reactions:

'Now, it's at night I work. From midnight to five. Last month, my room rue Monsieur-le-Prince looked out on a garden of the lycée Saint-Louis. There were some enormous trees under my narrow window. At three in the morning the candle faded; all the birds began chirping at once, in the trees: that's the end. No more work. I had to stare at the trees, at the sky, entranced by this inexpressible moment, the first of dawn. I could see into the Lycée dormitories, absolutely still. And already the rumble, deep, delicious, of the carts over the (cobbled) boulevards. I smoked my pipe, spitting on the tiles, for it was a garret, my room. At five, I would go down to buy some bread; this is the moment. The workers are on the move everywhere. For me, it's the moment to get drunk in the wine shops. I go back to eat, and into bed at seven, when the sun brings out the wood-lice from under the tiles. The first light, in summer, and December dusk, that's what has always delighted me here.

But at this moment I've a pretty room looking on a bottomless court, three yards square . . . There, I drink water all night, I don't notice the dawn, I don't sleep, I suffocate.'

It was out of such nights' work that *Matinée d'Ivresse* was created; the most revealing commentary on his 'magical' period.

Such concentration could not be indefinitely prolonged, and when Verlaine, sick of his domestic responsibilities, mooted a flight from Paris, Rimbaud, one may assume, was eager to set off.

It was July when the two friends, *Jolly Wandering Jews*, made their get-away. They had no itinerary and no plans except to enjoy the moments as they passed, wherever they might be.

Verlaine's motive was to escape from the unbearable tension which had developed between himself and his wife and her parents. If Verlaine was to be disciplined (it was not so hard to lead him) it must be by a grasp at once firm and powerful, like that of his later experience-hardened mistresses. The methods of his wife and mother-in-law merely infuriated him, for in their house he was subjected to a humiliating watch – even his drawers were rifled and his letters opened, he complained. This was the first cause of the separation, but later the Mautés saw in the intimacy with Rimbaud a pretext for permanently ridding themselves of this undesirable son-in-law. His wife had lost all affection for him, and we may guess that she would not have scrupled to exaggerate a point to save herself from a renewal of her repulsive bondage, for Verlaine drunk must have been a most unappetizing husband.

Rimbaud was in a state of mind which was half resignation and half unsatisfied ambition. He had said farewell to the world in some snatches of song and reached an isolation which he could not sustain. The rough draft of the *Alchimie du Verbe*, referring to this period, is quite explicit: 'After these noble moments, complete stupidity . . . I could do nothing more. The hallucinations overwhelmed me . . . I travelled a little. I went to the North. I wished to know the sea, as if she would be sure to cleanse me of a stain.' . . .

Verlaine had gained his mother's consent to withdraw some of his capital, and with this in his pocket and no one to answer to, he abandoned the past and the future in the absorption in the one present. Rimbaud lent him for the moment his extraordinary curiosity, and that he translated into his own terms:

> Let us be two children, two young girls
> Delighted with a trifle, astonished at everything . . .

But there was another side to Verlaine's character which was expressed only too complacently in his later poems, and balances against the ideality of *Romances sans paroles* the debauchery of *Parallèlement*:

> Among other blame-worthy excesses
> We must have drunk a great deal of everything.

After the first delicious month in which they lived with no thought for the morrow, sleeping in hedges, gutters, or hotels as the mood took them, even this comparative freedom became irksome to Rimbaud and he fixed on Verlaine as the cause of this constraint. Verlaine was the human-all-too-human, and his self-indulgence angered Rimbaud, merciless to himself, who boasted that he had strangled every human joy in his soul. But beneath Verlaine's childish sensuousness Rimbaud had perceived a native nobility netted in the habits of convention; before he himself went off to seek a freer freedom he wanted to restore him to his primitive condition as a son of light. But the chains of sentiment and of the desire for the affection of his wife were already pulling him back and drew down Rimbaud's angry pity. Read the complaint in *Romances sans paroles*:

> O sad, sad was my soul
> For love, love of a woman...

and then consider the impatience of Rimbaud as he expressed it in *Vagabonds*.

The incurable frivolity of Verlaine which forced Rimbaud finally to abandon him, his absolute submission to the emotions of the moment are plainly shown in every page of his biography; it is the price he paid for the sincerity of his later poems. If his wife's memoirs are ever published in full, they will doubtless add further instances of his weakness where none is needed. Such is her account of the conclusion of an attempt at reconciliation which took place in Brussels. Both his petulance and his apparently sincere repentances are as distant as may be from the anger of Rimbaud, which was implacable once he deigned to admit it. The anecdote in question, which is not absolutely reliable, considering its source, is probably substantially true. The younger Madame Verlaine and her mother kept a rendezvous with Verlaine in Brussels at which the conjugal situation was discussed. Verlaine was hankering after his wife, and the women made the desertion of Rimbaud a condition of his return. He must have given way on this point, for he went back with them as far as the frontier, but after the customs examination he was not to be found. At last, as the train was about to start, Madame Mauté saw him on the platform and called to him to get in quickly. 'No, I am going to stay,' he answered, squashing his hat on his head with his fist. They never met again.

The source of Verlaine's sudden courage was no doubt absinthe, and it was under the same influence that he sent this impossible note after his wife; impossible, one would have thought, from the poet of *La Bonne Chanson*: 'You wretched red-headed elf, Princess Sneak, you bug, a nip of the fingers and into the chamber-pot with you; you have ruined everything; you have perhaps broken my friend's heart. I am going back to Rimbaud, if he will have anything more to do with me after this betrayal you have forced me into.'

So, after having lived a little of every kind of life for nearly three months, and Verlaine's funds being far from inexhaustible – Rimbaud, of course, had no money at all – it fell to the hard-headed partner in this debauch to remind his friend of the inconveniences of poverty. It hardly mattered where they went so long as it was not back to the old monotonous life of Paris, and they decided on

London as the most inexhaustible and the most likely field to repay their suddenly industrious intentions.

They crossed to Dover early in September and found a lodging in Howland Street, off Tottenham Court Road, where Verlaine had a number of friends among the proscribed Communards. Soon the poets began to drift apart. Verlaine grumbles because he cannot get absinthe in a beer-shop, and he was alone on the occasion he describes. Rimbaud had prophesied a return to sobriety in a poem, *Comédie de la Soif*, some months before, and the renunciation of such artificial landscapes:

> No more of such landscapes.
> What is drunkenness, Friends?
>
> I would as soon, much rather even,
> Rot in the pool
> Under the fearful scum,
> Near some floating woods.

Though he had in all probability given up absinthe at this time, he was not yet abstemious or industrious. London had to be explored, and the friends penetrated the city and took a boat as far as Woolwich and Gravesend. The amusing *Croquis Londoniennes* in Verlaine's letters tell us all we shall ever know about these wanderings, but something of the impression made by the great confusion of the city will be found in such *Illuminations* as *Villes* and *Métropolitain*.

In the meantime a change was coming over Rimbaud. Just as in 1871 he despised his poems of the year before and had ordered a friend to destroy all those he had sent him in June, now he began to despise the ambitions of the months in Paris. 'One must be absolutely modern,' he said, and we can see a reflection of his teaching when Verlaine praises the interminable docks and says that his own poetic is becoming more and more modernist. Rimbaud slowly emerged from the trance-like condition in which he had lived so long, an emergence dictated partly by physical debility, partly by the failure to discover in it any essential satisfaction.

As he returned then to the ordinary life he became aware of its exigencies and of the insufficiency of Verlaine as a permanent comrade in arms. He used to go to the Reading Room of the British Museum, partly to satisfy his still active curiosity, partly to acquire that knowledge of negotiable value on which he now set his heart.

He bought a silk hat for ten shillings and conserved it carefully, caressing it with his elbow. He wore it in Charleville when he went back to his native town, and I see in this a desire, now newly sprung and later strengthened, to show the bourgeois that he could beat them at their own game.

If Rimbaud was bound to Verlaine now principally by material motives, the latter was no less an emotional parasite on his friend. He was miserable enough in London, which is such an inhospitable city to the poor stranger. There was no comfort in England but of the domestic kind, and the public-houses of the west central district were a poor substitute for the Paris cafés. Rimbaud's preparations for independence worried Verlaine, who was left alone for long stretches of time. The action taken by his wife now demanded a complete divorce, alleging in particular immoral relations between the two friends. Partly in response to his mother's advice to solve the situation by leaving Verlaine, partly for his own reasons, Rimbaud decided to return to Charleville. Poor Verlaine was faced with the loss of the two people whose affection he most desired. Whilst all the English families who could afford to were gorging themselves on Boxing Day 1872 he wrote from his cheerless lodgings, after a meal of 'exquisite goose', and said: 'I'm pretty miserable, though. All alone. Rimbaud whom you do not know, whom I am the only one to know, is not here any more. Fearful void. The others are all one to me, riff-raff.' . . .

Madame Rimbaud owned a farm at Roche, in the Ardennes, at some distance from Charleville. The farm buildings had been destroyed by fire and she moved there with her family to supervise the rebuilding. This did not suit Rimbaud, who grumbles, 'The *mother* [thus] has stuck me in a miserable hole.' He has to walk more than five miles if he wants a drink in the evening. He misses even Charleville and cafés and the Bibliothèque. The day before yesterday, he says, he went to see the 'Prussmans' – the German troops still occupying the frontier provinces – and adds 'that cheered me up a lot.' His hatred found this immense satisfaction in seeing his countrymen humiliated by the invaders. But now he is in revolt against himself and mocks his most delicious impulses; 'The contemplostate of Nature absorculates me altogether,' he jibes. And here is the way he announces the birth of *Une Saison en Enfer*: 'I am working quite regularly, however; I'm making up some little stories in prose, general title: Pagan Book or Nigger

Book. It's stupid and innocent. Innocence! Oh! innocence, innocence – inno-stench.'

He is as usual horribly bored – not a book, not a cabaret within
reach, nor any happening in the street. 'My fate depends on this
book, for which I've still to concoct half-a-dozen or so atrocious
stories. How invent atrocities in a place like this? I won't send you
any although I've done three already. Postage costs so much!'

Verlaine had proposed a rendezvous at Bouillon with Rimbaud
and Delahaye, and it was here, near the end of May, that the two
poets met again. Both were bored with the country. Verlaine was
disappointed of the absurdly hoped-for meeting with his wife, and
both needed some means of earning money. After a week's wandering in Belgium they took the boat from Antwerp to London – an
economical route. There they found lodgings at 8 Great College
Street, Camden Town, and set seriously to work. This, the third
stay of the pair in London, is undoubtedly described in *Délires I* –
the friendship with Verlaine and his own literary ambitions appeared to Rimbaud the two greatest follies of his life.

Rimbaud set out very seriously to earn his living. He was not a
bohemian, and horrible as it may seem, even his dissipation had
been indulged in for an ulterior motive. So when he turned his
energies in another direction – that of acquiring independence by
frenzied work – it did no violence to his nature. His mother had
only too thoroughly stamped out of him when he was young the
precious faculty for wasting his time. With Verlaine it was very
different. They quarrelled and Rimbaud says with simplicity in
his deposition, they quarrelled because they shared all their resources yet, though their existence depended on their mutual
exertions, he had to reproach Verlaine with 'his idleness and his
manner of behaving among our acquaintances' – the last being most
important as they wished to give private lessons in French, and for
this, of course, good recommendations would be essential.

At the best they earned a dozen francs a week, and such a paltry
life was not likely to ease Rimbaud's irritation. He plunged into the
study of English as a means of escape. Their quarrels were frequent.
Verlaine, if we may believe a sonnet of his, would wake Rimbaud
in the night to ask him if the soul were immortal! When his mother
wrote from Brussels to say she had arranged a meeting with his
wife, and that a reconciliation was almost certain, Rimbaud told
him that that was unlikely, and that it would be better to keep at

their work. Unable and unwilling to submit to a reasoning which did not please him, and perhaps to prove to his wife that he had done with Rimbaud, he flung off without any warning and took the boat to Antwerp.

Once on his way he felt remorse for his desertion of Rimbaud, who was left with hardly any money. He wrote to him on the boat saying that he had sent for his wife, and that if she did not come within three days he would shoot himself. Rimbaud wrote two letters asking Verlaine to return to London as he was stranded, or else help him to cross to Brussels. It was then Verlaine telegraphed him his address at Brussels and the money for the fare. On Tuesday, 10th July 1873, he rejoined Verlaine in the hotel where he was staying with his mother (it was not a house of ill fame, as George Moore characteristically describes it), and found him in a very nervous and undecided state. Verlaine could not fail to see that his wife's failure to accept his meeting-place was a final and definite refusal to have anything to do with him. He wanted to go back to London with Rimbaud, but the latter feared the ridicule from the friends who had seen their undignified departures; he himself had decided to go to Paris. As soon as Verlaine heard this he wanted to go to Paris himself and have the law on his wife and parents-in-law; then he wavered and would not go with Rimbaud because of the sad memories these old places would revive. The only thing that mattered now was that Rimbaud should stay with him, but as the latter remained determined to go away by himself Verlaine passed from rage to despair and back again: there was no coherency in his ideas. On Wednesday evening he drank excessively and went out at six o'clock on Thursday morning. He came back drunk at midday and showed Rimbaud a revolver he had just bought, saying, 'It's for you, for me, for everybody.'

Whilst they were in the room together with Madame Verlaine, her son went out several times to get a drink. He persisted in preventing Rimbaud from going to Paris alone, but the latter was determined, and as he had no money, asked for his fare from Verlaine's mother. Verlaine locked the door opening on to the landing and sat down in front of it on a chair; Rimbaud was leaning against the opposite wall. Rimbaud still refusing to stay with him, he called out something like 'That's for you, because you are going away,' and fired twice in quick succession. The first shot hit Rimbaud in the wrist, the second was not aimed at him and struck the floor.

This was the most dramatic moment of the quarrel, but it was not the definite rupture. It was only a repetition of the quarrels in London, the material difference – that Verlaine had a revolver – did not affect the moral situation. Rimbaud saw in Verlaine an image of the weaknesses in his own nature. Had he not said, 'Je veux que ce bras durci ne traine plus un cher image'? His mind was made up and the decisive action was taken by him a few hours later; Verlaine's pistol shot only hastened the break.

As soon as the shots were fired Verlaine fell into the depths of remorse and despair. He ran into the adjoining room, threw himself on the bed, and begged Rimbaud to shoot him. His mother calmed him, and about five o'clock they went to a hospital to have the wound properly dressed. Rimbaud would not be persuaded to stay any longer, but stated his desire to return to Charleville, and for this purpose Madame Verlaine gave him twenty francs. They all walked together towards the station, Verlaine talking very wildly, fidgeting with the pistol in his pocket, and beseeching him not to go away. When they reached a certain square Verlaine, who was a few steps ahead, turned suddenly round in such a way that Rimbaud feared another attack and turned to run. Verlaine followed him, waving, calling, threatening perhaps, till, happening at this moment to meet a policeman, Rimbaud claimed his protection and Verlaine was arrested. That was the action which determined their subsequent lives. It was done, perhaps in real panic by Rimbaud, perhaps from a calculation that this was the most effective way of getting clear from Verlaine. At worst he would not have expected him to suffer more than a night in the police-station. He could not have foreseen the absurd sentence of two years' imprisonment which was passed on Verlaine for this affair.

Rimbaud was obliged to remain in hospital, as the bullet was still in his wrist. It was there that the deposition was taken from which we have drawn most of the above details. This document gives a cold and concise summary of the affair, its tone is as disinterested as may be, as though he were narrating the actions of some ants or children. There is no accusation brought against Verlaine, and the general impression an intelligent judge would have drawn was that Rimbaud meant to imply the irresponsibility of Verlaine. 'I can think of no *serious* motive for the assault he made on me,' he says from his great distance, with that complete incomprehension of sentimental attachments which characterizes most of his work.

And is not this exactly in the tone of a nursemaid exonerating her charge: 'He was in a drunken state, he had been drinking during the morning, as he has anyhow the habit of doing when he is left to himself.'

On the 20th July Rimbaud rejoined his family at Roche; his arm was still in a sling and he appeared very depressed. He was, as usual, taciturn, and shut himself up in a loft to finish the *Livre Paien*, or *Livre Nègre*, of which he had written to Delahaye in May. 'Mon sort dépend de ce livre', he had told him, meaning no doubt at the moment, though the words have retrospectively a deeper meaning, that his mother was willing to pay for the printing of it, as an ordeal by the failure or success of which as a means of earning money she would conform her future discipline. In May he had written three of the prose poems which compose the *Saison en Enfer*. In London he had drafted *L'Alchimie du Verbe* and the *Prologue Abandonné*; the former appears much more highly wrought in its present state. Between the 20th July, then, and the date in August when he took the manuscript to a publisher in Brussels, he must have worked pretty hard.

Besides three short poems, Rimbaud saw nothing of his own in print beyond this *Une Saison en Enfer*.[1] He received some copies from the printer towards the end of October and sent one or two of these to the few people he thought still his friends – most certainly to Delahaye, a true friend, and a bundle of three or four to the artist, J. L. Forain, to give to Jean Richepin and Raoul Ponchon, young writers then in opposition to the Parnassians. It had long been rumoured that a mass of over 400 copies, the bulk of the edition, had been found in Brussels. This was confirmed about 1912 and contradicts the picturesque account of his wholesale destruction of his work. Certainly he burnt his early manuscripts, for not a poem has come to us from the family. He considered his poetry a folly and had printed a few specimens in *Une Saison*. But if he had really thrown on the fire the whole edition, on which good money had been laid out, the protest from his mother would surely have embedded itself in the memory of the sister who wrote her reminiscences of Arthur. Impatient, probably, that the fifes and drums

---

[1] *Une Saison et Enfer*, Bruxelles, Alliance typographique (M. de Poot et Cie), 37 rue aux Choux, 1873. It is a pamphlet, in-18, of fifty-three pages, with printed wrappers. The title is in red on this cover, in the centre. 'A. Rimbaud' on the top in black. The price is printed a little below the title, 1 franc.

of Paris delayed so long to mourn his departure from the world of letters, he disembarrassed himself of the incriminating early poems, and set off to the capital to find out the cause of the silence. His valediction to poetry was unalterably sincere, but in view of his chronic impecuniosity, it is not impossible that he may have thought of launching the booklet through acquaintances. The emotional life has its ebb and flow and it would be unrealistic to think that Rimbaud abandoned immediately every thought of publishing what he had already written.

In Paris he revisited the quarter in which he used to stay, and in the evening took a seat in the Café Tabourey, near the Odéon. Other young writers and artists whom he knew (they included even those to whom he had sent copies) were seated at tables near him, and pointed him out, and sneered, and circulated some garbled version of the Brussels affair such as George Moore picked up. They believed it was he who had ruined Verlaine. Rimbaud, of course, did not flinch and stayed at his table in his impenetrable silence. Presently a young Southerner, more generous, or more curious by temperament, left the crowd and introduced himself to Rimbaud as an admirer of his poems. Rimbaud told him that he was no longer interested in writing, that he would get his poetry travelling; that he had just looked in here (was this a magnificent improvisation?) on his way to London, where the people were more open-minded, and more truly intelligent. He displayed the advantages of London life so seductively that Germain Nouveau, the young man who had braved the dominant opinion, enquired eagerly when he was going to start and if he might join him. Rimbaud replied that he was leaving next day, that it was all the same to him if Nouveau joined him or not; that in any case their life would not be an easy one.

They reached London together and at first found work making wooden boxes. When he had thus extended his knowledge of English, Rimbaud found a position in a school through an educational agency and advised Nouveau to do the same. In this way, some time in 1874, they became separated. Rimbaud, now filled with a mania for learning languages, remained in England. He visited Charleville in January 1875 and persuaded his mother to give him a little money, and he lived on this with anything additional he might earn by giving lessons. In February he was at Stuttgart, apparently as tutor in a German family, discontented but determined to acquire his independence, even to the extent of having visiting-cards printed and inserting an advertisement in the newspapers.

During these many months Verlaine had been lying in prison, in Brussels and Mons. He continued to send Rimbaud specimens of his work, some of the poems of *Sagesse*, but only through their friend Delahaye, as the former would not communicate with him directly. In one letter he informed him that he had returned to the Catholic Church, and begged him to do the same. Rimbaud's comment was not sympathetic. Owing to good conduct Verlaine gained a remission of his sentence and was released in February, and, with hardly a friend but his mother, rushed at once to Rimbaud, whose address had been given him by Delahaye. 'Aimons-nous en Jésus.' Verlaine had written Rimbaud from prison. A few days after their meeting, the last, Rimbaud scribbles a note to Delahaye in which his one-time friend is, if not maliciously, then ruthlessly, disposed of. 'Verlaine arrived here the other day, a rosary in his claws . . . Three hours later he had denied his God and made the 98 wounds of O.S. bleed afresh. He stayed two and a half days, very sensible, and on my insistence he turned to Paris . . .' More fully, as soon as the two met they went to have a drink, with the result that Verlaine, after his long sobriety, quickly became drunk and Rimbaud's scepticism assumed its old ascendancy. No doubt he kept the upper hand all the time Verlaine was with him, and it was when he became bored with the latter's pleading for a return to life in common that, whilst they were walking in the Black Forest, he gave him that drubbing which he refers to as 'my insistence'. The day before this he had handed him some manuscripts to read and to pass on to Germain Nouveau, then in Brussels. In this way Verlaine and Nouveau became acquainted and met when the former was school-mastering at Stickney.

It is at this point that the question may be answered as to whether Rimbaud completely ceased writing when he finished *Une Saison en Enfer*. It is unlikely that so immense a vibration should have been stilled at once. Though for some time back he might have experienced a diminution of ambition, *Une Saison* is a genuine renunciation; he abdicates in the height of power, and with pain, not in exhaustion. If anything may be dated after August 1873 it is some of the *Illuminations*, especially those which reflect a vision of cities and societies of the future, which from the mental states to which they refer, could not have been written much before the *Saison*, though of course they may have been written at the same time and discarded as unsuitable: 'I am really from beyond the tomb, and no commission taken', is the sort of thing which he might have written in a posthumous struggle.

The man with whom he went to England, Germain Nouveau, was a fine poet, so it was not until after Stuttgart that he was completely cut off from literary relationship. Then, absorbed in the needs of the moment and his desire for a universal proficiency, he might have said, like Beddoes in the midst of his anatomical studies, 'I find literary wishes fading pretty fast.' His last words on poetry and letters are contained in a letter of October of this year.

'Je ne commente pas les dernières grossièretés du Loyola, et je n'ai plus d'activité à me donner de ce côté-là à présent, comme il parait que la 2ᵉ "portion du contingent de la classe 74" va-t-être appelée le trois novembre suivt. ou prochain,' and he scribbles a burlesque rhyme on the hungry conscripts whom he so much dreaded he might have to join.

The 'dernières grossièretés du Loyola' were the latest verses destined to form part of *Sagesse*, such as that beginning

O mon Dieu vous m'avez blessé d'amour[1]

which Isabelle Rimbaud, believing it to be her brother's, extracted from the latrine to which his contempt had abandoned it. So far as any written records show, that was the last thought Rimbaud ever gave to literature. Fear of conscription and the necessity of living freely are from now onwards his apparent motives. As the tremendous impulse which flung him out of the orbit of his heredity exhausts itself he returns more and more closely to the ancestral path. But for the restless spirit of his father, who could not submit to domesticity, he might have stayed in Charleville and made a fortune.

Whilst this unrest drives him ceaselessly through space, in other respects he falls under his mother's, his original, domination. It may be that because she held the purse-strings he had to court her favours, but I do not think that finally her cast of mind was uncongenial to him. His continual preoccupation with money is quite

[1] The *grossièreté* was, from Rimbaud's point of view, the humble and contrite tone of Verlaine's petitions and the proselytizing zeal with which he sought to save the soul of his one-time companion in Hell.

in her manner. At the Stuttgart boarding-house he will have nothing to do with inclusive terms at sixty francs a month; on his last agonizing journey in a litter, with his swollen leg, hundreds of miles, he yet has strength to include in his briefest notes the fines exacted from the carriers who set him on the ground carelessly; he does not forget to record the price of his artificial leg. Even in the letter from which we have last quoted he makes extensive enquiries, which show her influence, as to the conditions of the examination, which years ago he would have heartily reviled. He could not, after all, subdue his restlessness to that extent, but from time to time in his exile he cries out for rest and security. All that is left to sight is a smouldering exasperation.

LES ILLUMINATIONS: POEMS IN PROSE

Millions of golden birds, O future Vigour!
Million d'oiseaux d'or, ô future Vigueur.

One of the most superficial observations about this part of Rimbaud's work is not the least significant. That is, to point out the negligence of the poet as to the fate of his later manuscripts in contrast to the careful recopying which occupied him when he stayed at Douai. The 'man of letters' had given way to the seer or visionary, to whom it was enough to have perceived and to have fixed a vision for himself. Little matter if we others should be blind except to a narrow range of forms and grammatical constructions. His sacred ambition is a private one. 'If that which comes from down there has form, I will give it form; if it has no form I will leave it formless,' he said, and *Les Illuminations* is the result.

It is here that we are in touch with the poet as a psychological manifestation; the artist, a social development, being momentarily discarded. We touch the sources of inspiration. We may compare with Rimbaud's metaphor of *down there* the anecdote of Trelawney, about Shelley's first draft of a lyric. 'It was a frightful scrawl, words smeared out with his fingers, and one upon another, over and over in tiers,' etc., and Shelley's reply: 'When my brain gets heated with a thought, it soon boils, and throws off images and words faster than I can skim them off. In the morning when cooled down, out of the rude sketch, as you justly call it, I shall attempt a drawing.'

The mythical blindness of the bard, the poetic frenzy, the metaphor 'inspiration', are so many attempts to define the conditions under which poetic creation takes place, and on which, in fundamentals, Shelley's and Rimbaud's evidence agrees. At the period of Rimbaud's intensest concentration, however, his 'atrocious scepticism' made him question the authenticity of a drawing made after cooling down. In *Fairy*, *Being Beauteous*, and *Barbare*, for instance, I imagine we have an all but direct transcription of what was passing in his mind. It might be thought that this method of composition would be artistically worthless, as indeed it would be if the person submitting to it were not an artist. The subconscious which he touched in his trances, which all poets touch, being a mass without soul or personality, would be useless in art, except that no glimpse of it can reach the consciousness, even the semi-consciousness of dreams or automatic writing, without passing first the censorship of the poet's personality, and then that of his communal sense. These pieces are peculiar in that in them the second is inhibited.

'He is seeking the absolute, which the great artist, with his careful wisdom, has renounced seeking.' There is some truth in that dictum from Arthur Symon's early essay on Rimbaud; for the artistic sense is offended by botched work and by the shapelessness which comes from straining ambition above the natural powers. But I cannot think the great poets have been either so careful or so wise as many minor ones; their artistry, like their genius, has been an unconditional gift.

So though one appreciates Symons's criticism and sometimes regrets that there is much ambiguity in these pieces, one has also sufficient faith in Rimbaud to believe that they could not have been written otherwise. In any case, he did not ask us to read them, and had he published them he might have smoothed away some difficulties. But he would not have altered them in structure. If the forms made by the mind hamper the mind, then it must discard them or accept the eternal symmetry of ants and bees. No price was too great for him to pay to escape the death of formalism. 'What is my nothingness, compared with the stultification which awaits you?' he demands. But for all that, the writer of this prose never falters.

For it is in a sort of nothingness, as he says, that these moments of illumination end. As we thread each path of the maze we are brought up short by a gulf of light. That is the Absolute to which he leads us, from which in the later pieces we see that he has begun to retrace his steps. This gulf which stopped him so abruptly was not Nirvana, but the Fountain of Life. It will be suggested, because of the disintegration or annihilation of reality in which many of his poems culminate, that he aimed at the primordial, non-conceptual existence out of which rises the source of all psychic energy.

One tap of your finger on the drum releases all sounds
and begins the new harmony.

A word on the literary art of these poems in prose. Rimbaud, in the above quotation, defined this art in an example of it. Paul Claudel, in his enthusiastic praise of the prose of *Une Saison en Enfer*, lets fall a phrase which enlightens us as to the nature of these earlier pieces: 'The progress of the thought . . . does not proceed through logical development, but, as with a musician, by melodic form and the relationship of associated notes.'

That in this disuse of logic Rimbaud was bringing his art in much closer touch with the processes of thought, as distinct from the means of communication between members of society, will be obvious to anyone who has examined his mental life. Logic is a good servant, but the method of linking effect to cause which has resulted in material triumphs, has created grotesque monuments in the world of thought. May all poets be defended from the illogical, which is detestable, and may all critics recognize that the mental world is non-logical.

In reading these pieces, then, one must be content to be 'the drum'. Rimbaud's phrases are so created that their impact sets up a complex development of the thought which is directed, but not stilled, by each succeeding one. The effect of submitting to this process, for it is better not to attempt to follow it, is more exhausting than any argumentative reading. So does an excess of logic deaden the faculties and render them unfitted for higher exercises.

A biographical commentary is sufficient to elucidate much of the poems in verse. For the others this would not be so. To look in these pieces for the description of reality is to fail to perceive their nature, and to regard them as arbitrarily distorted pictures is equally to misunderstand them. Although certain objects or events may be recognized in them, it is only by regarding them as part of the pure subjectivity of the whole that their meaning appears. Rimbaud was continually (under hallucination often) duplicating his consciousness, and the essential part of him, shall we say the subconscious, took for its manifestation a form of scene, figure, or garments which translated its qualities, inexpressible except in images. Sometimes the identification is complete, and we have a unique poem; sometimes his self-consciousness impatiently obtrudes and the vision is flawed.

Aube is one of his most completely achieved poems, and at first seems to contradict what has been said about the absence of objective description in these pieces. The joy and wonder of the first light and its successive phases are captured in images of rare delicacy. It is as a moment of pure ecstasy, but under dissection it would reveal its kinship with the rest.

AUBE[1]

J'ai embrassé l'aube d'été.

Rien ne bougeait encore au front des palais. L'eau était morte. Les camps d'ombres ne quittaient pas la route du bois. J'ai marché, réveillant les haleines vives et tièdes; et les pierreries regardèrent, et les ailes se levèrent sans bruit.

La première entreprise fut, dans le sentier déjà empli de frais et blêmes éclats, une fleur qui me dit son nom.

Je ris au wasserfall blond qui s'échevela à travers les sapins : à la cime argentée je reconnus la déesse.

Alors je levai un à un les voiles. Dans l'allée, en agitant les bras. Par la plaine, où je l'ai dénoncée au coq. A la grand'ville, elle fuyait parmi les clochers et les dômes; et, courant comme un mendiant sur les quais de marbre, je la chassais.

En haut de la route, près d'un bois de lauriers, je l'ai entourée avec ses voiles amassés, et j'ai senti un peu son immense corps. L'aube et l'enfant tombèrent au bas du bois.

Au réveil, il était midi.

Though *Les Illuminations* is a fragment, it is a princely one. It is the creation of fervour and confidence in an inexhaustible fecundity of images. The visionary strikes unknown chords on the keyboard of prose, but he is never languid or voluptuously swooning. In his territory it is never afternoon, no lotus grows there. Strange that he should have been claimed as the chief of decadents. There is not in these poems a concession to weakness,

---

[1] For English translation see p. 165.

not a sentiment. Nothing but perception, sensual or psychological. He is among us like a young chief of barbarians who has sacked all the libraries of a purer world and scorns to warm himself at our fires and feed from our pot. Out of the books he has read he has picked the vision of a superior existence which might be achieved but for the figures of the present, his own inhibitions which obtrude themselves, rather than the incomprehension of his contemporaries. For it is technical learning which he has absorbed, he has leapt the centuries of intellectual effort at a bound, but the centuries of organized feeling cannot be leapt. He has cast out of his heart, as though they never existed there, all affections and greedy passions, all humiliating humility and superstitious adoration. To those sorcerers, misery and hatred, he entrusted the treasure of his sensibility that they might bring it to fruition, to a superhuman perfection before it was even human.

These pieces mark his attempts to define the conditions necessary to his existence without compromise, at the full intensity of his desire. So we find here and there the persistence of his belief that some new social order might be in harmony with his ambitions, that by means of the expansion of both the moral and the economic life a society might be created in which his immense energy could work unhampered. In *Génie* he announces the terms of a new morality, not weighing actions in the scale-pans of reward and punishment, but with the sense of the inevitable perfection of the deeds to which we spring:

> O ses souffles, ses têtes, ses courses: la terrible célerité de la perfection des formes et de l'action.
> O fécondité de l'esprit et immensité de l'univers!
> Son corps! le dégagement rêvé, le brisement de la grâce croisée de violence nouvelle!
> Sa vue, sa vue! tous les agenouillages anciens et les peines *relevées* à sa suite...
> Son pas! les migrations plus énormes que les anciennes invasions.
> O lui et nous! l'orgueil plus bienveillant que les charités perdues.
> O monde! et le chant clair des malheurs nouveaux!

That is a spiritual discovery such as one of the early Fathers might have made, Nietzsche might have envied. It is simple as a physical sensation, and bracing as the touch of a Northern sea.

In *Matinée d'Ivresse* Rimbaud has reached such a pitch of

egoism that he claims to have his own ultimate values, even his own Good and his own Beauty. This poisonous ideal he knows will remain in his veins even when, his intoxication having subsided, he is returned to the conditions of ordinary life.

O maintenant [he cries], nous si dignes de ces tortures! rassemblons fervemment cette promesse surhumaine faite à notre corps et à notre âme créés: cette promesse, cette démence! L'élégance, la science, la violence! On nous a promis d'enterrer dans l'ombre l'arbre du bien et du mal, de déporter les honnêtetés tyranniques, afin que nous amenions notre très pur amour.

The nature of this 'love' which he so characteristically associates with violence and knowledge begins to be apparent. In such a visionary Utopia as *Villes I* he creates the sort of community in which his desire might be appeased. It is an orgy of imaginative delight.

Des chalets de cristal et de bois qui se meuvent sur des rails et des poulies invisibles ... Des fêtes amoureuses sonnent sur les canaux pendus derrière les chalets ... L'écroulement des apothéoses rejoint les champs des hauteurs où les centauresses séraphiques évoluent parmi les avalanches. Au-dessus du niveau des plus hautes crêtes, une mer troublée par la naissance éternelle de Vénus ... Là-haut, les pieds dans les cascades et les ronces, les cerfs tettent Diane ...

The mental powers are raised to their extreme intensity, the impulses of the past and present reinforce the common vigour:

Des groupes de beffrois chantent les idées des peuples. Des châteaux bâtis en os sort la musique inconnue. Toutes les légendes évoluent et les élans se ruent dans les bourgs ...

But of the social organization on which this creative life is based we hear only in an echo in the tone of the ancient communist:

Je suis descendu dans le mouvement d'un boulevard de Bagdad où des compagnies ont chanté le joie du travail nouveau.

For he himself cannot grasp the secret of that existence any more than the child could fully clasp the dawn in *Aube*; and the vision concludes, like so many others, with the failure to maintain himself in this condition to which he aspires:

Quels bons bras, quelle belle heure me rendront cette région d'où viennent mes sommeils et mes moindres mouvements?

It would take too long to follow the theme throughout the *Illuminations*. In *Solde* we have perhaps the concisest expression of it. He offers for sale the riches of his genius, and among them 'l'éveil fraternel de toutes les énergies chorales et orchestrales et leurs applications instantanées! l'occasion, unique, de dégager nos sens!'

But that is apparently irreconcilable with the mutual concessions necessary for social harmony. 'Rimbaud was an unsociable creature,' said Charles Cros, who suffered from him, 'and shut all the doors of friendship as if he enjoyed doing so.'

Certain of the characteristics of hallucination may be recognized in these poems. The significance of objects has no relation to the normal order. The sense of duration has gone, and only that of succession remains. But the historical sequence is broken. There is no knowing whether a First Empire nymph or a barbarian horde will next appear on the scene. The stable appearance of things is dissolved and a breach is made like that through which the religious mystics have observed the splendours of Paradise. 'Un souffle ouvre des brèches opéradiques dans les cloisons – brouille le pivotement des toits rongés, – disperse les limites des foyers, – éclipse les croisées.' Rimbaud most frequently sees the tumbled universe of childhood, when the sensations are not yet aligned in a conventional perspective. His trances are invaded by memories from that inexhaustible world, 'Que le monde était plein de fleurs cet été!' Its painted toys and its legends mingle with the debris of the ordinary world with no regard for their relative dimensions, like the details in a Primitive painting. 'On tira les barques vers la mer étagée là-haut comme sur les gravures' is one of many instances. In the ruts of a damp track under the shadow of a hedge he sees this procession pass:

> Des chars chargés d'animaux de bois doré, de mâts et de toiles bariolées, au grand galop de vingt chevaux de cirque tachetés, et les enfants et les hommes, sur leurs bêtes les plus étonnantes – vingt véhicules, bossés, pavoisés et fleuris comme des carrosses anciens ou de contes, pleins d'enfants attifés pour une pastorale suburbaine. Même des cercueils sous leur dais de nuit dressant les panaches d'ébène, filant au trot des grandes juments bleues et noires.

He himself does not know to what he would attain; it seems that his satisfaction is simply in the destruction of the familiar world. But he is evidently seeking something, to recover something, or to return somewhere, for the sense of exile is often with him. He spoke of himself as 'Cette âme égarée parmi nous tous'. In his failure to achieve this return he came to worship the disorder of his mind as being a frontier state to his own kingdom. For his failure is very frequently expressed, even so early as *Les Déserts de l'Amour*, which concludes:

Puis O désespoir, le cloison devint vaguement l'ombre des arbres, et je me suis abîmé sous la tristesse amoureuse de la nuit.

Or in *Bruxelles*:

C'est beau, trop beau, gardons notre silence.

Or in the conclusion of *Aube*, or *Ouvriers*:

Un rayon blanc, tombant du haut de ciel, anéantit cette comédie.

Or again, as he stridently proclaims at the conclusion of *Parade*:

J'ai seul la clef de cette parade sauvage.

Rimbaud was impatient, but his fame rests securely on poems which can be enjoyed without commentary. Such is *Aube*, such is *Antique*,[1] a Bacchus of singular beauty, with a just agreeable distortion:

Gracieux fils de Pan! Autour de ton front couronné de fleurettes et de baies, tes yeux, des boules précieuses, remuent. Tachées de lies brunes, tes joues se creusent. Tes crocs luisent. Ta poitrine ressemble à une cithate, des tintements circulent dans tes bras blonds. Ton cœur bat dans ce ventre où dort le double sexe. Promène-toi, la nuit, en mouvant doucement cette cuisse, cette seconde cuisse, et cette jambe de gauche.

But if his art could function generally only at the expense of some confusion or distortion, there must be some great difference between his art and that which we call art. And there was, for with us art is the setting of limits where psychologically there are no limits. Rimbaud desired his art to disregard even this capital condition, even though chaos were the price.

If we discover the object which lies beneath the subjectivity of the majority of the poems in prose, and find that it is for something without limits, for something absolute, we shall understand why he wrote

Maintenant je puis dire que l'art est une sottise.

[1] For English translation see p. 164.

There is one characteristic which is common to all his poems in prose, and that is their subjectivity. All the personages of whom he writes are emanations of his own nature. In *Aube* he is the child pursuing his desire. Hortense, Hélène, and the figure in *Being Beauteous* are images of this Demon dissociated from his earthly self. Even the setting is a refraction through his mind of some scene remembered or imagined. External reality only enters the poem to destroy it. What was this ambition which drove him to a combat in which he was continually defeated? Naturally, he himself could not say, but the traces may be followed up with a little persistence; it is a combat like that of Jacob with the Angel.

Let us not attempt for the moment to name this Spirit which urges him and which he seeks to clasp. If we recognize it under its successive metamorphoses we may perhaps arrive at the point of perception. It is the x in an algebraic equation. On the surface *Angoisse* is one of the most baffling poems, but let us test it by this process:

> Se peut-il qu'Elle [the Spirit] me fasse pardonner les ambitions continuellement écrasées – qu'une fin aisée répare les âges d'indigence – qu'un jour de succès nous endorme sur la honte de notre inhabilité fatale?

The quashed ambitions, the periods of beggary, the fatal inability are all forms, as the conclusion of many poems has shown us, of the tyrannous reassertion of the real world.

The poem continues with a parenthesis of adoration which brings us a little nearer to the nature of the Spirit:

> O palmes! diamant! amour, force! – plus haut que toutes joies et gloires! – de toutes façons – partout, démon, dieu – jeunesse de cet être-ci: moi!

Love and Force, infernal or divine, are placed far above joys and glories, and this love and force we see quite plainly are qualities of his own nature, those predominant in – Youth.

Is it possible, he asks again –

> Que des accidents de féerie scientifique et des mouvements de fraternité sociale soient chéris comme restitution progressive de la franchise première?...

We know with what intensity he had flung himself into the struggle for social emancipation. It was not precisely from altruism that he had acted, but in the hope of restoring the conditions of original freedom, which are identical with those of individual youth:

> As free as Nature first made man
> When wild in woods the noble savage ran.

He is no longer assured of the efficacy of that means nor of the scientific marvels which his age regarded with such naïve satisfaction.

In the next paragraph the Spirit appears as the Vampire who has withdrawn from him these material means of salvation but still exercises her domination:

> Mais la Vampire qui nous rend gentils commande que nous nous amusions avec ce qu'elle nous laisse, ou qu'autrement nous soyons plus drôles.

And the poem concludes with the exhortation to fakirism indicated in the title:

> Rouler aux blessures, par l'air lassant et la mer . . . aux tortures qui rient dans leur silence atrocement houleux.

This gloss makes it appear that the *x* of the equation is a quality of its own, or an association of qualities, predominant in the early years of life, and which, in this instance, he hoped to regain by drastic self-torment.

In *Being Beauteous*[1] the figure is 'un être de Beauté de haute taille'. This is again our *x*. She stands against the snow, far from the world (Jacques Rivière has pointed out in his admirable study the obsession of the idea of *extremity* in these poems), and by the magnetism of her action the sensibility is re-born:

> Oh! nos os sont revêtus d'un nouveau corps amoureux.

Always we are drawn towards the beginning of life as the point of maximum intensity. The return to chaos, the end of the world, M. Rivière sees as the object of these poems. But he does not define which *end* of the world.

> Pour l'enfance d'Hélène [the Spirit again] frissonèrent les fourrées et les ombres, et le sein des pauvres.

Or again, there is Hortense, who has been '*sous la surveillance d'une enfance*, l'ardente hygiène des races'. We are told that 'sa

---

[1] For English translation see p. 164.

porte est ouverte à la misère.' Again we notice the dissolution of images, the frequency of words like shudder, as though the world were nothing but a vast system of vibrations – and again the sense of youngness:

> O terrible frisson des amours novices sur le sol sanglant et par l'hydro-gène clarteux!

It is quite plain that this spirit which draws him is something as primitive as Force, something on whose great bulk our restrictions and codes, our affections even, and our ideals are of no more moment than the clinging barnacles and trailing weeds on the whale's back.

Among our own poets Vaughan, Traherne, and Wordsworth have celebrated the purity and divinity of the child's vision. Rimbaud has but given the same convictions a metaphysical basis. Now does not the child's pursuit of dawn and his falling to slumber take on a new significance? And how simple appears the poem *Après la Déluge*.[1]

> Aussitôt que l'idée du Déluge se fut rassise . . .

So soon as we felt ourselves secure from a cataclysm, from any possibility of destruction and re-birth, all sorts of stupid things took place:

> Un lièvre s'arrêta dans les sainfoins et les clochettes mouvantes, et dit sa prière à l'arc-en-ciel, à travers la toile de l'araignée . . .
> Oh! les pierres précieuses qui se cachaient – les fleurs qui regardaient déjà . . . Madame *** établit un piano dans les Alpes . . .
> Les caravanes partirent. Et le Splendide Hôtel fut bâti dans le chaos de glaces et de nuit du pôle.

But these banalities obscure the vision of the poet who calls down the waters for their destruction:

> Sourds, étang – écume, roule sur le pont et par-dessus les bois – draps noirs et orgues, éclairs et tonnerre, montez et roulez – Eaux et tristesses, montez et relevez les déluges.
> Car depuis qu'ils se sont dissipés – oh, les pierres précieuses s'enfouissant et les fleurs ouvertes! – c'est un ennui! Et la Reine, la Sorcière qui allume sa braise dans le pot de terre, ne voudra jamais nous raconter ce qu'elle sait, et que nous ignorons.

So, having perceived the gulf towards which he was driving,

---

[1] For English translation see pp. 163–4.

hard-headed Rimbaud realized that he was a physical being, at least for the moment, and not a metaphysical hypothesis. As such he had been flirting with dissolution. His mental organism could no more withstand the touch of that fountain-head of energy than any fleshly creature the force of a high-voltage current: 'J'attends de devenir un très méchant fou.'

When exactly this crisis arrived we cannot say. There are several references which leave no doubt as to its occurrence, such as, for instance, 'Les hallucinations tourbillonaient trop' and 'Le terreur venait', etc. Most probably it was about the middle of 1872. There are at any rate a number of prose poems which show little, if any, trace of hallucination, and which might well have been written after that crisis. Such are *Conte* and *Royauté* and *Vagabonds*.

The first expresses most lucidly his character and his recognition of the failure of his ambition. It not only illustrates, as Claudel points out, the destructive side of his nature, but also the possibility of the co-existence of himself and his demon in the conditions of ordinary life. He has even an inkling that his absolutism might be an excess of virtue, an aberration of piety – this desire 'pour voir l'heure du désir et de la satisfaction essentiels. Néanmoins il le voulut. Il avait au moins une assez large pouvoir humaine.'

This poem was perhaps suggested by one of those called *Spleen* by Baudelaire, in which, too, there is a Prince who cannot find satisfaction:

> Rien ne peut l'égayer, ni gibier, ni faucon,
> Ni son peuple mourant en face du balcon...

But the malady of Rimbaud is the reverse of this, and the source of his profound originality. His desire is not too weak to be pleased, but so strong that it consumes whatever is put before it in a tireless pursuit of the essential satisfaction:

> Toutes les femmes qui l'avaient connue furent assassinées: quel saccage du jardin de la Beauté! Sous le sabre, elles le bénirent. Il n'en commanda point de nouvelles – les femmes réapparurent.
> Il tua tous ceux qui le suivaient, après la chasse ou les libations – Tous le suivaient... Peut on s'extasier dans la destruction, se rajeunir par la cruauté! Le peuple ne murmura pas. Personne n'offrit le concours de ses vues.

The world and all its treasures are but fuel for this desire. Nothing can be denied it and yet it is eternally unsatisfied. 'La musique savante manque à notre désir' he admits with a splendid frankness. Yet from this idea of the identity of the Prince and the Génie he drew the inspiration of one of the loveliest of his poems. In *Royauté*[1] it is the man and the woman, the individual in harmony whose wish is sufficient to achieve its realization:

> Un beau matin, chez un peuple fort doux, un homme et une femme superbe criaient sur la place publique: 'Mes amis, je veux qu'elle soit reine!' 'Je veux être reine!' Elle riait et tremblait. Il parlait aux amis de révélation, d'épreuve terminée. Ils se pâmaient l'un contre l'autre.
>
> En effet, ils furent rois toute une matinée, où les tentures carminées se relevèrent sur les maisons, et tout l'après-midi, où ils s'avancèrent du côté des jardins de palmes.

From this point of wisdom, this *bonheur*, this pinnacle from which he sang in the *O saisons, o châteaux*,

> Ce charme! il prit âme et corps,
> Et dispersa tous efforts . . .

he did not descend. It is identical with the concluding phrase of *Une Saison en Enfer*, when he says that it will be simple for him to possess the truth in a soul and a body.

The object of Rimbaud's desire may be compared with the state of identity with Nature or Reality which Lévy-Bruhl calls 'participation mystique'. It is a condition which cannot be expressed by verbal concepts because it evades the consciousness, whether reached through physical love or delight in a sunrise. Rimbaud's sublimation, by long looking-inward, of this erotic joy (from the girl in *Les Déserts de l'Amour* to the goddess in *Aube*; from the dawn-dewed violets of *Soifs* to the sunlit sea of *Eternité*) symbolizes the dissociation of his desire from sensuous objects, by which means he achieved the happiness of living constantly in the absolute of pure joy.

It was in this mood of self sufficiency (brutal, or angelical it may be, certainly inhuman) that he said: 'J'envoyais au diable les palmes de martyrs et les rayons de l'art.' His attempts to change the external world were superfluous now, his aesthetic as well as his social crusade. There was no more need to seek outside himself for the essential satisfaction he desired. But he found that the withdrawal of desire from objects (introversion) leads to mental disaster. 'Spring', he said, 'brought me the idiot's frightful chuckle.' It was

[1] For English translation see pp.164-5.

as if his beloved Nature had added her insult to Society's. In face of it his visions and his idealism seemed to be so many weaknesses and he held a bargain sale of all the promises of his genius:

A vendre ce que les Juifs n'ont pas vendu, ce que noblesse ni crime n'ont goûté ... Elan insensé et infini aux splendeurs invisibles, aux délices insensibles ...[1]

So, with that recognition of the senseless splendour of his vow we take leave of the visionary.

Six poems from *Les Illuminations*
translations by Edgell Rickword

AFTER THE FLOOD

As soon as the idea of the Flood had subsided, a hare stopped among the saintfoins and the swaying hare-bells, and said his prayer to the rainbow, through the spider's web.

Oh! the precious stones which hid themselves – the flowers which looked out already.

In the dirty High Street, stalls were put up, and the barges were drawn towards the sea shelved high above as in engravings. Blood flowed, at Bluebeard's – in the slaughter-houses, in the circuses, where God's seal paled the windows. Blood and milk flowed.

The beavers built. The glasses of coffee steamed in the estaminets. In the great house with panes still streaming, children in mourning gazed at marvellous pictures. A door slammed; and, in the village square, the child turned his arms, followed by the windvanes and weathercocks all round, under the sparkling shower. Madame *** set up a piano in the Alps. The Mass and the First Communions were celebrated at the hundred thousand altars of the cathedral.

The caravans started out. And the Hôtel Splendide was built in the chaotic, icy night of the Pole.

Since then, the Moon hears the jackals whining in the wildernesses of thyme, – and the wooden-shoed pastorals grumbling in

[1] See p. 165.

the orchard. Then, in the violet budding forest, Eucharis told me that it was spring.

Rise, pools; – foam, flow over the bridge and pass beyond the wood; – black sheets and organs, lightnings and thunder, rise and flow; – waters and sorrows, rise and bring back the Floods. For since they have been dispersed, – oh, the precious stones hiding themselves, and the open flowers! – it is wearisome! And the Queen, the Witch who lights her embers in the earthen pot, wants never to tell us that which she knows, and of which we are ignorant.

ANTIQUE

Gracious son of Pan! Around your brows garlanded with flowerets and with bays, your eyes, those precious globes, revolve. Stained with russet lees, your cheeks sag. Your tusks glisten. Your chest is like a cithar, tinklings pass along your golden arms. Your heart beats in that belly where sleeps the double sex. Roam you, at night, moving softly that thigh, that second thigh and that left leg.

BEING BEAUTEOUS

Against the snow, a Creature beautiful and tall. Hissings of death and dull vibrations of music make this adored body rise, swell, and tremble like a ghost; black and scarlet wounds break out in the superb flesh. The proper colours of life deepen, dance, and break loose around the vision as it forms. And the shudders rise and rumble, and the frenzied savour of these effects absorbing the deathly rattlings and raucous tones that the world, far behind us, darts at our mother of beauty, – she recoils, she draws herself up. Oh! our bones are clad with an amorous new body.

O the ashen face, the horse-hair shield, the crystal arms! the cannon on which I must fling myself across the medley of trees and the limpid breeze.

ROYALTY

One fine morning, among a most amiable people, a splendid man and woman cried out in the public square: 'My friends, I wish her to be queen!' 'I wish to be queen!' She laughed and trembled. He spoke to friends of a revelation. of an ordeal that was ended. They swooned one against the other.

Indeed, they reigned a whole morning, when the crimson hangings glowed upon the houses, and all the afternoon, when they moved towards the palm-gardens.

SUNRISE

I have clasped the summer dawn.

Nothing stirred yet on the palace fronts. The water was dead. The legions of shadows had not left the forest road. And I walked, breathing out warm, swift clouds; and precious stones looked out and wings rose without sound.

The first adventure was, in the path already filled with cool, pale flashes, a flower which told me its name.

I laughed at the pale waterfall as it tangled its hair among the pine-trees: at the silvered summit I recognized the goddess. Then I raised, one by one, the veils. In the lane, with a shaking of arms. On the plain, where I warned the cockerel of her presence. In the city she fled among the steeples and the domes; and, running like a beggar along the marble wharves, I chased her.

At the top of the road, near a wood of laurels, I gathered her within her heaped-up veils and I felt the touch of her vast body. The dawn and the child fell together to the bottom of the wood.

Wakening, it was noon.

SURPLUS STOCK

For sale that which the Jews have not sold, which neither nobility nor crime have relished, of which unholy love and the infernal honesty of the masses are ignorant! which neither the age nor science can perceive: Reunited Voices; the fraternal awakening of all choral and orchestral energies and their instantaneous application! The unique opportunity to free our senses!

For sale Bodies without price, beyond any family, class, sex, descent! Riches gushing out at each step! Sale of diamonds without control! For sale anarchy for the masses; irrepressible satisfaction for superior amateurs; atrocious death for the faithful and lovers! For sale habitations and migrations, sports, fairylands and perfect comforts, and the noise, the bustle, and the future they make! For sale unprecedented applications of the calculus and leaps of harmony. Lucky finds and terms never suspected, – immediate possession.

Wild and infinite leaps towards invisible splendours, insensible delights, – and for each vice its maddening secrets – and for the crowd its frightful gaiety.

For sale bodies, voices, immense unquestionable opulence, that which will never be sold. The sellers are not at the end of their stock! The travellers need not hand in their deposits so soon.

From *The Calendar of Modern Letters*
1925–1927

The Calendar of Modern Letters, edited by Edgell Rickword and Douglas Garman, appeared between March 1925, and July 1927. Rickword contributed poems, articles, reviews and comment. 'Instead of a Manifesto' appeared in the Comments and Reviews section of Volume I, Number I, March 1925.

A new impression of *The Calendar of Modern Letters* with a 'Review in Retrospect' by Malcolm Bradbury was published by Frank Cass & Co., London, in 1966.

INSTEAD OF A MANIFESTO

The reader we have in mind, the ideal reader, is not one with whom we share any particular set of admirations and beliefs. The age of idols is past, for an idol implies a herd – to each literary idol a herd of literary worshippers – and for the modern mind the age of herds is past. For some time after the breakdown of the Victorian religion of great men, disconsolate worshippers sought refuge from the rigour of solitary conviction in a succession of literary chapels, each of which claimed its patron as most efficacious to salvation. Scepticism as to the validity of choice has destroyed the comfort of this 'exclusiveness' except for a few simple souls. The slang use of 'exclusive' was one of the last tremors due to the poison of snobbery, before it was, as it is always in the end, fatal to its devotee. In all seriousness, apparently, a novel was advertised recently as *A Romance for a Few People*. (*11th Thousand.*) That is making the best of both worlds.

Today there is only the race, the biological-economic environment; and the individual. Between these extremes there is no class, craft, art, sex, sect or other sub-division which, it seems to us, can claim privilege of the rest. It is with the mind of the individual, the queer creature, rather new in geological time, which flaunts aggressively or smiles furtively behind the social mask, that literature communicates. Perhaps there are not so many individuals as there are men and women with names and addresses. Perhaps the streams of people in the street are no more dissimilar than autumn leaves, manure for next summer's generations. The artist, who can differ only in degree and in function from the rest of men, by revealing differences, creates realities. It is through him that we can perfect our individuality, our own shape, which under the comparatively crude strokes of actual experience might remain only roughly chipped out on the surface of that rock of ages, the folk-mind.

This view of society means the death of dogma. Parson may roar in the pulpit (and the lay preacher is trying hard just now to snatch a share of the old prestige) but the congregation turn round amicably in the pews to discuss the text with their neighbours. Agreement and disagreement are terms which mean little in such circumstances. The aim of writing is not to convince someone else (for that can never happen against the will) but to satisfy oneself. If, as well, the reader's pleasure is aroused by one of the many means which literature has to waken such a response, then the reader may make a gift of his assent or dissent to the conventicles founded on those wraiths, for the cycle of expression is complete without them.

In reviewing we shall base our statements on the standards of criticism, since it is only then that one can speak plainly without offence, or give praise with meaning.

THE RE-CREATION OF POETRY
THE USE OF 'NEGATIVE' EMOTIONS

An effect of the triumph of the romantic movement in the last century has been to separate the poet from the subjects which abound in ordinary social life and particularly from those emotions engendered by the clash of personality and the hostility of circumstances. A distinct bias has been created against the expression of particular grievances, which are supposed to offend against the proper attitude to poetry. This convention is as dangerous as the distinction which the French classicists drew between noble and vulgar emotions, and has a similar reflection in its effect on the poet's vocabulary – the erection of a literary language. Certain words become sacrosanct and are repeatedly invited to contribute, not for themselves but for the prestige they bring with them.

The same prejudice towards a specific poetic appropriateness accounts for the contemporary preponderance of 'nature' themes and imagery drawn from the back-garden of the week-end cottage. Under the pressure of this romantic theory personality and, still more, personalities have been squeezed out of contemporary verse.

This is partly caused, no doubt, by the extension of the audience. It is doubtful if subjective poetry (that is, poetry which is not communal like the epic, drama, or narrative) is, by its own nature, capable of being stretched over such a wide area as that covered by the modern publisher. If fact, it demands an audience homogeneous in culture, and to some extent in its attitude to life, otherwise the difficulties of communication cannot be overcome, and the poet must fall back on commonplace, coarse reactions, or invest his small genuine discovery with a theatrical grandeur in order to get it a hearing.

The modern poet is to his audience an author, not a man. It is interested in his more generalized emotions, not in his relations with the life and people round him. Yet to himself the poet should be in the first place a man, not an author. He should not be conscious of a distinction between the sensations he gets from his immediate contact with things and the sensations he uses as the material of his art. At present he is inhibited from expressing a set of emotions (those we call negative emotions) because of a prejudice against them which is based on a temporary social queasiness. With what consternation would the critics and the public receive from a reputable poet such furious but measured invective as that with which Churchill attacked the dying Hogarth! I shall not quote that passage on Hogarth's physical ruin, which begins:

With all the symptoms of assur'd decay . . .

since it is fairly well known. An assault from another direction shows exactly the kind of subject from which the modern poet is cut off, though not because he is unfamiliar with it:

Oft have I known Thee, Hogarth, weak and vain,
Thyself the idol of thy awkward strain,
Thro' the dull measure of a summer's day,
In phrase most vile, prate long, long hours away,
Whilst Friends with Friends all gaping sit and gaze
To hear a Hogarth babble Hogarth's praise.

Churchill has little verbal delicacy and none of the fatal wit of Pope; he stuns his opponent under the cumulate blows of the obvious. But he is also capable of varying the tone of his anger, and the impression we receive from the whole of the 'Epistle to Hogarth' is not that of a small dog snarling at a big one; it is really sensitive, and so poetic, indignation. Apart from the political issues involved, such as Hogarth's antagonism to Churchill's hero, Wilkes, it is a poem of the repulsion one personality may exert on another, the expression of the emotion with which one sophisticated social being may regard another, and made more poignant by the exploitation of Hogarth's decrepitude. Such material is taboo to contemporary taste; the artist is unable to approach it with an unprejudiced mind, since a low sort of agreement to universal solicitude has been reached by the modern community. In this respect the world of the eighteenth century is almost as remote from us as that of the *Satyricon*. Could we tolerate the innocent opportunism of the Matron of Ephesus except in the licensed playground of the classics?

Churchill is not pre-eminently a satirist; he has not sufficient detachment. He is a poet of invective, passionately absorbed in his subject. He cannot forget the miserable condition of Hogarth, and the thought of the venom which this almost extinct monster had the audacity to breathe out, stirs him to fresh indignant eloquence:

> I dare thy worst, with scorn behold thy rage,
> But with an eye of pity view thy Age;
> Thy feeble Age, in which as in a glass,
> We see how Men to dissolution pass.
> Thou *wretched Being*, whom on Reason's plan,
> So changed, so lost, I cannot call a Man,
> What could persuade thee at this time of life
> To launch afresh into the sea of strife?
> Better for thee, scarce crawling on the earth,
> Almost as much a child as at thy birth,
> To have resigned in peace thy parting breath,
> And sunk unnoticed in the arms of death.

Verse like this, though not often so fine as this, formed a not negligible part of the reading matter of the eighteenth century, today it has no survivors, and by some canons of criticism it would seem that we are well rid of it. It would most commonly be censured as unpoetic, since the term 'poetry' tends to be narrowed down to expressions of certain kinds of experiences. Blake, who is qualified as an authority here, drew without immediate discrimination on his mundane comprehension as well as on his celestial apprehensions:

> When Sir Joshua Reynolds died
> All Nature was degraded;
> The King dropped a tear into the Queen's ear,
> And all his pictures faded.

There is no doubt that literature suffers from the absence of a socialized medium to carry off these reactions, explosions of the spleen or long-rumoured fulminations, and bring about that relief and cleansing of the mind which is one of the functions of expression. Such 'negative' responses, which religion has exiled in forms of demons, are essential components of any fully satisfying work. So long as they are ignored we may continue to have a poetry fit for adolescents, but not for men; and the judgement of the common person, that poetry is 'sloppy', will be quite justified.

Emotion acts not unlike such a fluid as the early scientists invented to explain the effects of electricity; it has really one continuous circular movement, but to the subject it appears to have two, parallel and in opposite directions. That is to say, it has a positive and a negative pole; it can be orientated, at its extreme, in either of two ways: as delight in, or disgust with, an object. Romantic poetry is geared to the expression of extremes, but since our reactions are rarely pure ecstasy or sheer revulsion a great deal of such poetry (of Shelley's, for instance) fails to satisfy modern consciousness. We need a poetry in which the moods are subtly balanced. But, the more discordant the elements of a poem and the more freely they are associated, the greater becomes the difficulty of creating an aesthetic entity to bring about the catharsis which is its function. In the romantic convention this is achieved by an assertion transcending the values of ordinary emotional experience, and very effective this may be, but, like all phantasmal satisfactions, in its continued employment it leads to impotence; the abused nerves are stretched beyond the limit of responsiveness.

The poetry of the negative emotions, of those arising from disgust with the object, provides the means for a whole series of responses in parts of the mind which have been lying fallow for nearly two hundred years. This contemporary value is greater than its absolute value, for it shares with the romantic lyric the paucity of the too-sharply differentiated response, the facile catharsis. Even, since delight is more valued socially than disgust, an aphrodisiac more than an anaphrodisiac, it is likely to be always underestimated by criticism; but this natural prejudice should not be allowed to obscure, as it too frequently does, the perfection of expression the negative poem may achieve, as for instance in the concluding lines of the *Dunciad*.

Swift is a great master of this kind of poetry. His verse has no pleasure-value beyond that of its symmetry and concision, but it is the most intricate labyrinth of personality that any poet has built round himself, not excepting Donne. It is characteristic that the study of 'negative' emotions in poetry should tend to centre particularly in the fact of personality. That Swift was morbid is a commonplace; his verse would supply a text-book of pyscho-pathology with as much material as it could use. The interest for the literary critic lies in Swift's success in transforming this material into forms of art. As a preliminary, we may examine the conclusion of one of his most repugnant descriptions, 'The Lady's Dressing Room':

> When Celia all her glory shows,
> If Strephon would but stop his nose . . .
> He soon will learn to think like me
> And bless his ravished eyes to see
> Such order from confusion sprung,
> Such gaudy tulips raised from dung.

After the long and exhaustive inventory which precedes them, these lines produce an expansion which is of the nature of a catharsis. It is effected by the sudden breaking of the monotonous revulsion with the introduction of a mass of irony and the final completely satisfying plastic image. Without sacrificing the integrity of his disgust he draws up the blind on a landscape towards which the mind may leap with justified delight, since the idea of erecting order out of chaos is an absolutely valuable one, whatever the implication in this particular instance. After this momentary concession Swift brings down the shade again with the last word, rhyme-enforced, but the image floats on in the consciousness. A similar process of expression, more complex aesthetically, and with the positive bias uppermost, may be observed in such of Baudelaire's poems as the 'Hymne à la Beauté' or in 'L'Amour du Mensonge', which concludes:

> Qu'importe ta bêtise ou ton indifférence?
> Masque ou décor, salut! J'adore ta beauté!

Catharsis is a term which should perhaps be limited to works in which the emotion is objectified in characters and action. Yet an analogous process is the essential of success in a poem. A poem must, at some point or another, release, enable to flow back to the level of active life, the emotions caught up from life and pent in the aesthetic reservoir. Otherwise the poem is an artifice, a wax effigy in a glass case, a curiosity. In a poem there may be several such points of release, or of partial release, and it seems necessary that the predominant release should take place sufficiently near the end of the poem to be held in the consciousness till the poem is concluded. It need not take place in the last lines of a poem, though in fact it often does, but this is an effect which becomes mechanical and may be tiresome to sophisticated readers. The final couplet of the Shakespearean sonnet imposes this localization on a poet; it is a demand which is sometimes disadvantageous to Shakespeare himself. All fully-evolved formalistic structures, like the heroic couplet and the ballade, are susceptible to this automatism; lacking the element of surprise, their effectiveness as agents of the release is quickly diminished.

It seems that an early step to be taken, if poetry is to be liberated so that it may become a natural form of expression in the modern world, is an examination of the kinds of effect which have been employed to bring about the essential release.

LANGUID STRINGS

The vulgar prejudice against the minor poetry of the eighteenth century may be defended so long as it does not attempt to include the period that may properly be called Augustan. When, therefore, Professor Nichol Smith, in his preface to *The Oxford Book of Eighteenth Century Verse*, says that the century was not merely one of decadence and preparation but one of 'definite achievement', we have to distinguish periods of poetic fertility from simple measures of time. His adherence to the limits of the chronological century certainly helps his thesis, for by this means he has Pope, Swift, Prior and Lady Winchilsea at one end of his anthology, and Blake and Burns at the other. Wordsworth and Coleridge are there too, of course, but in their early manner they are scarcely distinguishable from several of their predecessors. By using the time-limit in this straightforward way, those who condemn the 'eighteenth century' are disproved in their own terms; unless they respond more attentively to the challenge and consent to stigmatize a narrower period. Such a period, which no anthological charity can do much to rehabilitate, may be dated from about 1720 (for Pope assimilated all the elements of his style from much earlier sources) till 1780. Whether English poetry, in spite of the individual genius that worked in the next fifty years, has ever recovered as an organism from that period of depression is too long a question to be discussed now. At least we can say that, for sixty years, the instrument of English verse was thumbed with very little aptitude by men who seem to have had very little excuse for handling it at all; and the prejudices of literary criticism, which, for the sake of the system, will praise anything that is not positively incorrect, should not oblige us to pay homage to mere inoffensiveness. Verse, in each of its modes, is a medium which must be realized to the limits of its possibilities, or it is nothing. The writers of this middle period had not the excuse that they were engaged in forming an instrument, for they subscribed no technical innovations (though some revival of forms) to the equipment of their successors. To the formation of a conventional romantic sensibility, to the School of 'Nature', they contributed earlier and more abundantly than is generally supposed, as this anthology clearly shows. But, if some excuse be necessary for their uninventiveness, it may, perhaps, be found in the fact that they were aware of three fully developed verse forms – spenserian stanza, miltonic blank verse, and the couplet. They are like men numbed among machinery of great precision and high speed, who dare only hope to keep the workings smooth. The names of Thomson, Johnson, Gray, Collins, and Smart must be in part excluded from these strictures. It is the smaller men, writing in a semi-romantic strain in a semi-urbane manner, whom it is difficult to consider with much respect. Their appearance coincides with the petering out of the metaphysical influence. It is clear that Pope could not have evolved his style without a knowledge of the processes by which Donne worked his transmutations, but his own creation was so brilliant and so adaptable (and so readily assimilated, it must be said) that the already unfashionable metaphysicals were completely obliterated. So English poetry gradually entered the Stage of Sentiment which advertised itself as the Age of Reason – whose decease in the greenest youth had escaped notice. In the finest seventeenth-century poetry it is possible to say that the idea or thought is the immediate subject of expression; the feeling derives from the expression. In mid-eighteenth-century verse, feeling becomes primary and the thought derives from it. Consequently, the thought, which must be (whatever its order in the writer's processes) the subject of expression, is slack and pendant among a diversity of objects. An example:

> In youth's soft season, when the vacant mind
> To each kind impulse of affection yields,
> When Nature charms, and love of humankind
> With its own brightness every object gilds
> Should two congenial bosoms haply meet,
> Or on the banks of Camus, hoary stream,
> Or where smooth Isis glides on silver feet,
> Nurse of the Muses each, and each their theme,
> How blithe the mutual morning task they ply!

These writers approach their theme with compunction but tackle it without audacity. If their verse rarely displeases, it seldom elevates satisfaction into active pleasure. The gift of complete expression is rarer than it had been even among the minor writers of the Restoration decline.

Such are the results, perhaps, of working on the axiom that in a good style all must be congruous. This negative injunction is valueless without its completive axiom – that an element of strangeness is necessary to beauty. The only method of reconciling these two claims is the use of the conceit, or, more generally, the metaphor, wherein the maximum amount of apparent incongruity may be resolved instantaneously. The consequent pleasurable surprise is, as it were, an amount of energy liberated for the use of the poet in influencing his reader further, and, if we may say that the presence of metaphor is the sign of the poetic nature, this handling of it is a measure of poetic power. Personification, so freely used in this period, is generally a debased substitute for that *thought* which alone can create genuine structural, as apart from ornamental, metaphor.

Our reproach, then, to the poets of the middle period is not the romantic one that they did not *feel* enough; but that they did not *think* enough. The contemporary parallel is obvious.

THE RETURNING HERO

The representation of the Hero, and of the heroic in action, is the achievement towards which great poetry has always moved. Is it possible, in the absence of pathetic elements from the universe, as we see it now, to project such a figure? Perhaps, for the purposes of this metaphysical poetry, the anthropomorphic is obsolete.

Mr. Wyndham Lewis suggests that there is a similar hold-up in the plastic arts:

'As already his body in no way indicates the scope of his personal existence (as the bear's or the barnacle's indicates theirs) it cannot any more in pictorial art be used as his effective delimitation or sign.'

It was with the invention of language that man's capacity outgrew his physical form, and in poetry we find continually the purpose to represent him as other than he looks; fundamentally, as more powerful than he is. Wistful literature is simply this desire turned upside down (as certain Orientals will say, 'Oh, what a beautiful child!' and in parenthesis, 'The ugly little brat', to deceive any maleficent spirit that may be eavesdropping), primarily under the influence of Christian ethics. But, at bottom, creation is the attributing to a suitable figure the extraordinary powers our super-animal vitality demands, which are inhibited from physical expression under present, biological conditions. From Ulysses to Don Juan and to Hardy's Napoleon this mechanics holds good, only with the de-humanization of nature it becomes more and more difficult to represent the vehicles of power in concrete forms. Hardy's Spirits share the modern fate. In the poignancy of the actual fables there is nothing to choose between the *Iliad* and the *Dynasts*. Where are we to find, or how tap, that immense fertility of invention which makes the ancient poem so eminently superior?

We can at least be sure that even if the *Iliad* had been *composed* by one man, the labour of *creation* was by no means his alone. His labour was an aesthetic choice out of the mass of folk-imagination, so that most of his energy was spent simply in arrangement, to which a very great part of art may be reduced. The trouble for our modern poets is not any lack of sensibility or technical gifts, which several possess in high degree, but the necessity of creating entire any mythology they may want to use. The only living mythology is that of the nursery, and though one or two poets have relapsed on this, the result cannot deeply affect a healthy adult community. Since poetry should give the illusion of control over circumstance, in one obvious activity these childhood fantasies baulk us – in the realization of sex.

As far as the texture of verse is concerned, the actual descriptive imagery, the modern poet could be very well off. The sciences, industry and engineering, the habitual activities of common life, are all waiting to be drawn from, and provide a variety of material not surpassed by any period. The effort which still seems to hang fire is that of conceiving the poem itself in a modern metaphor, as Marlowe seized on the broad-sheet reports of a case of German charlatanism to embody his lust for absolute power. In this he was helped by the race-consciousness, or subconsciousness, and we must look to this elaborately grotesque tailor of deep-seated desires to provide the costumes for our Hero and his Antagonist. It is none of the poet's business (the attempt is fatal to his art) to supply the Cosmos with mask and cod-piece.

The literature of disillusionment is reaching its last stage; it is becoming popular with the reading-public. Mr. Strachey and Mr. Huxley have replaced Ruskin and Carlyle. No doubt, too, all young men of poetic ambition have their version of *The Waste Land* in their wash-stand drawer. If this is not quite the same thing as popularity it means at least that Mr. Eliot's inspiration was not merely personal; in its coarser manifestations, if not in its ultimate delicacy, it tuned in with an emotion common to the best spirits of the age, a fastidious and anguished rejection of the various forms of satisfaction offered by the Spirit of Historical Culture. The passion for sophistication is only one of the forces of life. The determination not to be fooled is, a young Frenchman said, the disease of our time. But that is no reason for taking the first turning back to divine simplicity. The hefty heroism of Mr. Masefield's narratives is meretricious. The stoicism of Mr. Eliot's middle-aged lover is as tense heroics as the material of his art will bear.

Though we are not likely to cut any more ideals for a good many years, being hardly convalescent from the wholesale extractions of the last century, we cannot imagine the poets remaining content to cultivate the drugget-fields of genteel discontent. A Hero would seem to be due, an exhaustively disillusioned Hero (we could not put up with another new creed) who has yet so much vitality that his thoughts seize all sorts of analogies between apparently unrelated objects and so create an unbiased but self-consistent, humorous universe for himself. The form of him is naturally still in question, but we can be pretty sure that he will not be a Watts horseman in shining armour. Possibly he will be preceded (I should say that he is being preceded) by some tumbling, flour-faced harbingers to the progress (for we cannot grow serious all at once) just as the death-facing wire-walker in the circus is led into the ring by clowns who mime his tragedy. Perhaps the Hero will be one of these loons himself, for the death-defying gesture is a demoded luxury in the modern State. So long as the social mind has no coherent expression like that given it by a supernatural explanation of the universe, the fantastic and the comic, disintegrating forces, will continue the most reputable of styles. They need by no means be inimical to heroic poetry, to which not dignity is essential, but a conception of power: and the further this can be removed from conventional erotic, ethical, or other social values, and the more deeply it can be resolved into its abstract elements, a diagram or skeleton of impulses (like the bare tremendous Sign of the Hero of the Dance of Death), the nearer it will approach a reality underlying the surviving fabric of the old culture.

T. S. ELIOT

Poems, 1909–1925. By T. S. Eliot (Faber & Gwyer)

If there were to be held a Congress of the Younger Poets, and it were desired to make some kind of show of recognition to the poet who has most effectively upheld the reality of the art in an age of preposterous poeticizing, it is not possible to think of any serious rival to the name of T. S. Eliot. Yet, to secure the highest degree of unanimity, such a resolution would have to be worded to the exclusion of certain considerations, and it would concentrate attention on the significance of this work to other poets, rather than on its possession of that quality of 'beauty' for which the ordinary reader looks; though we do not doubt that on this count, too, perhaps the final one, it will slowly but certainly gain the timid ears which only time can coax to an appreciation of the unfamiliar.

'That Mr. T. S. Eliot is the poet who has approached most clearly the solution of those problems which have stood in the way of our free poetic expression', and 'that the contemporary sensibility, which otherwise must have suffered dumbly, often becomes articulate in his verse', are resolutions which express a sort of legal minimum to which individual judgements must subscribe.

The impression we have always had of Mr. Eliot's work, reinforced by this commodious collection in one volume, may be analysed into two coincident but not quite simultaneous impressions. The first is the urgency of the personality, which seems sometimes oppressive, and comes near to breaking through the so finely spun aesthetic fabric; the second is the technique which spins this fabric and to which this slender volume owes its curious ascendency over the bulky monsters of our time. For it is by his struggle with technique that Mr. Eliot has been able to get closer than any other poet to the physiology of our sensations (a poet does not speak merely for himself), to explore and make palpable the more intimate distresses of a generation for whom all the romantic escapes had been blocked. And, though this may seem a heavy burden to lay on the back of technique, we can watch, with the deepening of consciousness, a much finer realization of language, reaching its height in passages in 'The Waste Land' until it sinks under the strain and in 'The Hollow Men' becomes gnomically disarticulate.

The interval is filled with steady achievement, and though the seeds of dissolution are apparent rather early, there is a middle period in which certain things are done which make it impossible for the poet who has read them to regard his own particular problems of expression in the same way again; though he may refuse the path opened, a new field of force has come into being which exerts an influence, creates a tendency, even in despite of antipathy. Such a phenomenon is not in itself a measure of poetic achievement; Donne produced it in his generation; much smaller men, Denham and Waller, in theirs.

Let us take three main stages in this development of technique, the three poems which are, in essence, Mr. Eliot's poem, 'The Love Song of J. Alfred Prufrock', 'Gerontion' and 'The Waste Land.' (The neo-satiric quatrains do not raise any fundamental queries, they are the most easily appreciated of Mr. Eliot's poems, after 'La Figlia che Piange'.

'Gerontion' is much nearer to 'The Waste Land' than 'The Love Song' is to 'Gerontion'. The exquisite's witty drawing-room manner and the deliberately sentimental rhythms give way to more mysterious, further-reaching symbols, and simpler, not blatantly poetic rhythms. As an instance, we have in 'The Love Song':

> For I have known them all already, known them all:
> Have known the evenings, mornings, afternoons,
> I have measured out my life with coffee spoons.

But in 'The Waste Land':

> And I Tiresias have foresuffered all
> Enacted on this same divan or bed;
> I who have sat by Thebes below the wall
> And walked among the lowest of the dead.

The relation, and the differences, between these passages hardly need stressing, but, though I had not intended to enter into an examination of the psychological content of these poems, I find that this subject of fore-knowledge is cardinal to the matter. Fore-knowledge is fatal to the Active man, for whom impulse must not seem alien to the end, as it is to the vegetative life of the poets, whose ends are obscured in the means. The passage in 'Gerontion' beginning: 'After such knowledge, what forgiveness?' and the remainder of the poem are such profound commentary on the consequent annihilation of the will and desire that they must be left to more intimate consideration. The passage is a dramatic monologue, an adaptation one might hazard of the later Elizabethan soliloquy, down even to the Senecal:

> Think
> Neither fear nor courage saves us. Unnatural vices
> Are fathered by our heroism. Virtues
> Are forced upon us by our impudent crimes.

'Gerontion' is a poem which runs pretty close to 'The Waste Land', and it is free from the more mechanical devices of the later poem, but lacks its fine original verse-movements. In the Sweeney quatrains, especially in the last stanzas of 'Among the Nightingales', the noble and the base, the foul and fine, are brought together with a shock; the form has little elasticity, and tends to become, like the couplet, stereotyped antithesis. In the fluid medium of 'The Waste Land' the contrast may be brought about just as violently, or it may be diffused. This contrast is not, of course, the whole content of the poem, but Mr. Eliot has most singularly solved by its means the problem of revoking that differentiation between poetic and real values which has so sterilized our recent poetry. His success is intermittent; after a short passage of exquisite verse he may bilk us with a foreign quotation, an anthropological ghost, or a mutilated quotation. We may appreciate his intention in these matters, the contrast, the parody, enriches the emotional aura surrounding an original passage, but each instance must be judged on its own merits; whether the parody, for instance, is apposite. On this score Mr. Eliot cannot be acquitted of an occasional cheapness, nor of a somewhat complacent pedantry, and since we cannot believe that these deviations are intrinsic to the poetic mind, we must look for their explanation elsewhere. We find it in the intermittent working of Mr. Eliot's verbal imagination. He has the art of words, the skill which springs from sensitiveness, and an unmatched literary apprehension which enables him to create exquisite passages largely at second-hand (lines 60–77). It is when this faculty fails of imaginative support, as it must at times, that certain devices are called in; the intellect is asked to fill in gaps (possibly by reference to the notes, when they are, as they rarely are, significantly helpful) which previous poets have filled in with rhetoric, perhaps, but at any rate by a verbal creation which stimulates the sensibility. The object of this verbal effort is not merely to stimulate the sensibility, since disjunctive syllables can do that, but to limit, control, and direct it towards a more intense apprehension of the whole poem. That is where a failure in verbal inventiveness is a definite poetic lapse. In a traditional poet it would result in a patch of dull verse, in Mr. Eliot's technique we get something like this:

> To Carthage then I came.
>
> Burning, burning, burning burning.
> O Lord thou pluckest me out
> O Lord thou pluckest
>
> burning.

Whether this is better or worse than dull verse I need not decide; that it is a failure, or the aesthetic scheme which would justify it is wrong, can I think be fairly upheld.

Though we may grasp the references to Buddha's Fire Sermon and Augustine's Confessions, and though Mr. Eliot may tell us that 'the collocation of these two representatives of eastern and western asceticism, as the culmination of this part of the poem, is not an accident', we find it difficult to be impressed. It is the danger of the aesthetic of 'The Waste Land' that it tempts the poet to think the undeveloped theme a positive triumph and obscurity more precious than commonplace. The collocation of Buddha and Augustine is interesting enough, when known, but it is not poetically effective because the range of their association is only limited by widely dispersed elements in the poem, and the essential of poetry is the presence of concepts in mutual irritation.

This criticism might be extended to the general consideration of the technique of construction used in 'The Waste Land'; it is still exploited as a method, rather than mastered. The apparently free, or subconsciously motivated, association of the elements of the poem allows that complexity of reaction which is essential to the poet now, when a stable emotional attitude seems a memory of past grandeurs. The freedom from metrical conformity, though not essential as *Don Juan* shows, is yet an added and important emancipation, when the regular metres languish with hardly an exception in the hands of mechanicians who are competent enough, but have no means of making their consciousness speak through and by the rhythm. Mr. Eliot's sense of rhythm will, perhaps, in the end, be found his most lasting innovation, as it is the quality which strikes from the reader the most immediate response.

LAURENCE BINYON AND ALFRED NOYES

The Sirens, an Ode. By Laurence Binyon (Macmillan)
The Torch Bearers (Vol. 2). By Alfred Noyes (Blackwood)

The failure of either of these books to make any strong impression is linked up with certain ideas which we have found to be in the air about the audience for modern poetry, and also, and in particular, since each has an heroic theme, with our suggestions as to the qualifications necessary to the modern hero.

As to the audience first. There are, I know, certain groups which respond to these works as fully as they respond to *Prometheus Unbound*. There is also a smaller group which must be sensible that Mr. Binyon's faculty for manipulating words and rhythms is superior to that of Mr. Noyes. Here and there are individuals like ourselves who do not find in these poems the satisfaction they get from classic poetry, or the sympathy with common preoccupations which they feel in much now obscure modern verse. There may be technical objections to be made to these poems, but it will only come from the quarter where the response was faint in the first place. Technical criticism can never gain a clear verdict; the case is to a great extent prejudged when we call in the expert, our technical knowledge, to find reasons for the condemnation. As each group reacts to the poem as a whole, it will find the technique proportionately adequate or not.

Humanity is in each case the Hero of these poems: to Mr. Noyes the Seeker after Truth; to Mr. Binyon, less specifically, the Adventurer. Destiny the background, History the foreground. Mr. Noyes has a simple narrative scheme in which men of science pass the torch of knowledge from hand to hand. Really, of course, it is no narrative, because there is no end, no aim, and no form therefore. It is the negation of art, like Creative Evolution: a simple getting infinitely better, with one naïve moral idea behind it. Mr. Noyes is a social asset; but in a well-regulated state he would have been made a lower-form master, for his conception of the nobility

of purpose is simple enough to be intelligible only to the uncorrupted. Even considered as a versification of the *Heroes of
Science* series which used to be given as school prizes, the result
does not seem to justify the labour. The poem does not communicate knowledge, at least no more than is contained in any shilling
manual, nor initiate to any experience, except to the vague glamour
of 'discovering truth', which is the stock-in-trade of every hagiographer of science. These torch-bearers are allotted the most
insignificant experiences. Of the particular sensuous experience
which individualizes the poet's idiom and demands fresh metaphors, there is no glimmer.

A few gleanings:

> Shone like a dream in the Eternal mind.
>
>   ... black
> As night ...
>
>   like the foundered spars
> Of lost Atlantis.
>
> The dawn-wind, like a host of spirits, ...
>
> A bird cried, once, a sharp ecstatic cry
> As if it saw an angel.
>
> Blind throats ...
>
>   (A Miltonic parody!)

If 'science' had really meant anything, poetically, to Mr. Noyes,
it would have altered his universe; would have created metaphors.
As it is, he sails his pretentious kite with rags of literature and
superstition in its tail.

To drag Mr. Noyes out of his group in this way is unfair; he loses
all his beauty, like a fish on the bank. It was necessary though, in
order to show the unimportance of this sort of connexion between
poetry and knowledge.

The hues and graces of *The Sirens* will also suffer from similar
treatment, but we have only to put these poems back in their
village pond and they will regain their natural freshness. What we
are showing is simply this, that the 'knowledge' of any period is as
much a reflection of its sensibility as its poetry, and its poetry will
share and show the qualities and consequences of its knowledge,
so far as it is alive, and of any other outstanding and common
experience, such as the war. Poetry will deal with it in such a way

as, generally, to avoid factual references, and the reader will take up these references unconsciously; the texture, idiom, rhythm, and imagery of the verse all helping, and all dating. Mr. Turner's *In Time like Glass* succeeds Einstein as obviously as *The Waste Land* succeeds Sir James Frazer.

Dating helps to explain our group system. Mr. Noyes and his audience are roughly 1880 minds, Mr. Binyon and his about 1900. We base these figures not on the facts referred to in the subject of the poem – there are none in Mr. Binyon's poem – but to the way in which the poet approaches the Universe – by his sensibility to heroism. Mr. Binyon is all on; he is a straight backer. It is characteristic of the contemporary poet to put his money on each way. I mean that irony has come back to the attitude; it is the opportunism of the disinherited. For Mr. Binyon, however, Man, the mediaeval Son of God, is still in possession of the universe; he, of course, admits the evil of industrialism:

> Hark to the hammers endlessly hammering!

and of the Sirens who lure our animal nature—

> Eternal woman, wonderful, with a bosom
> Heaved as with love, and with warm, white eyelids
> Over eyes cruel and young,

but the doubt is transcended in a realization of our supraterrestrial destiny.

Can a poem with such a theme claim to be a contemporary poem? I would say that is possible, since such an emotional constitution is by no means rare, but unlikely, because the more vital people, including the poets, do not see in the universe at present the material for such a structure. If such a poem were to be written, the terms of reference would all have to be re-created, and the result would, no doubt, be very obscure and unfamiliar and it would have to wait for proper appreciation till our generation, too, were out of the way. There is, however, no sign of such a re-creative faculty in Mr. Binyon. We can follow all his references as fast as he can make them. That is to say, there is no sign of his having apprehended any non-literary experience, no sign of contemporary speech to his idiom, or of contemporary life in his imagery. His foundry scene in the lurid Brangwyn manner refers us back to wine vats and Titans. When he would rise to rhapsody, it becomes apparent that Mr. Binyon possesses an emotive sensibility to words, not the sensuous appreciation common to the articulate poet. To Mr. Binyon words mean states of soul, not things or sensations. Hence preference for the general term prevents the mind from being stimulated through the senses. The eye slides over the metaphors and perceives them no more than the books on a familiar shelf; or accepts them dutifully like the promises of a politician. This style, indeed, is the journalese of poetry, a real decadence. In this phase of a poetic convention, words are no longer used to define objects, to circumscribe and make palpable a sensation, to direct the maximum intensity to a point, but to diffuse an emotional prejudice over the largest possible area. The language of *The Sirens* is representative of much that is accepted as poetry at present, a parasitic growth supporting its brief existence with the sap of earlier aspirations. It is so like the language of poetry that the unsophisticated are deceived. The emotional associations of the vocabulary are so strong that it does actually produce an effect; that is why we cannot refuse *The Sirens* the title of poem. Today, to a number of people, it is one, but as its effects are derived from a series of rapidly dissolving combinations, the chances of its surviving long enough to be called a modern poem are very few. And a poem which was never modern will not pass into that curious state of suspended animation by means of which the poems we call classic are preserved active to the palate.

AN EARLY AMERICAN POET

Selected Poems of Carl Sandburg. Edited by Rebecca West (Cape)

Sandburg writes in his own way; you can tell a poem of his by the feel of it and that is more important than your liking or disliking it. Style is not everything the poet needs, but it is the first thing and a substantial beginning. Sandburg is the most obvious fact in the great literary Wish of the last decade – for real American poetry free from the traditions of what, for propaganda purposes, was called the English tradition, but which was really the mannerism of a small colonial clique. It is easy to understand the irritation of the younger intellectuals with the moribund New England reputations which gave them nothing which could possibly look like a foundation for a national poetry. Poe and Melville apart, as too wide-seeing for the moment, Whitman, with all his limitations, is the first milestone on the way out. But the road is longish and the Americans have been impatient. Possessing everything that Europe has in an abundance which has reduced large tracts of many other-wise agreeable cities to the level of entertainment-caterers for their garrisons of spoilt children, it has seemed to some of them that they ought to have already a poetry as distinct and superlative as their civilization is of its kind. They have wanted to have a distinctive poetry before they have existed as a distinct community long enough to absorb all their alien blood. For a poet has to be born into a language and a way of thinking that language. An immigrant Englishman would no more make an American writer than an immigrant Italian; our idioms are distinct, and it is through the realization of its automatic uniqueness that American literature is coming into existence.

In the early stages, a national literature is likely to be regional, impregnated with the tang of the speech among which the writer has grown. This is always a virtue, even in an era of metropolitanism; but, when a nation has only a second-hand literary language, it becomes of first importance. The exiled and vacationist Americans have, perhaps, from this point of view, retarded their country's emancipation; for they have drained it of a good deal of its talent, and an increased dexterity in the handling of ideas is not an efficient substitute for the writer's absorption in his environment.

Though it would be sentimental to advocate a return to re-gionalism at the present stage of English literature, such a con-dition is a sign of health in contemporary America. Localization is Sandburg's strength. As the middle-west, with its metropolis Chicago, is the materially dominant section of America, it may well be that its idiom will be the determinant of the continental language. It has more vigour, if at present less delicacy, than the language of the rustic Frost and the urban Robinson, and it is incomparably more vital than the jejune nomenclature of the imagists.

Sandburg has succeeded in doing, within the limits of his per-sonality, what has long been recognized as the thing that has to be done. He has accepted his environment as material for his poetry – the things that surround him for imagery and the names by which people call them for the texture of his verse. It is surprising how much rhythm he gets simply by accumulating naturally-pointed speech units. He is not psalmodic as Whitman becomes, nor does he often adopt recognizable metrical units unless they derive from rhythms of the vernacular. Sandburg's rhythm, though, is often not sufficiently emphasized, and might benefit by a higher degree of formalism.

Sandburg has been helped to do what he has done by a simplicity in his nature; he has found the marvellous in the growth of the middle-west. He can praise Chicago for being what it is:

> Laughing the stormy, husky, brawling laughter of youth, half-naked, sweating, proud to be Hog Butcher, Tool Maker, Stacker of Wheat, Player with Railroads, and Freight Handler to the Nation.

But this titanic happening is realized against the frieze of events. Dead civilizations mock the blatancy of this fervour, or their case is simply stated:

> A thousand red men cried and went away to new places for corn and women: a million white men came and put up skyscrapers, threw out rails and wires, feelers to the salt sea; now the smokestacks bite the skyline with stub teeth.

A strong sense of tonic values, a particular feeling for consonants (perhaps the Scandinavian blood counts here) helps to give cohesion to Sandburg's periods. And the Scandinavian nature-awe gives the needed reaction from constant optimism. Sometimes this in-bred tension, suddenly released in an environment less inimical, swings over to a sentimentalism which is definitely too sweet.

It is stated that Sandburg 'expresses' the middle-west. Miss Rebecca West's preface does not tell us if the populace or any section of it appreciates the fact that it is being made articulate. They can have no excuse for refusing to popularize Sandburg – his vices and many virtues are equally of their sort. Perhaps they do, but we should like to know.

RICHARD HUGHES

Confessio Juvenis. By Richard Hughes (Chatto & Windus)

The traditional supremacy of verse is more seriously threatened by recent achievements in prose than it ever was by the polemics of the free verse movement. Verse has not been able to retain that immediacy in the expression of reality which has been its essential quality in the past, and poetic theory has rather flattered its tendency to easy emotional gratification through uncurbed phantasy. Prose, on the other hand, in various lesser currents and supremely in the 'foul chaos'[1] of *Ulysses*, has realized contacts which had not previously been possible outside the field of influence generated by regularly rhythmic control. In Mr. Joyce's prose the concept achieves its maximum vitality, whereas in most modern verse it exists as an anaemic parasite.

Verse is unnecessary for a great many purposes for which it is used, from the inertia of habit. But it would be a rash assumption to suppose that verse was not still the most powerful instrument for certain narrowly defined ends . . . which would not be by any means trivial ends, word gymnastics or amorous imbecilities, but as it were quintessential ends, of which one is envisaged in *The Waste Land*.

The direct rivalry of prose should stimulate the writing of genuine verse, for plainly such a very vigorous competitor cannot be met with obsolete strategy. Which of the various new tendencies in technique will finally predominate cannot usefully be discussed, but a movement towards an economy of means seems to be definitely established.

A writer in *The Times Literary Supplement*, however, complains that 'there is a constant intellectual teasing to have verse approach the current use and enunciation of words.' It is this teasing, overcome but never annihilated by the stronger verbal sensibility of the poet, that has kept our poetry, to the extent it is, pure and vital. Any movement towards poetic creation contains two elements, a reaction against the unintellectual use of debased poetic idiom, an effort to re-define the content of words; and the creation of a new idiom (which in its turn will be debased and destroyed) not referable to the immediate intellectual obligations of language.

It is an accident of the time, a limitation that must be admitted, that there is at present more evidence of the first of these processes being at work than the second. The verse of Mr. Hughes is an example to the point, it is purged of the grosser emotional conventionalities, for a rather laborious virility. But, in the creation of a style, he shows little personal sensibility. Was it not Mr. Robert

[1] I have seen this immortalizing phrase attributed to Sir Edmund Gosse – how unjustly I do not know.

Graves who, in an unguarded moment, loosed on us this trotting stanza, of which *Confessio Juvenis* contains several specimens:

> Robin stark dead on twig,
> Song stiffened in it:
> Fluffed feathers may not warm
> Bone-thin linnet.

'Glaucopis' is a tragedy in jingle which is comic in its affected economy of language. There can be a mock concision as well as a false exuberance in poetic style:

> John Fane Dingle
> By Romney Brook
> Shot a crop-eared owl,
> For pigeon mistook.

Richard Hughes's longer pieces are more accomplished. 'The Rolling Saint', 'Unicorn Mad', and the two odes on 'Vision' have a metrical dexterity which is quite uncommon. But in these last two the actual poetic content, realized experience, seems very small in proportion to the verbal energy expended in the elaboration of a rather commonplace metaphysical proposition. A public claim to vision, to a perception of the very structure of the universe, ought to be backed up by something less trite than these literary lucubrations:

> Naked of words alone we pass:
> We hang our names upon a tree,
> Pile epithets upon the grass
> In useless heaps: our restless verbs
> We chain – they stalk uneasy.
> Naked of words we enter in
> Where formless beauties walk in threes,
> And soundless music stirs no trees,
> And thoughtless knowledge bursts no mind,
> And uneyed senses thin as wind
> Swim on the darkness with no fin,
> No light wing-fall;
> And speechless Joy in Sorrow's arms
> Engenders Nothing: and the hours
> Flatten and shine like pigments on the wall.

Thus the pretension to vision, however genuine in private, lacking a creative sense of words, turns to prettiness. At every step

the verse form, not of itself but because it is not mastered, leads
away from the immediate object of the experience, whatever it was,
to conventional verbal equations, which, though they may remind
the writer of what it was, do not evoke a fresh sensation in the
reader's mind. It is good, it is ingenious, but it does not convince.
Samuel Butler's blunt diction is really more poetic:

> He had First Matter seen undrest:
> He took her naked, all alone,
> Before one rag of form was on.
> The Chaos too he had descried,
> And seen quite through or else he lied;
> Not that of pasteboard, which men show
> For groats, at Fair of Barthol'mew,
> But its great grandsire, first of the name.

'More poetic' is a comparison which cannot be used in the present
dilapidated state of critical terminology, without an attempt at
definition. I mean *poetic* simply to designate a definite stylistic
quality, and I do not see that it can be usefully applied in any
other way. To use it of the kind of effect (as when people talk of
Coleridge's *poetic* imagination or of certain *poetic* stories), and not
of the means, is to open ultimate problems which can only obscure
the contemporary issue. An expression, in prose or verse, is poetic
when the object is immediately realized. To classify objects, which
in the last analysis are feelings, into poetic and non-poetic is to
plunge into endless and meaningless labour. A number of feelings,
those associated with the idea of destiny for instance, are perpetually interesting and it is not surprising that they should be the
subject of a great deal of poetry; unfortunately, they are also the
subject of an infinitely greater mass of stuff which is simply negligible. On the other hand, feelings not generally regarded with
passionate interest will impel this interest when realized in poetic
style; not because the subject has been made more 'important',
blown-up, idealized, but because it has been exactly apprehended
in its particular implications; without this, any pretension to universal significance will be a sham.

HUMBERT WOLFE

Humoresque. By Humbert Wolfe (Benn)

In considering Mr. Wolfe's verse, we are in no danger of being deluded as to its real value by ambitious subject matter. His 'feelings' are also the subject of the sentimental verses to be found in the popular magazines, but he has read the poets with rather more artistic consciousness than those humbler laureates of the heart. But his attempts to stylize the banal are frustrated by an ingrained banality of style. The obvious may yield exquisite fruit, if cultivated with the devotion and intelligence of, say, Toulet, Pellerin, or Derème. But, when the expression is anything less than consummate, there is obviously nothing there to break the hideous fall. Mr. Wolfe is not well qualified to be a *fantaisiste*, for he seems to have a merely elementary sense of irony, a defect which is reflected in his technique:

> In the wonder month of May
> a German and a British
> poet threw their verse away
> to decorate a fetish.
> That was May. A little later
> both philanderers
> having found the spring a traitor
> broke their hearts in verse

O qui dira les torts de la Rime? Are these ugly noises the result of Art, of a deliberate apprenticeship to Verlaine's suggestion, *'rien que la nuance'*? Or, perhaps, they are the work of modernist ambitions, like the absence of capitals at the beginning of lines?

Really the traditional great-poet manner demands less of the writer, and Mr. Wolfe might do well to cultivate a vein in which he shows some facility. One does not often come across such a perfect example of the naïve-profound as in these stanzas:

> Some call this God, and some the hopeless cry
> of death to the unborn. I do not care.
> I only know the day that you passed by
> whatever men may call this, it was there.
> It was not only that the deathless bond
> was tied between us by a single word

but something in us both had passed beyond
into that incommunicable surd.

It is a pity that such experiences are not permanent and complete.

POETRY CALENDAR

The Best Poems of 1926. Edited by Thomas Moult (Cape)

As no one else seems to have done so, it is left for us to state that
this book is a disgrace to compiler and publishers. There is no
particular reason why Mr. Moult should not name, and reprint,
annually the poems he has liked best in the year's periodicals, but
he might well keep his selection private. It has already been so
thoroughly demonstrated that he has neither taste nor judgement
that it is quite unnecessary for him to go on exhibiting his de-
ficiencies year after year. If he must publish, however, and this is
also the publisher's concern, a more modest title would be becoming. The book might then rest in decent obscurity. As it is, it is
necessary to protest, not merely that Mr. Moult's 'Best Poems' are
very nearly the worst, but that for any person, or even committee,
no matter how well-qualified to offer to make any such choice is a
pretension deserving ridicule.

Very few of Mr. Moult's poets have even a manner of their own.
One or two contributors, however, achieve lonely eminence. Only
Mr. Noyes, pausing momentarily from the composition of epics,
could throw off the following lofty and original sentiments:

> Know'st thou where that kingdom lies?
>   Take no lanthorn in thy hand.
> Search not the unfathomed skies,
>   Journey not o'er sea and land,
> Grope no more to east and west,
> Heaven is locked within thy breast.

The superbly poetical 'know'st thou' and 'lanthorn' could proceed from the pen of this master alone, while Mr. Humbert Wolfe's
friends, the elves, with their silver flutes are clearly responsible for:

> The echo of a song
> makes all the stars a gong.

They would never ask in fairyland whether every star is transformed into a gong, or all the stars into one gong, since there they

> ... are impatient of truth, that is no more
> than finite stain upon the infinite.

I. A. RICHARDS

Principles of Literary Criticism. By I. A. Richards (Kegan Paul)

We are not often privileged to follow so lucid a discussion of the
fundamental conditions of aesthetic judgement as that with which
the above volume presents us. Its analysis of current methods of
evaluating works of art is delicate, destructive, and final; the
mechanism with which it replaces them may not have the same
quality of finality, but its adaptation to the needs of our time is so
nearly complete that we cannot imagine its essential modification.
The tone of the book is astringent, and its comment uncompro-
mising, but it is not dogmatic; it offers us 'not a rock to shelter under
or to cling to, rather an efficient aeroplane in which to ride the
tempestuous turmoil of change' to which the human mind is
native.

It is in definiteness of statement rather than in any novelty of
conception that Mr. Richards's preliminary destruction is valuable.
Anyone who has already freed himself from the system of values
imposed on literature by the Kantian metaphysic, with its cate-
gorical imperative of judgement, will have been teased by the unreality of such terms as ideal Beauty or pure Beauty, and its
derivative, the specifically aesthetic emotion. This dissatisfaction is
the first step to a real appreciation of literature, but it provides no
effective instrument for the organization of the responses evoked
by the impact of actual specimens of the literary 'stuff'. Mr.
Richards arrives at a basis for the judgement of value by examining
the processes of psychology. He does not differentiate between the
kind of stimulus which we receive from raw life and the kind
which we receive from the representation of life in the arrangements
recognized as artistic forms.

He shows, in fact, that there is no basic difference (though there is a
difference of degree) in the quality of response which we receive from

certain arrangements rather than from others; it is this difference of degree which determines his scale of values. The created work is valuable when the response to the impulses which it sets up is the satisfaction of an appetency, or of appetencies, which does not involve 'the frustration of some equal or *more important* appetency'. It is obvious that if this definition of value is to be anything but a dodge round the problem, the critic must particularize the hierarchy of appetencies, must state the positive from which his comparative *more important* is derived. One could wish that Mr. Richards had been more explicit on this point, though, if I understand him rightly, it is a matter which is determined by biological evolution, a fact which naturally follows from his abandonment of an absolute point of reference. The physio-psychological entity, the individual, is continually changing under the constant impact of sensations, so that the same work can never evoke the same response; hence 'there are specialist and universal poets, and the specialist may be developing in a manner either consistent or inconsistent with general development, a consideration of extreme importance in judging the value of his work.' Here is an opportunity for a false syllogism – to assert that the poet who is in line with the general development is a better poet than the one who is not, when really all one can deduce from the premises is that he will exist *as a poet* for a longer time.

This existence of poetry *in* the audience is the crucial point in Mr. Richards's theory of value. It has an obvious affinity with the Augustan conception of poetry as the supreme social attitude, and similarly, in spite of his codicils, his reasoning tends to diminish the importance of the solitary illuminant who is the natural outcome of a metaphysical theory of criticism. Mr. Richards admits the possibility of 'admirable though utterly eccentric experience', and claims the right to neglect work which may be 'admirable in itself' if 'a general approximation to it is impossible'. He says, too, 'what is excellent and what is to be imitated are not necessarily the same', though his criterion of excellence is that which we tend to imitate. His definition of value does not admit of a thing being 'admirable in itself'. In his anxiety, which one appreciates, to assert the 'normality' of the poetic mind, he has inadvertently put in juxtaposition the mentality of 'the usual and ordinary man' and that of Blake, Nietzsche and the Apocalypst, and naturally recoils at their incompatibility. Certainly this difference must be only relative, not one of kind, yet Mr. Richards seems to underestimate the gap, and, for the moment, though only for the moment, to threaten us with a dynasty of 'occasional' poets.

It would give an inadequate notion of the wealth of ideas in Mr. Richards's book if one neglected to draw attention to the chapters of technical – more particularly literary – criticism. His analysis of the effect of metre, which he concludes to be 'for the most difficult and most delicate utterances . . . the all but inevitable means', is an example of the heightened understanding which is reached by his way of approach to the subject:

'Metre adds to all the variously fated expectancies which make up rhythm a definite temporal pattern, and its effect is not due to our perceiving a pattern in something outside us, but to our becoming patterned ourselves. With every beat of the metre a tide of antici- pation in us turns and swings, setting up as it does so extraordinarily extensive sympathetic vibrations.'

The chapters on 'Imagination' and allied subjects are extremely illuminating, and many ideas are set down which should yield very profitably to a fuller exposition. There are a couple of pages on the nature of Tragedy which are a much-needed antidote to the usual comments which that breeding-ground of sentimentality brings forth.

A suggestive assertion is that 'irony is constantly a characteristic of poetry which is of the highest order.' Certainly there is a high per- centage of irony in the poetry which we most admire at the present time. It would need longer space than a review to discuss such a problem, which as Mr. Richards states it, is made of fundamental importance. Since it is only one of a multitude of fine perceptions, it may, perhaps, stand as a sort of colophon to an appreciation which is far from exhaustive.

ROBERT GRAVES

Contemporary Techniques of Poetry: A Political Analogy. By Robert Graves (Hogarth)

A pamphlet war might do a good deal to improve the modern race of poets; at least there is room for a literary analogy to Bern- hardi's too-abused theory. Toleration or indifference has gone so far, and so prostituted the terms of praise, that it is impossible to tell from an ordinary review whether a book of poems contains really original work or if it just avoids the more obvious commonplaces. Under this wadding the feebler shoots are protected from the contempt which would naturally cut them off, and live to blossom in collected mediocrity – absorbing so much sun and air from the healthier growths. The task of pruning is such a delicate one that autocratic statements are not to be recommended; it is by personal evaluations, such as this essay of Mr. Graves's, backed up by the knowledge of practice, that some order may be introduced into the present muddle.

He draws his analogy from contemporary politics by dividing the poets into three parties – Conservatives, Liberals, and Left-Wing reformers, revolutionaries and exiles. His comments on the techniques of the two constitutional parties are mischievous and mildly destructive; they have the wisdom-in-humour, the disarming smile which always saves Graves's prose divagations from becoming portentous, but at the same time open a path for casual evasions which does not always tempt him in vain.

'I am the historian merely; but having regard to the enormous dead-weight of prestige behind the Conservative view, and to the popular success of the Central Party, I shall possibly find myself making out the clearest case for the party which is least vocal, the Left Wing.'

A most courteous assassin. But is it simply the desire to champion the oppressed which enables Mr. Graves to make out the best case for the less-appreciated of the younger poets? Do not their merits entitle them not merely to an equalitarian, but to a preferential judgement? To get itself said, any new thing has to break up, more or less, and re-model, the old forms of expression. All the poets lumped together as the tradition were innovators in their time and none of the new modifications of verse technique quoted by Mr. Graves seems to me incapable of being absorbed into the English tradition. It is rather too much of a sacrifice to surrender to merely conventional versifiers the title of traditionalists, so that those who have real vigour of expression must be branded, though honourably, revolutionaries. The blood of Donne and Milton is more likely to be found in these apparent throw-outs than in the approved stereotypes which crowd our sumptuous anthological mausoleums.

I differ rather in approach than in conclusions from Mr. Graves, and must commend his essay as a timely and valuable piece of propaganda. His chapter on 'Structure' is most suggestive, though condensed. The psychological basis of verse is a subject which has occupied him before and led to interesting statements. Changes in the physiology of verse, diction and rhythm, are manifestations only of the more elusive renovation of the core of the mind.

The outlook for poetry, if it can find its audience and assert true values, is certainly more encouraging than it was twenty years ago. Many powerful conventions have been realized to be demoralizing, and experience is seen to be pretty well autonomous within the conditions of successful expression. The war of attrition against critical inertia still needs speeding up, and for this short raids into the opposing trenches are most efficacious.

VIRGINIA WOOLF

The Common Reader. By Virginia Woolf (Hogarth)

There is no explicit link between the literary essays which make up this volume and to be just to Mrs. Woolf it would be necessary to criticize each of them separately, the longer ones at any rate, for it is a great virtue in these pieces to stimulate a sort of private discussion in the reader's consciousness. If however, the reader is of the sort that finds discussion harsh and unprofitable, the picturesque is sufficiently in evidence to enable him to ignore very comfortably the deeper implications of Mrs. Woolf's criticism. The essay called 'The Pastons and Chaucer' is to my mind the most substantial in the book and it shows as clearly as any what is constantly the subject of her inquiry, the influence on a writer of the society in which he lives – the relation of artist and audience.

Analysing the freedom with which Chaucer absorbs into his verse every kind of experience, ignorant of our uncomfortable distinction between the poetic and the unpoetic subject, Mrs. Woolf says:

'He could sound every note in the language instead of finding a great many of the best gone dumb from disuse, and thus, when struck by daring fingers, giving off a loud discordant jangle out of keeping with the rest.'

And of course, this freedom from any necessity of verbal compromise is simply the reflection of an unprejudiced relationship to experience, of an 'unconscious ease' . . . 'which is only to be found where the poet has made up his mind about the world they (his women) live in, its end, its nature, and his own craft and technique, so that his mind is free to apply its force fully to its object'.

This happy state has been, in some considerable degree, the lot of the writers of any age remarkable for its literature, the Elizabethan, the Augustan, and the Victorian. In spite of internal dissension, the writers of these periods had a solid stratum to which finally they could refer to give value to their emotional utterances. For the Elizabethans it was the passionate life, for the Augustans the social life, the 'honnête homme' of polite scepticism replacing the chivalrous knight of the literature of religious idealism. The Victorians, of course, lack the serenity of their predecessors; the protestations of Carlyle and Browning are symptoms of the insidious ravages of the will-to-believe which replaces inbred conviction. Still, they took advantage of the lull before the storm and produced the last examples of the literature which retains its expressive value along the whole scale of group sensibilities.

Since then, the reading-public has split. We have the small body of educated sharp-witted readers from whom a small spark of intelligence sometimes flickers; but being passionate, if at all, only about values and not experience, ultimately uncreative; and themselves so frequently practitioners as to be unsatisfactory even as audience. Beyond lies the vast reading-public which is led by the nose by the high-class literary-journalist-poet type; and its tail tweaked by the paragraphist with pretensions not rising above personal gossip. Mrs. Woolf sketches this gloomy scene with a restraint and delicacy which we cannot emulate. But her essay, 'How It Strikes a Contemporary', coming as it does at the end of a volume which begins with Chaucer, flings the contrast of then-and-now into unmitigated light and shade. Mrs. Woolf concludes that as all the signs point to this as an off-season the best thing the critic can do to fill in the time is 'to scan the horizon; see the past in relation to the future; and so prepare the way for masterpieces to come'.

This is advice which the middle-aged will perhaps welcome; but we doubt if those studious evangelists are of much use as path-straighteners for the Messiah. If the past is any guide, he will come with none of the signs of grace and perhaps attempt to borrow five pounds from the ladies and gentlemen scanning the horizon. For what, in fact, does all the present fuss about literature amount to? It is the disease of an age which has no proper outlet for a great deal of its energy and so directs the surplus into forms which retain a certain amount of prestige from the time when they were the ornaments of the life of educated aristocrats. It should be clearly understood that creative literature has nothing whatever to do with the mass of material which in books and periodicals is produced as literary criticism. The public has never been so confused and debased in its tastes as during the fifty years in which the discussion of literary questions has become general. The only useful criticism must be technical, but the stuff the public swallows now is, like pap the mother-monkey provides for its young, a masticated product easy of digestion; only, the parent monkey does not extract all the nourishment.

If the discussion of literature is of little help towards the production of masterpieces, in itself not an inspiring aim, the admission of boredom from the public might lead to better results. In its present tendencies literature is far too destructive, too anti-social, or at least enquiring, to be appreciated by those whose appetites are sufficiently keen to enable them to relish the contemporary spectacle. Modern work appeals necessarily to a restricted audience, of no particular class but with a common sensibility, and there is no object in trying to expand this audience artificially. It is certainly to the advantage of literature, now, to fall below commercial standards of value. If the common reader could really be identified with the author of these essays we should not have been able to make them the excuse for a tirade. Unfortunately the sensitiveness which is common to them is a quality with which we rarely meet in contemporary criticism. Perhaps we may hope it is a property of the inarticulate, who silent and unnamed, form the real modern audience. Whether or not Mrs. Woolf's title be an appeal from the self-styled *illuminati* to the anonymous throng, at any rate she may claim the attribute which is the most valuable of those in Johnson's definition of the common reader, one whose sense is 'uncorrupted by literary prejudices'.

'A CHARMING PARASITE'

Authors Dead and Living. By F. L. Lucas (Chatto & Windus)

Mr. Lucas prefaces his book with a shoddy sort of apology for the indeterminateness of his own criticism, summarizing the lack of agreement among Aristotle, Coleridge, Wordsworth, and others of his more ambitious predecessors. No doubt the pedantic don is a bore, but he is sometimes useful to lazier but more intelligent men; the same excuse cannot be made for the man of learning, who, with the affectation of familiarity, flatters the common audience by discrediting the apparatus of critical thought.

But for Mr. Lucas criticism is not an instrument; it is an entertainment, or, more precisely:

'Criticism then is a form of art which deals not primarily with life, but with other art – a charming parasite; it is a form of expression which allows us to overhear the introspection of an intelligent person into his own reactions in response to a work of art.'

Mr. Lucas uses the shirt-sleeve style of the popular University lecturer, and the elaborate facetiousness that goes with it. 'Second best bedlamite lives of Shakespeare', and 'a veritable somnambulance corps of poets' are, perhaps, no more than the penalty of forced picturesqueness; his fondness for the journalese of the higher journalism is constant, a permanent disability . . . 'the calm, relentless, bitter logic, as of destiny itself' . . . 'the feeling that for all the agony of transience, all the disillusion of hopes in vain fulfilled, there are no consolations, but the bitter beauty of the Universe and the frail human pride that confronts it for a moment undismayed'. These clichés are staple matter of Mr. Lucas's introspection, with little regard for the particular poet who is under examination; calculation of the proportion of sibilants to open vowels would be as pertinent.

These big, noble, tragic emotions which Mr. Lucas paraphrases indefatigably, are for him the substance of poetry, and this fact gives his book an emotional, if not an intelligent, coherence. So the book might be called criticism even in our sense of the word, for he does, from that basis, generalize from his experience, though the results we generally disagree with.

He has read widely, but not so profitably as if he had thought more. On the subject of the decline of poetry in the eighteenth century he drops this hint without picking it up again:

> Hence Dryden's remark, amazing when one stops to think what it implies, that the composition of poetry is and ought to be of wit.

He does not tell us what he thought of it when he stopped to think, whether he was amazed at its profundity or stupidity; the fact that he stopped to think is left to our reverent contemplation. But surely Mr. Lucas, who must know the sense in which 'wit' was used by Dryden and his contemporaries, saw the strength of the notion behind that thought. Again, he says, 'Rosenberg's idea of poetry as an "interesting complexity of thought", while it serves to describe some kinds of it, is a perilous guide for practice.' So are all guides, for that matter. He misses the significant point, the parallelism with Dryden's remark and its peculiar relevance to the contemporary aesthetic of poetry.

'The Progress of Poetry' (bones of Swift) is a long, ambitious and fantastical attempt to bring modern poetry to its senses.

'In the tom-tom lying silent now in some museum gallery the dreaming imagination may discern the cradle of Shakespeare. When some hairy object in a wilderness first found that making a regular series of noises somehow gave vent to something he felt . . .' the flatulent anthropoid was no doubt a lineal ancestor of Shakespeare. 'The mother of music came now into the voice of man as she had come, even then, thousands of centuries before, into the cry of the cuckoo amid the woods of a yet unhuman world.' No matter that birds are a later development than man, 'Genesis' is good enough for poets and literary critics. After a little anthropology, we reach solid ground and the threshold of history. 'Verse had at first been improvised – like those hoarse raven-croaks of sudden song uttered by the men of the Icelandic sagas, when their steel has bitten into the foemen's brain, or their foemen's steel to their own.'

So we have the familiar romantic view of the primitive, comparatively free and uncontrolled; 'but, as time goes on and men think more and act and feel less violently, some of the old giant vigour dies away.' And, in the end, tradition becomes almost too much for the poets. A pretty picture, but from all we know of surviving poetry the early poets had to walk in very narrow conventional paths. We are much freer; in fact, at the present time we suffer from having no master-convention. When we get one, poetry may revive again. We agree with Mr. Lucas that this poetry will say very much the same things as the old. But, in order to say the same thing in a different environment, the way of saying it must be different.

His indictment of the younger poets is pointless because indiscriminate. If he objects to certain tendencies, he should have named the exponents of them instead of tarring everyone with the Dada brush. But at the end we do at least know what kind of emotions Mr. Lucas likes to imbibe with his poetry and this gives us the key to the wants of most readers, perhaps; they demand that poetry shall present them with a magnified replica of a nobly suffering self. Their optimistic protestations are faint, muffled by the presentiment that this sort of poetry cannot long survive the collapse of the egocentric universe. Hence his Canute-like attitude in face of the advancing tide, which he exhorts by all the corpses in the Pantheon and Mr. Humbert Wolfe, to hold 'with a Roman strength' to 'its sense of form and order, of unexpected beauty and sudden pity, of certain standards, mistaken it may be, but genuine, amid the chaos of the world'. At which point in a pious but precarious pose, half-threatening and half-propitiatory, Mr. Lucas leaves the reader to the mercy of the future and makes the best use of his heels, vanishing in a consolatory cloud.

EPIC POETRY

God, Man, and Epic Poetry. By H. V. Routh (Cambridge University Press)

Epic poetry has not been much written about by the younger critics and it is doubtful if genuine enjoyment of it is at all common nowadays. If it is not enjoyed, it is obviously a good thing that it should not be written about, but the neglect, with the consequent concentration of criticism on the lyric and shorter forms, is, perhaps, responsible for most of the more extreme propaganda which has infected our attitude towards all forms of verse composition during the last thirty years. It is difficult to see how the tenets of all the more or less subversive schools from symbolist to surréalist could have seemed at all plausible to any but those who were ignorant of, or for some reason antipathetic to (as was Poe), the more extensive and exhaustive experience of epic poetry.

Yet, without identifying ourselves with those contemporary 'lovers of verse' who, Mr. Routh says, 'now expect to dissociate the purest and most felicitous poetry from any story of men's earthly pursuits, such as are portrayed in dramas and satires; and to look for it in glimpses of the poet's own soul': or that we come 'more and more to search in the words for what their author feels but cannot say'; without identifying ourselves with such contemporary 'lovers of verse' and their generous quest, we confess to a certain ceremoniousness in approaching the vaster monuments of fame. One has not the same expectation of spontaneous enjoyment as in the creations of more restricted and intensive actions.

But, if we look at its productions without regard to their poetic quality, we shall see that there has been no diminution in the quantitative energy of the epic spirit. Simply, the poets with any glimmering of talent seem to have left the most ambitious themes to those who had none at all, or at least who drowned what they may have had in the infinite extension of their meagre narrative. In other words, given a man sensitive in the way a poet must be, would not the modern epic theme involve him in the necessity of representing such general and socialized emotions, that he would instinctively avoid the attempt?

The whole *raison d'être* of epic is its presentation of an heroic type in which the particular conflicts which most beset the consciousness or semi-consciousness of the race may be resolved. The fact that the earliest surviving creations of this kind were records of the achievements of the Heroic Age set all the poetasters copying the martial type of hero. Yet even as early as the *Odyssey* he had been succeeded by the 'intellectual' hero, as Mr. Routh shows. (Of course, martial heroes appeared again in the Northern Heroic Age.) But more important than this copying of externals is the fact that the products of the Heroic Age have a quite peculiar homogeneity – the poet's heart is beating in time with the great heart of the public in a way which is impossible in a society where the survival conditions are not so narrow as absolutely to stereotype the valuable forms of action.

But, even in the Heroic Age, we must remember that the poet only spoke for a caste, *Beowulf* is as much restricted to the aristocratic warrior as the *Iliad*. Where are the peasants and craftsmen on whom these civilizations depend? Probably they were not deliberately hidden, but no one thought they were worth making a song about. It was the *comitatus* that had to be worked up to the point at which the idea of its own heroism would involve it inextricably in heroic action in the next day's scrap. Epic, or heroic poetry, is strictly utilitarian; that is where it differs most from the lyric, and, as most theory has lately been based on the lyric, Mr. Routh's elaborate study should do a great deal towards getting critics to pull themselves together and reconsider the whole question of poetic composition. And we must remember this caste origin of epic poetry when we ask, in a sentimental moment, where is the modern epic which has thrilled and inspired the race, from the highest to the lowest? Probably there never has been one (religious myths, perhaps, excepted). Certainly, various castes within the community have had their own epic cycles, though except for Dante's and Milton's poems, out of these no poem of pure literary proportions has crystallized since the Heroic Age. In this respect, Mr. Routh might have touched upon the huge, multi-tongued cycle of which our Reynard the Fox was the central character. Here we have, definitely the 'intellectual hero' of a rising caste, the bourgeois (not the serf), which was beginning to get the better of its rather heavy-brained feudal lords – a ruling type surviving from the age of conquest, and of no use in a settled community.

Mr. Routh's study of the subject is crammed (too crammed, perhaps, for clarity) with material and with observations. He is particularly good in the way he brings fresh and significant matters to the discussion of the subject – for instance, he has a chapter on the 'Inception and Significance of the Doctrine of Original Sin', and his references to Hades-literature are striking and suggestive.

FOUNDATIONS

The Mentality of Apes. By W. Köhler (Kegan Paul)

This book is not an attempt to prove that the chimpanzee is capable of miracles of thinking. For this reason it is a very valuable document in the study of intelligence, and the claim which, with all modesty, Professor Köhler makes for the chimpanzees, after four years' close and affectionate observation of *untrained* animals at the Teneriffe Anthropoid Station, is that thought definitely enters into their mental processes. The experiments he conducted were of the simplest form, but the problems he set the animals were designed with a nicety which excluded, ultimately, the possibility of solution by an animal such as the behaviourists postulate, a complex of motor reactions. The basic problem set the animals, in many different ways, was to reach some fruit they desired, which was so placed that they could only get to it, or get it to them, by the invention of a new process. One example must suffice.

Sultan, a young and particularly bright chimpanzee, wanted to get a banana which lay outside his cage. He had already taught himself the use of a stick in dragging an object to him, but neither of the two sticks in his cage was long enough, in the present instance, to reach the fruit. He tried each of the sticks in turn, even tried pushing one stick with the other till it touched the fruit, but as they were not joined together this was of no practical use, though it was a good error, from the point of view of rational conduct. At last he admitted that he was baffled and sat back in his cage and played with the sticks, one of which was hollow, and the other thin enough to fit in it. He joined the two sticks together, and immediately turned to the bars and raked in the fruit. Whether the joining was an accident or not does not really matter, for he at once made use of the new stick, so that he must have had in his mind what we should call an idea of length, though only as *long enough* and *not long enough*. The author has a chapter on 'Chance and Imitation' to which we refer the sceptical reader.

The ape, like the man, is not continually rational. Most of his life is, no doubt, governed by affective relations. One of the saddest sections of the book confesses that the apes try to solve a problem, which is only superficially the same as an earlier one, by the repetition of inappropriate solutions remembered from earlier problems. Periods of inertia, mental fatigue due to unsuccessful grappling with the problem, laziness, age, and personality, all affect the efficiency of the ape's mental processes just as they do those of human beings. The tendency, particularly strong under certain conditions, to repeat old solutions, whether practicable in the circumstances or not, is a human trait with which the critic of civilization and culture will be very familiar. Another interesting point is the frequently repeated observation that the elements of the successful solution are associated in a flash; however much work may have been spent on a problem, the answer comes as an inspiration – a fact also observed by mathematicians (Poincaré is a familiar example) and poets. The apes may serve to remind us that the most intelligent people are those susceptible to 'inspiration'. They may also remind us that 'inspiration', poetic or otherwise, has nothing to do with emotional frenzy, which, when it overtakes the chimpanzees, renders them incapable of a correct solution. Professor Köhler's observations of the social life of the animals are full of interest, and, it must be said, charm. We really begin to accept our relationship to these creatures with some emotional warmth, not as with the vague assent to a hypothesis. Their behaviour as a loose political group is most instructive, and it is a pity that there was no opportunity of observing family relationships. In spite of this, there is enough information in the book to make one say of these particular apes not 'how almost human', but 'how very human'. Actually, of course, millions of our fellow-countrymen go through life without ever solving a problem so difficult, relatively to the achievement of Galileo or Newton, as that of Sultan when he made two short sticks into a long one.

THE ORIGIN OF MAN

The Origin of Man. Man and His Superstitions. By Carveth Read (Cambridge University Press)

Although there is undoubtedly a difference in intellectual power between individual apes, on Professor Read's theory we should expect to find it less strongly marked than in civilized man. His hypothesis traces the rise of man from the movement which led the ancestral anthropoid out of the forest, and a vegetarian diet, to hunt his living meat over lightly wooded plains. It follows that the form of human society developed out of the organization of the hunting-pack, and this is a view which Professor Read sustains with skill and erudition and a sense of style, and without that forcing of the evidence which so often accompanies the discussion of hypotheses.

It would have been during the early days of hunting that the utility of leaders became apparent, both to the leader and the led, but it is evident that even in a highly-organized pack there is still almost as great a demand for initiative on the part of subordinate members of it as there is on the leaders. It was probably after the invention of agriculture, which introduced the possibility of living by routine, that the gap between the individual and the mass became seriously wide. And it remained more or less constant until the industrialization of civilization, by drawing the arts and crafts (previously the refuge of initiative) into routine production, made life a matter of automatic functioning for almost everybody except the poet and the scientist pure. Society still depends on these two for new modes of feeling and new directions of activity. The apparent leaders, the financiers and commercial magnates, are mere functionaries, organizers of effort with politicians for their subalterns, in whom a remnant of the primitive urge to leadership still survives.

Professor Read's second volume contains a detailed account of the surviving instances of animism and magic as they exist among primitive peoples (and incidentally among ourselves). An examination of the conditions which gave rise to these fallacious, but momentarily useful, explanations of the order of natural phenomena, is of the utmost importance, since through it we can attain to some knowledge of the constitution of the mind of contemporary man. The reader will find Professor Read of the greatest assistance in clarifying his ideas, in giving historical perspective to his conceptions of different levels of culture, and his bold exposure of contemporary barbarisms will attract those who wish to emancipate themselves completely from the no longer acceptable myths of the past. This is not, as it may seem, remote from the subject of literature, nor of poetry, even.

Poetry is not directly concerned with myths, as romantic practice might seem to imply, but only with myths which are capable of symbolizing the poet's reactions to the life he actually lives; that they should be familiar to his audience is, of course, a necessary condition of communication. I believe that the modern poet will tend to a more frequent use of the myths peculiar to our own civilization, the accepted body of scientific theory (for its absolute truth is neither here nor there), which is bound to replace the theological myths surviving from the last great effort of human intelligence, the scholastic philosophy. For this reason we have drawn attention to Professor Read's volumes, which discuss these fundamental matters with integrity, and with the charm which complete sincerity and lack of pretentiousness bring with it. Our readers will, no doubt, be able to bridge the gap between the work of Professor

Köhler and Professor Read. To us the path of transition between the ape Sultan and the modern engineer appears to need only a little clearing done on it to become quite plain, and the fact need be no discredit to the engineer. Whether we shall ever have any but a hypothetical bridge between the ape and the animistic savage is, perhaps, not to be hoped for, but we see a very fruitful field for investigation in the connection between animism and idealist philosophy, between the savage 'soul-stuff' and, for instance, the Kantian 'thing-in-itself'. It would do no harm at present if the prestige of certain of these metaphysical concepts, which are commonly made the basis for a judgement of poetic values, should be diminished.

TOTEMISM

Australian Totemism: A Psycho-Analytic Study in Anthropology. By Géza Róheim (Allen and Unwin)

The works of the older school of anthropologists affect the reader like an excellent travel film. Indeed, no travel film is comparable to *The Golden Bough* as a pictorial and emotional representation of the beings separated from us by time as well as by space. Yet if the meaning for the savage of the complicated and often painful ceremonies to which he so earnestly devotes himself was often brilliantly exposed, their relation to the living phenomena of higher cultures remained obscure. This was necessarily so until psychology had constructed an instrument sensitive to the actual movements of the mind, and the method of psycho-analysis provided this instrument. The perception of the similarity between the (so-called) Unconscious of the civilized adult and the savage or child mind was a great step in the direction of the association of psychology and anthropology. The fact that totems, with the corresponding taboos, are instruments of repression will naturally give rise, at least in the mind of a Freud, to the hypothesis that the behaviour of a savage under a system of taboo will resemble that of a civilized person under the repressive influence of a neurosis. As the clues to the real thoughts of the neurotic are looked for in the person's dreams and in any fixed forms of irrational behaviour (ceremonial), so those of the savage will be looked for in his myths (where the real content can effectually escape censor in fantastic forms) and in his ritual (that is, those performances which have for motive an end not naturally that of the means employed). The most remarkable fruit of this identification of the contemporary Unconscious with the archaic mentality was Freud's 'Totem and Taboo', a work to which, as to that of Sir James Frazer, Dr. Róheim fully declares his indebtedness. 'Totem and Taboo' gave a theoretical interpretation to the bewildering mental system revealed in 'Totemism and Exogamy'.

'Australian Totemism' brings such a mass of facts into line with Freud's main theory (and, in addition, many fine developments of the author's own) that it will require nothing short of a synthetic genius to suggest any other equally valid arrangement of the material.

The explanation of taboo as an incest-inhibition is, of course, with its corollary, the identification of the totem-animal with the 'father' of the tribe, the essential fact on which the further analysis proceeds. In the days when the human group was organized as one male with his mate and offspring, the young males were prohibited intercourse with any of the females. This is the original form of the Œdipus-complex (though psychologically the impulse may be analysed not as a desire to possess the mother, but to return to the state of pre-natal omnipotence). The resulting struggle of the generations, in which the sire was killed, was followed by a sudden realization of the deed done and fear of his revenge. So, Dr. Róheim says, an interval was created between the sinful deed and the enjoyment of its fruits. In this interval, occupied with ever more elaborate precautions against the revenge of the sire, we recognize the earliest form of religion.

This seems a slight foundation for such a prodigious structure, but it receives remarkable reinforcement from the great many myths of the aborigines which are given here. (These myths, it may be emphasized, were taken down by travellers who had never heard of the Œdipus-complex.) In one of the most startling we actually see the sire (the grey kangaroo) pursued by the young males, at first condensed in the symbol of Lakalia, but afterwards appearing in their real form:

A big grey kangaroo lived at a place near Finke George... There came one day from the west a man belonging to the totem of the Grey Kangaroo who was called Lakalia (the Pursuer); and he came to kill the grey kangaroo with a big stick. The kangaroo ran away, hotly pursued by the kangaroo man, who tried to kill it with his pointing-stick, but the kangaroo quietly turned round and looked his pursuer in the face . . . It ran on to the east, and everywhere where it stopped to feed or sleep there is a totem-centre at the present day. At last it came to Tanginta (Ironwood-tree place), where a rukuta (a young man after circumcision who must keep hidden) noticed the kangaroo and tried to stop its flight. The rukuta threw a stick at the kangaroo but missed it: the animal charged and squeezed the rukuta so that he remained there in a helpless state with broken bones. Lakalia came up and dressed his wounds. The kangaroo met a lot of women, stopped, and wanted to lie down there, but the women compelled him to continue his flight. He came to Tjuntula where there were many rukuta. One of them stood in the way of the animal and broke the kangaroo's leg with a stick. Then all the young men united to kill the kangaroo and take the Churinga (symbol of potency) from his head. They could not move the corpse when wanting to roast it; Lakalia, who had arrived in the mean-time, managed this with ease. After consuming the flesh it re-appeared on the bones and was cut off a second time.

This sacramental feast, followed by a resurrection, is completed by a sort of apotheosis of both pursuer and kangaroo. Such a vivid re-creation of the past is comparable to the reconstruction of extinct animals from fossil-bones, but even more far-reaching in its significance.

The chapter on Intichuima ceremonies (superficially fertility rites, but with much underlying psychological meaning) is particu-larly rich in general ideas, and, in fact, the whole book gives evidence of a very powerful conception of the nature of the savage mental life to which it is impossible to do justice in a review. The author's suggestion that the use of stone cairns in many parts of the world to mark the place where persons met violent or unlawful death, grew up out of the stones which the young males flung at the parent (vide the anthropoids' use of missiles), is an illuminating detail; especially the analogy he draws with the stoning of Hermes by Zeus for the murder of Argos (Zeus-of-the-night-sky) which enabled him to obtain Io. The legends of the soul's journey to the other world are also essentially interesting, as they reproduce the struggle with the father, and also tend to verify the theory that the root-impulse of the Unconscious is the return to the condition of fœtal bliss.

So much must suffice to indicate that Dr. Róheim has produced a book fascinating for the general reader; that it will rouse the combative instincts of the scholars goes without saying. Yet it is very far from being a work of mere speculation. It is imaginative; that is to say, the material is arranged in a significant structure and not merely amassed. To such work, so finely carried out, literature itself may legitimately look for the direction in which to apply its new but so far unorientated impulses.

NOTES FOR A STUDY OF SADE

The terms of the social contract have not become any less obscure since Sade analysed the conditions of existence down to a basis of mutual extermination. The corpse is for Sade the beginning just as truly as the end of life, for he could see no justification for a scale of values in which the human organism came out on top, but humbled men to the level of the vermin whose existence is bounded by the limits of their putrefaction.

He ordered that his own grave should be dug in a coppice on the edge of his estate, that no stone should mark the place, and that acorns should be strewn on the earth to hasten the obliteration of his memory. There is here both pride and sensibility for, though his systems were built on an assumption of unbridled egotism, he had so sincere a vision of the procession of phenomena that he realized even his own destruction as the return of so much energy to the plastic force of the universe. It would not be difficult to gild with a little rhetoric the tarnished reputation of Sade; to exhibit him for his integrity, which is such a contrast to the opportunism of the ordinary self-deceiving man, as a hero or a saint. But that is a paradox which could only please the sheep of the speculative flock who merely transvaluate the moral judgement, gnawing the fresh-turned side of their transcendental mangel-wurzel. It is therefore a matter for indifference whether the aberrations Sade depicted were intended only as illustrations to an intellectual argument (which purpose in fact they serve) or were phantasies which he would have enacted in flesh and blood had he had the power and the liberty. Herman Hesse says of the Karamazoff brothers, that 'they were prepared to commit any crime, but they only commit them exceptionally because as a rule it suffices for them to have thought of a crime or to have dreamt of it, to have made their soul a confidant of its possibility.'[1] But the road to action must be left open or the problem of conduct will have been side-tracked.

Sade's two recorded offences (committed under the old régime) for the second of which he was imprisoned in the Bastille, are not conclusive evidence against the view that he was by nature introverted; their conception was comparatively unambitious, their execution unexpectedly clumsy. Sade was not at all cunning, but rather naïve, as is shown by his earnest attempts to get his social ideas embodied in the republican code – such for instance as the view that the man who was robbed should be punished and not the thief – a spartan revision which did not catch the fancy of the army-contractors as it should have done. Sade, as a political prisoner, was released from confinement by the Revolution, and he might have retained his liberty had he not been so rash as to publish, in 1800, a novel called *Zoloë et ses deux Acolytes*, in which the characters of Napoleon and Josephine, who filled the principal rôles, were drawn with more acumen than a dictator finds tolerable in a contemporary, This episode cost him confinement in a mental hospital for the remaining thirteen years of his life, though he had invited it by a previous folly, no doubt the effect of his proselytizing fervour; that of sending an illustrated edition de luxe of the notorious *Justine* to each of the five chiefs of the Directorate. Napoleon is reported to have flung his copy into the fire with expressions of disgust:

> Qui fait le dégoûté montre qu'il se croit beau.

But there are not fewer corpses on the road to (and back from) Moscow than even in Sade's imagination.

· · · · · · ·

Most of Sade's surviving romances were written during his stay in the Bastille 1784-9. In his interim of freedom he wrote plays, one or two of which were put on without much success. In the hospital at Charenton he enjoyed a good deal of liberty, and could even entertain people of his own social position. The theatre was his principal consolation at this period, a fact which roused the spleen of the chief medical officer, owing to whose complaints Sade was moved to a place having fewer amenities. An extract from an

---

[1] *In Sight of Chaos*. Translated by Stephen Hudson.

official letter written by this doctor gives a notable impression of Sade's circumstances at the time.

'M. de Sade enjoys too great a liberty here. He is in touch with a considerable number of people of both sexes; he can entertain them in his apartment or visit them in their respective rooms. He is allowed to walk in the park and there he meets invalids who have the same privilege. He preaches his horrible doctrine to some, to others he lends books. Moreover, it is rumoured in the institution that he lives with a woman who passes as his daughter. Even this is not all. They have been imprudent enough to arrange a theatre in this institution with the intention of having plays performed by the mentally afflicted without considering the dreadful effects such an exciting display must necessarily produce on their imagination. M. de Sade directs this theatre. It is he who chooses the plays, casts the actors and leads the rehearsals. He is elocution instructor to both actors and actresses and teaches them the art of the stage. When there are public performances he always has a certain number of entrance tickets at his disposal and from his position in the middle of the audience he does in part the honours of the place. On great occasions he is even author; on the birthday of the Superintendent, for instance, he always takes pains to compose an allegorical piece in his honour or some complimentary verses at least.'[1]

. . . .

Sade is, of course, by no means the originator of the premisses which he carries to their logical extreme. Moralists have never been lacking who would expose to incredulous men the selfish roots of their apparently disinterested actions and prove that morality is the slave of custom, like itself bred of physiology and environment. Montaigne and La Rochefoucauld are obvious predecessors among the moderns, and a remarkable and hardly accidental parallel may be found in Bernard de Mandeville. 'The Fable of the Bees' was very well known in France in the first half of the eighteenth century (the translation was burnt by the common hangman), and his perspicacious pamphlet, *A Modest Defence of Stews*, had a wide circulation as *La Vénus populaire*. This work may very well have suggested to Sade his much more elaborate scheme for the

[1] Quoted by Guillaume Apollinaire in his 'L'Œuvre du Marquis de Sade', in the series *Les Maîtres de l'Amour*, from which book the other quotations are taken, unless a different source is noted.

provision of public brothels. Mandeville though, is much subtler in his analysis of social stratagems, he has a lively humour and is without the confounded didacticism which is always breaking out in Sade; in fact, he understood the complications of human emotions much better than Sade did. He was an empiricist where Sade liked to proceed from principles.

· · · · · · ·

The anti-social hero, who is such a prominent actor in later nineteenth-century literature and thought (Dostoevsky, Nietzsche, Rimbaud and Lautréamont come to mind at once), is always present as the starting-point of Sade's sociological divagations. A paragraph on law in 'La Philosophie dans le Boudoir' summarizes what is elsewhere elaborated, illustrated and extended:

> Laws are not made for the individual but for the generality, which sets them perpetually in conflict, seeing that the personal and the general interests are always contradictory. But the laws that are useful to society are very hurtful to the individual. Even though they may now and then protect him or safeguard him, for three-quarters of his life they hinder and restrict him. So the sensible man must despise them, and put up with them only as he does snakes and reptiles which, though harmful and poisonous, may be useful medicinally. He will ward off the laws as he would those venomous creatures; he will ensure his safety by precautions and stratagems, measures which come readily to the intelligent and far-sighted.

· · · · · · ·

A rough and ready, but for the purpose, efficient metaphysic can be found. In Sade's *Justine, ou les Malheurs de la Vertu*, a robber-chief tries to persuade the heroine to his perverse desires by an argument more abstract than seems called for in the actual circumstances:

'No, Therese, no, there is no God, Nature is self-sufficient! She has no need of a Creator, this supposed Creator is only the decomposition of her own forces, is only what we call in the schools a petitio principii, a begging the question. A God supposes either a Creation, a moment when there is nothing, or else a moment when all was chaos. If one or other of these states was an evil, why did your God allow it to subsist? If it was good, why did he change it? But if all is well now, your God has no longer any purpose: so, if he were useless could he be powerful, and if he is not powerful could he be God? . . .' and so on to the peroration, which is an examination, far from cold-blooded, of the 'deistic phantom'.

It follows that Nature, defined as the universe of matter in movement, is the sum of all possible experience, and that sensation is the sole possible mode of experience; the sentient organism must be a purely autonomous unit. The only attribute of Nature being movement, all values are indifferent to it, since sooner or later every organism must return to the common stock the energy which it has stored up for its individual satisfaction. But there is, perhaps, a greater mystery beneath this delirious circulation of destruction and growth, the contemplation of which excites Sade to the pitch of visionary speech:

'The horrifying project of the previous evening (a plan of large-scale incendiarism), was put into execution. The 37 hospitals were consumed in the flames, and more than 20,000 souls perished therein. "Oh god-in heaven!" I said to Olympe, "how delicious it is to yield to such wayward impulses as this! Oh mysterious, incomprehensible Nature, if it is true that such crimes offend you, why bestow on me such delectation? Ah, bitch, perhaps I am taken in by you as I was long ago by that infamous chimera of a God!, who is said to have you under his control! We are no more dependent on you than we are on him!" '

. . . .

Sade places his positive value on the destructive impulses because, he would say, they ensure a swifter return to Nature of the raw material of which it is in need, breaking down the more complex organisms into simpler ones. But this seems to be a value derived from sensibility alone, for there is no reason to believe that the energy pent up in the body of a man is abstracted from Nature; rather, the more complex organizations enable more energy to be expended, mass for mass, than simpler ones. If the end of existence is the running down of this primordial, universal movement to zero-level, stillness; then for this a poet would seem to be more effective than the same weight of maggots.

The illogical judgement is a clue to temperament. In spite of Sade's appearance of being a sensationist, a pursuer of whatever may excite or stimulate the nerves, his implacable hostility to the object of passion shows that he is actually seeking to annihilate the concept of perception. Freud suggests in 'Beyond the Pleasure-

Principle' that when an organism ostensibly seeks pleasure, its desire is a release from the pressure of, physically, the sexual glands, metaphysically, the world of phenomenon . . . a womb-like state in which there would be no differentiation between the subject and the concept, such as would exist in Sade's cosmos with the cessation of the individual consciousness.

A similar nostalgia for a paradisal condition, when the burden of identity seems to be accentuated beyond the tension which the organism is meant to bear, is frequent in modern art. In Baudelaire, for instance,

> Je jalouse le sort des plus vils animaux,
> Tant l'écheveau du temps lentement se dévide!

and, less directly, but more subtly, in many other poems; as in the later verses of Rimbaud; or in the scoriant vision of Maldoror where he imagines that he has sat motionless for so long that his lower limbs have sunk back into the vegetative life. The popularity of Schopenhauer is, perhaps, due to his expression of a similar sensibility. His Will, the root of all evil, does not differ essentially from Sade's 'Nature', and his doctrine of asceticism as a means of circumventing the pain of consciousness is only sadism seen the other way round – directed inwards to frustrate impulse instead of outwards to disperse it – that is, masochism. Both terms have an evil sound to popular prejudice, which is rather unreasonable as in one or other of these directions all impulses must move.

. . . .

In the phantasmal world of Sade's romances the moral platitude is elaborated and illustrated with the audacity and inventiveness of the dream-power. The futility of virtue, its fatal contradiction by the actual workings of the world of matter, which makes it a source of pain and disappointment to those who try to carry out its ludicrous code, and the fact that this virtue is, after all, only a roundabout way of getting what we want, persuade him that it is better to yield directly to impulse, no matter what the consequences to others. Compassion is a bug-bear against which the Marquis exerts all his eloquence:

'Reject, reject with disgust the perfidious advice of the Chevalier, when he urges you to open your heart to all the imagined ills of the unfortunate! He seeks to burden you with a weight of misery which, not being your own, will lacerate you to no purpose. Ah! believe me, Eugenie, believe me, the pleasures that arise from indifference, from callousness, are much more worth while than those derived from sympathy. These merely touch the heart, whilst the other excites every nerve and overwhelms the whole being.'

This certainty of the absolute identity of the individual, his isolation, is the basis of the sadistic morality; on the other hand, Schopenhauer says, 'it is precisely the (this) recognition of oneself in an alien phenomenon from which, as I have so often proved, justice and human love directly proceed, which leads finally to the surrender of the Will.' Fusion, brotherhood, self-sacrifice, humanitarianism and so many of the emotional currents which have swept modern European democracies, from Rousseauism onwards, can be traced to this source – English middle-class Socialism (distinct from proletarian envy-revolts), Toc H., Keyserling, etc., are all forms of expression in which the identity can be diffused, almost lost touch with, in a blissful anonymity. The devastating humility which floods sometimes a character in Dostoevsky or Tolstoy, e.g., Pierre in *War and Peace*, is another current from the same stream, but in these great men it is matched against such a powerful identity sense that great works are produced in the struggle.

In Dostoevsky, the sadistic element gained in force as he developed, *vide* the terrific character of Stavrogin. For an early sketch of the *dual* nature, insight into which makes Dostoevsky so profound, see *Letters from the Underworld* – in some ways unsurpassed.

Schopenhauer constructed a positive moral value out of the fact of sacrifice, an achievement which seems hardly possible to us now:

'Every benevolent action practised from a pure motive proclaims that he who practises it stands in direct contradiction to the phenomenal world in which other individuals are entirely separate from himself, and recognizes himself as identical with them. Every quite disinterested service is accordingly a mysterious action, a *mysterium*.'

It must be admitted, without cynicism, that there appear to be no sufficient grounds for assuming the purity of any motive; the unique voluptuousness of self-sacrifice covers a multitude of these so-called disinterested actions – Sydney Carton's Bargain: or All for Nothing, is the *beau idéal* of emotional commerce. Charity, of course, is positively repulsive because it pretends to be what it is

not, but Schopenhauer's pure benevolence assumes a donor without desire, and that, though it accords with his sole criterion of
virtue, hardly seems to us to hold the notion of a moral action.
Further, he says of Kant, 'to support morals by means of Theism
is equivalent to reducing them to egoism', but equally so is his
own theory that in our fellows we see the 'I once more', and that
in a case of self-sacrifice for another individual 'the true essence of
the perishing being remains untouched, continues in the other . . .'
But though, like all the would-be not-empirical moralists, Schopenhauer leads us into a blind alley, his peculiar psychological acumen
discloses a means of escape from the extreme rigidity of the pure
sadist principles. He who performs a 'purely' benevolent action, he
says, 'stands in direct contradiction to the phenomenal world'.
What could be more flattering to the ego or more advantageous to its
neighbours? That is an ambition which should surely result in a
further differentiation of the ego and not in its absorption in the
amorphous flock of those chosen people – the children of nature.

.   .   , ...

As nothing exists in ordinary life in a pure state, it is right that
Sade should have given his name to a concept in psycho-pathology.
Equally, his antagonist, the ubiquitous small Polish squire, von
Sacher Masoch, is an abstraction, a re-agent for use in analysis
which will obscure instead of revealing, unless used in appropriate
quantities. Taken together, they form a picturesque diagram of the
ambivalence of emotion, of the two poles towards which all impulses
are orientated – life and death, fulfilment and frustration, love and
hate, and all the other emotional twins. In life generally and in art
particularly, it is the compound, the relation between the elements,
which is the object of perception. In society it is the perpetually
precarious balance in the polarity of these two forces, a balance as
unstable in and between groups as between individuals, which
gives that unreliable, volcanic humour to the endless spectacle we
watch as we help to create it. At one moment we may bask in an air
of tolerance and sweet reasonableness, in which nothing seems more
certain than the elaboration and extension of the achievements of
the past; the next, as in 1914, and, perhaps, more sinisterly today,
the inoffensive individual is caught up in a whirlwind which has no
more regard for any mental equilibrium he may have reached than a
Bank Holiday char-a-banc. For society must have a positive sadistic

tendency if it is to exist in a healthy state, or the surrounding egos, races, or 'lower' forms of life will absorb it for their own purposes. The policy of state-craft, probably most effective when least cognisant of the ends in view, is to sift the natural givers and the natural takers, those who suffer and bestow, and those who exert and assert, into positions where they can satisfy these tendencies, and to provide a system of easy compensations for the dualistic majority. For the latter purpose, ideas (of honour, etc.) are not less powerful than material rewards; combined with them, they are irresistible. Thanks to the idea of justice, a wig and a slight charge on the Exchequer, we are able to cajole one anti-social element into eliminating the other. The hangman, too, is an honest citizen, though he has been getting a little queasy of late. In America, in England and even in Russia there have recently been examples of neurasthenic executioners; one of them tried to hang himself; others simply sent in their resignations on grounds of health. But so serious does the position seem that a humane paragraphist in an evening paper suggests that citizens should fill the office in rotation, like jurymen, to relieve any single person of so much responsibility. Nature is full of beautiful adjustments, the Victorians used to say, and certainly it looks as if the decline of torture and the rise of dentistry might be an example of compensation; in place of heretics and highwaymen, the Sunday papers.

In normal conditions, in a nation of industrial workers, the masochist tendency must obviously be exploited at the expense of the sadistic. So suppressed is the latter, in fact, that it rarely dares to show itself, except under cover of a crowd-emotion:

> But when the blast of war blows in our ears,
> Then imitate the action of the tiger;
> Stiffen the sinews, summon up the blood,
> Disguise fair Nature with hard-favoured rage . . .

War, the greatest of all crowd experiences, probably owes its irrationally prolonged existence to the provision it makes for both tendencies in human emotion. Under the excuse of patriotism, manliness and courage, the masochist can hug his exquisite bundle of thorns and win decorations for exceptional bravery in the discharge of his temperament. The sadist will not be found where there would seem to be most reason to expect him; those, at least,

who have any intelligence remove themselves early in the programme to posts of minor or major authority in the Base Camps and
bull-rings of the Back Area and the 'glass-houses' of permanent
cantonments. These provide more docile subjects than the fear-crazy
men of the enemy line, made dangerous by despair.

. . . . . .

I have not attempted in these few notes to distinguish between the
historical Sade and the derivative symbol used in psycho-analytic
terminology. The evidence necessary to an extended study of the
subject exists only in the stupendous compilations of Sade. 'Any one
who has read only the books of Sade which are readable, might as
well have read none of them.' [M. Blanchot]

In the meantime, there is abundant evidence, in literature and in
experience, for the view that the impulse which in him was developed
to the degree of mania, is an essential component of the most
commonplace, as well as the most exceptional, expressions of
vitality. Such a conclusion can only be accepted or rejected finally
by a scrupulous examination of personal motives; 'instinctive' revulsion is no argument against it.

THE LAUTRÉAMONT AFFAIR

A good deal of the emotional energy which would have been
absorbed, in an age of religious faith, by the exercises of religion,
the formulation of doctrine, or the criticism of heresies is today
discharged through the medium of literary theory. A parallelism
with the early stages of a new cult is apparent in recent poetic
propaganda in France; the fulfilment of a prophecy – the theory
of the psychology of the unconscious; the possession of certain
sacred writings in which the prophecy is anticipated by revelation
(i.e., by inspiration, sheer genius or some such other term) and of
which the signification is not so clear that it prevents the divination
of hidden or esoteric truths. And if, in order to equate literature
with religion, it is necessary to balance an unknown quantity (an
illogic, or super-logic) against the divine mysteries, it is no less
essential to approach the sacred ground with the slippers of reason
balanced on the devotee's head.

There is an aroma of mediaeval hagiolatry in the issue of *Le Disque Vert*[1] consecrated to Isidore Ducasse, self-styled Comte de Lautréamont. M. Phillipe Soupault owes to him a kind of conversion, which he records with the circumstantiality of St. Augustine: 'I was lying in hospital when I first read *Les Chants de Maldoror*. It was June 28th. After that day, not a soul recognized me. I myself can no longer tell whether I have a heart.' He prostrates himself in an ecstasy of contrition and humility: 'Thou, Isidore, hast forgotten nought, and suddenly I want to pour out my soul, in excuses, in recantations. With all humility I would be your chiropodist.'

M. René Crevel would salute him with a hymn of gratitude: 'It would seem sacrilegious' (the term is significant) 'to attempt a mosaic of critical pebbles around *Maldoror*.' M. Derème credits Lautréamont with having added a fresh string to the modern poet's lyre, 'the rope of one who hanged himself for love of life', and he, too, concludes in religious phraseology: 'all of us, we poets of today, innumerable as lice, express our gratitude in lengthy prayers to him.'

M. Pierre-Quint informs us that Lautréamont discovered the method of automatic writing. 'The pen notes down, without the intervention of consciousness, the associations of ideas or images. The phrases succeed each other, without any preconceived plan, without any logical premeditation, solely under the impulse of inspiration.' This rhapsodical technique is not such a novelty as the writer assumes. We must all have suffered from it in one form or another. But it seems to me that it bears little resemblance to Lautréamont's characteristic work, except that it goes on and on. Lautréamont slumps when he cannot bring his dream material into consciousness. When he can do so he realizes some magnificent visions, the atrocities proliferating over the page till the reader is numbed. For example, the evisceration of a little girl with a clasp-knife; the gibbet with its perishing victim and the two women hurrying towards him with buckets of tar; the Creator, supine on a rutted country road, running with blood, wine, and vomit; and many more such tableaux are both very horrible and very remarkable. And indeed there is no need of a New Dispensation to recognize Lautréamont's qualities – though one is certainly required to

---

[1] *Le Disque Vert* was edited by Franz Hellens and Henri Michaux in Paris and Brussels. A new series (Troisième Année, 4ième Série) appeared in 1925, No. 1 devoted to the theme of suicide and No. 2 to dreams.

glorify his defects, the confusion, the rhodomontade, the piling-up of anguish.

M. Hytier is less than just when he says in his contribution 'I forbear to make any comment on the genius of Rimbaud and the incapacity of Lautréamont, one does not have to resort to an arch-angel to demolish a hump-backed dwarf.' He makes a point, how-ever, when he traces some of Lautréamont's extravagances to his romantic reading, the 'school of terror' novelists deriving from our 'Monk' Lewis and Anne Radcliffe. But he far outstrips them!

M. André Malraux alleges that it is all done by a simple process of transposition. It is not Satan but God who flays a boy in a brothel and a hair of His head which narrates His monstrosities of behaviour. Malraux asks in conclusion, 'Even when it leads to such very peculiar results, what is the literary value of the procedure?'

From the literary-political standpoint the method is justified by the contemporary reaction. Modernists are thrilled by these simple transpositions; flesh-creeping is a recurrent vogue, provided the idea-associations are a little changed. Lautréamont left a vivid scar, an echo of his desperate blasphemy, which will not soon be smoothed away, but does this suffice to give literature a new direction and the pretensions of a cult? The phenomenon goes far beyond the bounds of a legitimate enthusiasm for an under-rated talent. It is an attempt to stampede a timid literary public into the private stockade of a few theorists, whose creed is a novel and obviously not ineffective medley of flattery and coercion.

THE APOLOGY FOR YAHOOS

Gulliver is all very well as an anthropologist, he had genius, but he wrote before the observation of primitive races had been de-veloped into a science. His generalizations are very open to error, as he lacked the knowledge of a rigorous method of cross-checking, such as that perfected by the Cambridge school for penetrating the private lives of primitive folk. Gulliver might even have found inapposite that spirit of devotion to an abstract ideal, to the ideal of certified scientific statements, which will impel an educated gentle-man to spend hours crouching in thorny scrub (like a Christian martyr in his burning bush) simply to decide whether the Fuzzy-wuzzies turn themselves N.N.E. or N.N.W. when urinating.

It is chiefly in his description of the two races inhabiting the island of Scatophilos, the Yahoos and the Houyhnhnms, that the critics have discovered inaccuracies, and this may be accounted for by his unreasonable prejudice, which is quite unworthy of a disinterested lover of truth, against the subordinate race. Dr. Samuel Johnson even goes so far as to assert that these accounts were written 'in open defiance of truth and regularity', but we cannot admit so strict a censure when we know that Gulliver lived for a considerable period on the island and enjoyed exceptional opportunities for studying the people, great and small, in their unsophisticated state and whilst unaware that they might be observed. No, we must attribute his defects, first, to a lack of method and, then, to that atrabilious temperament which never allowed him to respond to the suggestions of beauty and natural affection. As regards his insensitiveness to beauty, an editor of his works has actually established his complete ignorance of the part played by the Fine Arts – that greatest of civilizing influences – in the spiritual existence of the yahoos; for he classifies virtuosos, or, as we should call them now, artists, among 'bawds, attornies, ravishers, and pickpockets'.

I can only refer here to one or two of the many apologists who have come forward in defence of what might almost be called our common humanity. It should be noticed that the epithet most commonly applied to Fielding's ideal yahoo creation, Tom Jones, is *manly*. On the other hand, Thackeray's character of Richard Steele, by pointing out the existence of sentimental refinement in this apparently grossly selfish and timidly sensual nature, has done much to reserve him a place in the sympathy we bestow on the weak, the dirty, and the irresponsible.

So, though I do not claim to be the first to put in a good word for a shockingly misjudged people, I do assert that my study, when it is complete, will be such a vindication of this amiable and unpretentious race that we shall not hear any more about the mythical virtues of the houyhnhnms, the insufferable prigs on whom Gulliver heaped all the fulsome and even sycophantic euology of which he defrauded the humble yahoo.

It will be remembered that the last houyhnhnm died a few years ago in one of our magnificent metropolitan asylums for the insane, and, though the carcase, properly dried and eviscerated has been placed in the Museum, it is clear that the only reliable source of our information about this extinct people must be the historical researches and the criticism of their hereditary enemies, the yahoos themselves. After the opening up of Scatophilos, which followed Gulliver's accidental discovery, the yahoos showed themselves much more sensitive to European ideas than their quadruped tyrants, who ultimately paid the penalty for their inability to adapt themselves to the new conditions. It appears from the arguments of the brilliant school of historians instituted when the yahoos seized the reins of state about one hundred and twenty years ago that the houyhnhnms had been in a decadent condition for many centuries. As they studiously concealed from Gulliver the existence of their literature ('all their knowledge is traditional', he says), he had no material on which to base a comparative judgement, and this must be supposed to excuse his preposterous veneration for a race content to consider its evolution complete when it still existed in a state devoid of all civilized amenities.

From the studies which the younger yahoos have made of the ancient texts of the houyhnhnms, it seems to be pretty well established (though the significance of certain abstract terms remains to be defined) that, for the last three thousand years of their existence, they suffered from the delusion that their most spiritually exalted individuals were those in whom the idea of perfection reached the pitch of urgency and rendered worldly delight and even the joys of fellowship utterly insipid to their fantastic and uncharitable tastes. This vice was very far from infecting even the partly brutalized yahoos observed by Gulliver, suffering though they were from generations of the cruellest slavery, for he frequently describes them as he had seen them in the ardent and unaffected enjoyment of the few pleasures left them. Such a vignette as that of the yahoo devouring the lump of putrid asses' flesh refused by Gulliver is in striking contrast to the joyless vegetarianism of the effete autocrats.

A vigorous propaganda was put in motion as soon as the yahoos acquired the faculty of articulate expression, and many volumes of their works may be consulted in which the subversive paradoxes of the degenerate houyhnhnms are categorically refuted. These writings inculcate a spirit of courageous self-assertion, of hope, energy, progress, complacence, and tolerance, and an example may not be out of place here. A houyhnhnm had propounded a series of maxims in which the contradictions of the earthly state, contrasted with this idea of perfection they had, was made the excuse for many morbid and unsociable conclusions. He envisaged the individual as if lost in a remote corner of the universe without help or guidance as to his conduct in this world or his fate in the next. 'Contemplating this condition,' he says, 'I am seized with terror like one who has been carried on to a desert island whilst he slept and who awakes without knowing where he is and without any means of escape, so that I wonder how one does not fall into desperation at such a miserable condition.'

To which the spirited and travelled yahoo replies,

'For my part, when I observe Pom or Loobstck, I see no reason for falling into that state of desperation of which our author speaks; I see a city which in no way resembles a desert island, but one which is opulent, well-policed, and where the inhabitants are as happy as their nature comports. What reasonable person would despair because he does not comprehend the nature of his thought, because he knows only some few of the attributes of matter, because God has not revealed his secrets to him? One should equally despair at not having four legs and a pair of wings. Why should we be horrified at our condition? Our existence is not so despicable as some would have us believe.'

These are brave words and they are not empty ones, as any one who has had the privilege of living as long as I have in several of their cities will agree. Gulliver's observation that the yahoos 'appear to be the most unteachable of all animals, their capacities never reaching higher than to draw or carry burdens' is most obviously contradicted by the evidence these places afford. I do not refer to such professions as those of Cabinet Minister, literary journalist, or sanitary inspector, though it is obvious that all these are the creation of a superior intelligence, of one which ought to be called human rather than animal, but to the common occupations and amusements of the middle sort of people. Here is a list of some of those which lead to fame, fortune, or civic approbation:

Chiropodist, scavenger, sandwichman, toilet-paper manufacturer, clairvoyant, hangman, broker, chucker-out, justice of the peace, pip-carver in jam factory, bum, satirist, man-about-town, *imagiste*, lay preacher, gentleman's corset maker, butler, major-general, commissionaire, shop-walker, bishop, private detective, sporting peer, charity worker, strike-breaker, film censor, socialist millionaire, auntie, contortionist, poet, publicity agent, anthologist, hanger-on.

Their various amusements would present an almost more imposing list, but, as it is exceptionally difficult for an outsider to comprehend the nature of the enjoyment they derive from the ingenious pursuit of trivialities, I must defer this list till I can deal at length with the psychology of the yahoo at play.

In the meantime, I can give some particulars of their domestic ideals from a chapter of my forthcoming volume, *The Idea of an Earthly Paradise*, in which I examine the vast quantities of material I have gathered on this subject from the quasi-sacred writings which have replaced the archaic mundane literature of the houyhnhnms, the advertisement pages of their periodical publications.

The fundamental constituent of their ideal existence is a kennel, generally of brick, sometimes treated so as to resemble stone or wood, and sometimes of corrugated iron. This building may vary in size from one containing two or fewer small compartments to one of fifty or more, but all such distinctions are merged in the term *home* which is always applied to the places where the yahoos breed. This appears to be the difference between the largest kennels and the *hotels*, which they use in common, for, though couples voluntarily resort to the latter for intimate approaches, they are never, unless by accident, the scenes of parturition.

It is the ambition of the male yahoo to persuade a female of the species to occupy this *home* with him and to accord him her favours exclusively, without exceptions even in the case of his warmest friends, either for the propagation of offspring or for their mutual delight. When the female agrees spontaneously to this arrangement she is said to be *in love with* this particular yahoo.

The idea of love is the one most discussed among the yahoos and there are a hundred controversies as to its real nature. An extreme but very popular school affirms that this idea is peculiar to the yahoos and differentiates them from all the rest of the animal creation. This view is based on the fact that the yahoo is, ideally, monogamous, a virtue which does not extend to any other of the lower animals with the possible exception of the whale. To decide this important point they have just fitted out a marine expedition which will shoot silver arrows, marked with an identification number into all the pairing whales they come in range of. Next year they will kill all the pairing whales bearing these arrows and observe if the numbers still correspond. There is, however, a modern and rising school of empiricists who claim that love is not actually monogamous (and they have obtained a good deal of experimental evidence for this view), and even that it is not a desirable ideal, the better thing being always to conform to natural instincts; this is known as the intellectual school.

There are many shades of opinion between these extremes, but all are united in an unshakeable belief in the superiority of love to hatred. Love is beautiful, they say, hatred is ugly, and they are never tired of contrasting the benign expression of contented lovers with the distorted mask of gratified evil. Love delights to share its pleasure in youth and in old age its consolation, but hatred remains aloof and solitary, and its self-sufficiency falls like a reproach over the prostrate couples.

Before concluding this hasty sketch of the subject, I should like to put in a word for the extreme decency with which the yahoos conduct their discussions of these matters and the practical details of mating. Although the intentions of the pair are known for months ahead in the better sort of families, they permit none of those discreet jocularities, those oblique references to the physiological functions such as sometimes disgrace our publications. Their superior newspapers have trained observers whom they send out to describe for the common delight the coupling ceremony known among them as the *wedding*. But, as the utmost decorum prevails throughout the ritual, so I assure my readers the printed account will let fall no hint that a more than friendly arrangement has been concluded. This shame, for I cannot call it fear, of the physical is associated with an idea which is the second of the great triumvirate on which the stability of the yahoo *home* is based. This is Luxury, which, with Love and Law, is the mainstay of their universe, for, symbologically, because their metaphysic is matriarchal, they identify the universe with *home*. Luxury with them is not what it was with the decadent bourgeois of Greece and Rome, a means of intensifying or subtilizing the sensations, but simply the process of eliminating the physical reminders of their animal origin. As a proverb of theirs has it 'Mum's the word', or as the canonical *Home Journal*, Vol. 43, No. 6, page 182, expands the phrase,

'Mum is the word! It is so simple to use "Mum", the snow-white cream deodorant. A touch to the underarm, and wherever perspiration is closely confined, assures you that no matter how much you may perspire throughout the day and evening, there can be no unpleasant, unfeminine odour to detract from your charm.

'The use of "Mum" is not mere fastidiousness. It is a matter of good breeding and common sense.

'"Mum" is 25cs. and 50cs. at stores.'

The houyhnhnms had a very discouraging idea called original sin, which involved the conception of a fall from grace or perfection. A distinctive contribution of the yahoos to international culture is the identification of original sin with the fact of the animal origin of their species, so that fashionable luxury and intellectual awareness, remedies easily disseminated in rich modern democracies, have replaced the old, laborious methods of spiritual regeneration of the individual. Luxury supplies the necessary motive for this reform and, though the female was in the old days the snare of damnation as well as the mother of the Saviour, now she is solely the single instrument of salvation. The effort of the males to create the luxury that is to erase the bar sinister from the yahoo escutcheon is stimulated and intensified by the females' incessant rivalry in luxurious display. Unsullied with passion for luxury itself or for discrimination between its forms (for any evaluation of forms would necessitate a regression to the exploded metaphysic of the absolute), their unrelenting jealousy is the humble instrument which has lifted the yahoo from the cave to the hut, from the maisonnette to the villa, from a furry hide to artificial silk and superfluous hair. Still further improvements are expected in the near future.

If Love creates the yahoo home and Luxury adorns it, it is Law that secures it. Of all his inventions, Law is the one the true yahoo contemplates with inexhaustible satisfaction. Law is based on the idea of justice, of which they recognize two distinct varieties: one pertaining to the relations between the yahoos themselves and the other involving their relations with Providence.

The more intelligent of the modern yahoos are convinced that, by this time, the indifference of the universe to yahoo emotions has been amply proved, and they are naturally very impatient of their poetical writers who attribute joy, grief, hope, despair, rage, and benevolence to the vegetable, geological, and meteorological features of the landscape. Piety is by no means extinct among them and even their sceptics recognize that in the face of undeserved catastrophe criticism must be superseded by resignation.

> If this is as it ought to be,
> My God, I leave it unto thee,

concludes the eloquent author of a poem 'On an Infant Yahoo Dying before its First Meal', which is one of the gems in their national anthology.

The non-sectarian yahoos have a deity which they call the Whole or whole, which must not be confused with *hole* meaning an empty space. The Whole is an entelechy in which all opposites are reconciled, though, of course, without ceasing to be opposites. The expression of this state, in which they apprehend what is called the 'Wholeness of the Whole', generally approaches the condition of music, that is to say, it is non-conceptual, but here and there a flash of intuition illuminates their literature, such as this,

> Transcending self, myself becomes
> The larger self that moves the whole.

This kind of enthusiasm is very popular among them as it is always at the command of those who have no more immediate satisfactions. I shall have more to say about this when I describe their ideas of aesthetics. I shall also have something to say about their Practical Justice, which is quite distinct from Providential Justice, being designed to protect the weak against the strong. Within its protecting circle, the delicate flowers of culture, honour, and virtue enjoy a perpetual summer. In what these ideas consist we shall explain at length, for without an understanding of their meaning the yahoo psychology cannot be appreciated at its true value.

A NOTE ON FICTION
By the late C. H. Rickword
I

It is certainly wise, when tackling such an extensive, often camouflaged, subject as the novel, to defer the frontal attack. But such sporadic flank manoeuvres as Miss Drew initiates must be undertaken with the ultimate objective very much in mind. So if, as she says, 'the problem of language, the use of the medium in all its aspects, is the basic problem of any work of literature', then the relative merits of the attitudes to sex, of D. H. Lawrence and Michael Arlen, are not especially relevant. And it is to topics of that kind Miss Drew devotes most of her space.[1] Admitting that the pretensions of most novels to an aesthetic status collapse as soon as scrutinized, the fact that Miss Drew still considers them worthy of attention shows that she has not realized their insignificance, or else has alternative standards.

In pronouncing a bare verdict of good or bad, the critic of fiction is in no worse case than the critic of verse. And so far as giving a plausibly objective air to his judgement goes, he has at his disposal such speciously technical terms as character, situation, incident, narrative, etc. But, if he would give his judgement further validity by centring it in the work under consideration, he will find such terms only approximately descriptive of the impressions to be organized. For, whereas rhythm corresponds to an actual excitement in the reader's mind that can be traced to its source in the means employed, character corresponds to nothing so definite. Rhythm is a property of words, character a product that needs analysis before a satisfactory account of its effect can be given in terms of its constituents, and a product, moreover, that invites extra-literary scrutiny. Such scrutiny is fatal to criticism, for, though it may be that the critic's ultimate concern is with the conception of life (the 'values') of which the novel is a vehicle, yet he is only so concerned in as far as that conception is made active through art. That that conception is inadequate, to take the negative, which is the more frequent case, is only revealed by a break-down in the ex-pression, a flaw in the technique, for it cannot be known apart from the form in which it becomes manifest. Obviously, a right appre-hension of that 'form' depends on a right apprehension of its elements – of which character is generally considered the principal.

However, the impossibility of ignoring this diversity leads to the perception that character has two aspects, a static and a dynamic, 'character in repose' and 'character in action', each of which can be further sub-divided, as to whether it is the 'inner' or the 'outer man' that is presented. But these terms are descriptive, not critical, and indicate the angle of presentation – not its success or failure. They assume, too, that at whatever level it is presented, character is to be regarded as the portrait of an imagined human being. If that is the assumption, criticism may either deal with the degree of illusion as such or the significance of the illusion as a symbol of humanity. To praise a novelist for his 'knowledge of human

[1] *The Modern Novel*, Elizabeth A. Drew, Cape.

nature' is plainly irrelevant; a psycho-analyst or a parish priest might possess as much. Mere degree of illusion, however, provides no adequate test; novelists who can do nothing else are able to perform the trick with ease, since 'nothing is easier than to create for oneself the idea of a human being, a figure and a character, from glimpses and anecdotes.' Nor does depth of illusion matter: Raskolnikov is 'deeper' than Tom Jones, in the sense that more of his interior is directly exposed, but he is a figure of different not greater significance.

On the other hand, the judgement of 'values' arrived at through a consideration of the symbolic aspect of character is unreliable because of the danger, almost the certainty, that attention will be diverted from the symbol to what it may be guessed to symbolize, which, if the artist is incompetent and the critic hospitable and sympathetic, will be much. It is for no other reason than that Conrad's heroes have been discerned by many earnest people to stand for something really tremendous in the matter of soul, that that writer has been so overestimated. Moreover, a novelist who is capable of 'staging' a figure of tragic possibilities (by making use of the reader's readiness to objectify that has been noted above) may utterly fail to realize those possibilities.

But this conclusion is reached without any direct examination of character as an illusion or as a symbol at all, for 'character' is merely the term by which the reader alludes to the pseudo-objective image he composes of his responses to an author's verbal arrangements. Unfortunately, that image once composed, it can be criticized from any angle and its moral, political, social, or religious, significance considered, all as though it possessed actual objectivity, were a figure of the inferior realm of real life. And, because the annual cataract of serious fiction is as full of 'life-like' little figures as drinking water is of infusoria, it passes critical filters in undiminished volume and unrectified impurity; while the meagre stream of genuine literature, being burdened with 'the forms of things unknown', is anxiously traced to its hypothetical source – a veritable psychologico-biographical bog.

In this connexion, the main thing to be noted about the new 'subjective' novelists is their increasing tendency to rely for their effect not on set pieces of character-drawing, but directly on the poetic properties of words. The idea of a character's consciousness is created in the reader by the exploitation of the emotive powers of language used to evoke concrete imagery and sensation. The idea so created has unusual reality; the idea of Dedalus, for instance, that is obtained from the compulsory experience of Dublin Beach as he himself would have experienced it, is not disauthenticated by any suspicious connivance of Nature, as when the thunder rumbles conveniently over Egdon Heath.

Miss Drew calls this the 'stream-of-consciousness' method – rather pointlessly, for under such a head Henry James must be included – and is inclined to condemn it because 'the concern . . . being entirely with the immediate in consciousness, the result must of necessity lack all proportion or perspective as a vision of anything beyond the immediate.' Since it cannot be seriously contended that the past is not, in effect, present in the immediate consciousness to be reported if reporting were the whole matter, the fault must be, not in the method but in the writer using it, as, in fact, is shown by the success of those chapters of *Ulysses* in which it is applied. It is unfair to blame the defenceless consciousness for its lack of an 'artistic relevance' to which it has not aspired, and one gathers Miss Drew does not really wish to do so. Her label led her astray.

II

Having briefly considered the notions commonly attached to the term 'character', it may be profitable to examine the almost antithetical set of ideas customarily included under the equally vague term 'narrative'. The word has a quite specific sense when it is used of the method of a book. Then it signifies that a course of events is related directly by the author or his mouthpiece, and contrasts with 'dramatic' or 'scenic', which indicate that events are rendered more immediately by dialogue or other representational devices. In this sense, which is technical rather than critical, the word is quite unambiguous.

The case is different when it is applied to the whole book to denote the action, as distinguished from the characters. It has an apparently greater critical relevance than the latter term on account of the more genuine objectivity of the quality it designates. But this advantage is only apparent, for the actual story of a novel eludes the epitomist as completely as character; few great works are not ridiculous in synopsis. And for this reason – that the form of a novel only exists as a balance of response on the part of the reader. Hence schematic plot is a construction of the reader's that corresponds to an aspect of that response and stands in merely diagrammatic relation to the source. Only as precipitates from the memory are plot or character tangible; yet only in solution have either any emotive valency. The composition of this metaphorical fluid is a technical matter. The technique of the novel is just as symphonic as the technique of the drama and as dependent, up to a point, on the dynamic devices of articulation and control of narrative tempo. But, though dependent, it is dependent as legs are on muscles, for the *how* but not the *why* of movement; and, interesting as functional technique may be to the mechanical-minded and to workers in the same medium on the look-out for tips, the organic is the province of criticism. More important, then, than what may be called the tricks of narrative is the status of plot and its relation to the other elements of a novel, particularly its relation to character, in solution.

Modern opinion, commonly assuming that the novelist expresses himself primarily through character, tends to regard story as more or less incidental; either it is scorned as part of the 'good old compromise . . . for the entertainment of the reader' or it is looked on as merely the expository structure – the Aintree, as it were, of character or, in less serious connexion, a modiste's parlour elegantly set for the mannequin parade.

Hence, though it is stipulated that plot be organic, it is required to be so in the sense that it may be said to arise out of, or be determined by, character. When a book is found satisfactory, this fundamental condition is said to be fulfilled, and 'value' is attributed to it or quarried out of character. Only when an imaginative failure is perceived will the plot be scrutinized and then only for the, as it were, temporal location of the lapse, whose occasion is still sought elsewhere.

This position is vulnerable from several points. In the first place, in any sense in which the terms used have a meaning at all, it is plain that character, that is, the idea of a human being which is carried away from a play or a novel, is a product of the narrative. Whereas it is impossible to attend to the barest recital of an event, or series of events, without calling up for oneself an idea of the persons concerned, an equally bare description of character invokes no such animated notion. In fact, it is impossible to acquire from words any idea of a person unless that person is defined in time as well as in space. That is to say, action of some sort is indispensable. But, though this be admitted, it may still be maintained that value, nevertheless, resides in the character thus created.

This is, in fact, the usual contention. Professor S. Gaselee, in an Essay on the Greek Novel in the *Daphnis and Chloë* volume of the Loeb Classics, remarks that 'fiction is one of the very few of the inventions of man that have improved in the course of the ages'. 'Brought up', he declares, 'on good novels, we are bored with their rude predecessors of antiquity . . . Of psychology there is barely a trace . . . any attempt indeed at character-drawing is faint and rough.'

I am not concerned to defend Longus and his fellows against their detractor. Certainly, they and their English imitators such as Barnaby Riche and Robert Greene very soon become tiresome. No more speedily, however, than does Maurice Hewlett, whose *Forest Lovers* is instanced in the same essay as an example of the good novels that formed the Professor's taste. But the reasons he gives for the condemnation are interesting. In part, of course, they are the indignant outcry of a sophisticated palate at being fobbed off with thin and pastoral fare. More than that, they are also the sincere lament of an unsatisfied appetite. The Professor would like some sauce, but he really needs meat.

If he were offered Homer, even Homer in an English prose version, we should hear, instead of these wails of hunger, the happy noises of prolonged mastication. Now, it cannot be contended that the addition of a little psychology and character-drawing to a chain of events makes all the difference between aesthetic starvation and satisfaction, it must be some quality inherent in those events. And it is this quality that is common to all great works of literature, in no matter what genre. It is a unity among the events, a progressive rhythm that includes and reconciles each separate rhythm. As manifested in the novel, it resolves, when analysed, chiefly into character and plot in a secondary, schematic sense, – qualities that are purely fictitious. Neither of these is an active element in the whole work in the way that melody and harmony are elements in a piece of music. Perhaps it would be less ambiguous to designate this basic, poetic quality by some such term as rhythm or development; on the other hand, plot or story do indicate its nature – that it is primarily a sequence of events developing in accordance with an inner necessity.

And it is the recognition of this inner necessity that constitutes the recognition of value. To call this organizing principle 'character' is to attribute essential importance to what may be no more than a secondary manifestation and is often, even on the face of it, inaccurate. Obviously, the *Odyssey* has this unity; but it does not proceed from Ulysses. So, too, has *War and Peace*; yet Tolstoy makes it, perhaps, even too plain that events develop quite independently of the people they affect, as well as of those who are trying to affect them. And Hardy, in this at least, resembles him. Ultimately, this rhythmic coherence springs from the writer's conception of life and the adequacy thereto of his vehicle.

Actually, then, character is, to borrow biological jargon, an emergent quality of the novel. It emerges from the story, which is itself structurally a product of language, eloquence. An attempt, however, to cut out this intervening stage is marked by the assumption that the novelist's primary creation is of character. And this also indicates what is peculiar in the scope of modern fiction.

By the classic writer, elaborating a given pattern, the individual is seen included within the metaphysical hierarchy, symbolized as Fate, gods, and mortals. To the romantic, however, the individual appears containing within him that hierarchy, so that the writer is compelled to invent his own pattern. And the remoter his experience from the common, and the more personal his values, the more difficult will it be for his creation to make contact with an audience. This task, however, may be left to the character who, however highly specialized, is to be assumed to be a human being with the emotional, etc., equipment common to such. Whether a sceptical audience that, unmoved by assertion, demands sensible proof will be convinced is another matter.

Historically, character, as we now understand it, is an outcome of the Romantic Revival, a movement that has been discerned by some as one of escape from the indifferent universe of science into the fastness of the individual soul, and of an attempt to locate there the limitations that constitute value. In Professor Whitehead's words: 'The independence ascribed to bodily substances carried them away from the realm of values altogether. They degenerated into a mechanism entirely valueless except as suggestive of external ingenuity.' (There is no reason, however, to suppose, as this phrasing implies, and as it so often suggested, that developments in the aesthetic sphere proceed as effects from developments in other departments of thought. The imaginative faculty being supreme, poets themselves, neither science nor philosophy, are to blame for any decay of sensibility.)

Such an abstraction of values from the objective universe involves a corresponding restriction of the scope of significant action. In the epic, it is the completed action that animates the bare recital of events and, by unifying them, gives it structural vitality. Since the end is ordained by Fate operating through the wills and passions of gods and mortals, their deeds and speech are adequate to the poet's purpose. There is no need to go behind them to explain their meaning; that meaning is what happened and its inevitability. (The epic poet, like the historian, has also the advantage that, since the events he deals with actually occurred, his narrative cannot be doubted on the score of historic truth, but has only to satisfy as to its imaginative truth, or arrangement, whereas the feigning novelist raises questions of probability. But he, too, pretends to the authority of the past tense, and no one is likely so far to forget the rules of the game as to object unless there is a defect in his arrangement also.)

Problems arise, however, when the overt subject of a narrative is, not the fore-doomed destruction of Troy, but the integration of a Richard Myrtle. The scene of action being removed from the external to the psychological world, a technique is required that will manifest the otherwise imperceptible events. Further, a principle is needed that will unify those events when manifested. This principle can be identified with the individual, the 'character', and located, by the romantics proper in the emotions, by Henry James in the intelligence, by the followers of Freud – gentle Ruths, gleaning psychology's alienist fields – in the sub-conscious.

Linked to these questions is that of authority – the angle from which the story shall be presented. Henry James was the first to realize consciously and to state that the interior drama must be shown to the inner eye if it is to be emotively efficient. But it is not vision alone that confers authority; Homer owes his to no sleight-of-hand with the 'seeing-eye', but to the internal consistency of that which he offers to it. Nevertheless, visualization is necessary, and it it is the problem of objectifying and setting in disciplined motion the subjective narrative that has occupied nearly all English novelists of importance since Fielding, and Richardson before him.

It is curious that, though the Romantics destroyed the poetic forms of the previous tradition, yet the novel continued for a considerable period to be written on Fielding's plan. This was, perhaps, largely due to the fact that in England the novel has rarely been the medium of first-rate creative minds and to the not unrelated lack of self-consciousness in the matter of technique on the part of its practitioners. And Fielding's extraordinary effectiveness encouraged such inertia. But the effectiveness of his method proceeded from its entire adequacy to its content, which did not include the individual sensibility. Fielding's attitude was primarily social; he saw people as units in society and estimated their actions by the resultant effects on that organism. Secure of an audience that shared his views, he was able to use objective narrative with authority, though only types emerged from it. Further, being conservative of a tradition that accepted the whole of life as material for art, he was able to base his story very firmly on experience. But for all its permanence and solidity, his art was not heroic, as he himself admitted in calling *Tom Jones* a comic epic. Fielding's single-mindedness, which enabled him to retain so firm a grasp on the more immediate aspects of existence, was dependent on a spiritual crassness that allowed him to remain content with the stuffy metaphysics of his day. The difference between tragic and comic art lies partly in the different attitudes adopted towards the catastrophes ensuing on a collision between individual and collective values. Of course, the great comic artist, such as Congreve, takes his stand above society; his standards are absolute and his own, not those of the herd.

Now, it is the weakness of an art such as Fielding's that it is almost wholly typical. It operates by the setting in opposition qualities abstracted from men, so that the response it arouses is only partial. It has the veracity of correct analysis and the further truth of coherent re-combination, but the appeal is limited mainly to admiration. If the romantic attention to the individual had meant an extension of the field of perception, the attempt to particularize and subtilize Fielding's structure might have succeeded. Unfortunately, it meant not an extension, but merely a shifting of that field. Consequently, though along with Fielding's method, some of his immediacy was retained, it became increasingly more necessary to expound the meaning of action. Thus the plots of the Victorians became cumbered with a vast amount of not strictly relevant matter, essential to them for their 'meaning', but quite un-resolvable. For the difficulty in exteriorizing the movements of the individual sensibility is twofold. Outward actions have to be invented that will re-create, and not merely illustrate, inward happenings, and these highly particularized actions have at the same time to be universalized. The necessity for having regard to these two aspects constitutes the real problem. Dostoievsky solved it by the violent conjunction of extreme realism in manner to extreme ideality of attitude, but he did so only at the expense of a tremendous amount of will that might advantageously have been liberated for other purposes.

Henry James is often given credit for having been the first to assert that events within the mind might be just as important as those without. The claim is hardly just, but he certainly was the first to realize that the interior drama might be rendered immediately by language, without the intervention of circumstantiating physical action at every stage, that the word was as capable of embodying mental as physical movements, and that its latter function was useful only because of its superior vividness.

But James's, like Fielding's, was primarily a social art. Truly, the society James contemplated was composed of members far more differentiated and sensitive to others' individuality than any Fielding could conceive, and it was his own creation. It is one, however, in which the maximum development is assured for certain impulses only at the cost of the almost complete omission of others – roughly, the grosser appetites Fielding handled so vigorously.

Thus, though James's narrative is autonomous, it is so only within the boundaries of a limited experience; his action is complete and self-sufficing because it springs from a single source, but it is ultimately invalidated by a latent dualism that is not explicit only because the intractable factor is altogether suppressed. (This suppression is not complete until his last period, but its progress can be observed in his earlier books.) Hence the much extolled purity of his plots is actually of less worth than the impurity of those of the 'great' Victorians, in which the presence of large masses of unassimilated matter is evidence of at least an attempt to be comprehensive.

But James's skill in the manipulation of incident, the intricate technique by which events were arranged in varying degrees of relief, so that the climax stood out in the round with the maximum intensity and immediacy, was one elaborated to dispose the most attenuated substance in the most substantial manner possible; and it was dependent on the prose that, apparently aimless, yet with certainty isolated and held up to view the fact on which James

wished to dwell. Without it none of James's other devices is sufficient to give more than mechanical form to a novel, as appears from
his imitators.

It is notable that Joyce uses no such devices. Nothing in *Ulysses*
is, to use Mr. Lubbock's distinction, reported; everything is shown
or dramatized. But Joyce contemplates not only the discrepancy
between actuality and individual values, between things as they are
and as they appear modified by the sensibility; his irony springs
from a more profound opposition — that within the subject, the
contrast between actual impulse and the appearance which that,
too, assumes in consciousness. From this profoundly critical standpoint, he is able to exteriorize and objectify vast psychological tracts
that as a rule lurk shapelessly outside the action of a novel, perceptible only as unaccountable influences that distort and hinder
its progress. And regarding with an equal eye the response both to
external and internal stresses, attributing no more value to the one
than to the other, he is able to compel both into the same perspective
and so set in motion events that, occurring simultaneously on both
planes, are in themselves adequate and self-sufficient. Thus the
authority and directness of objective presentation is secured for the
subjective narrative, Joyce's unit being the consciousness, not its
social crystallization, the character. Dedalus and Bloom are but
symbols of disintegration; the imminent, never clearly apprehended Ulysses is the hero of this Odyssey, whose significance lies
wholly in the completed action and its organic relation to the events
of which it is composed.

Reviews from the *Sunday Referee*
1929–1931

POEMS OF TWO DEANS

Complete Poetry and Selected Prose of John Donne. Edited by John Hayward (Nonesuch Press)
Swift's Verse. By F. Elrington Ball (Murray)

Although circulated only in manuscript during their author's lifetime, Donne's poems were then the admiration of every cultivated reader. A brief period of posthumous fame was brought to an end by that ascendancy of French or pseudo-classical taste that followed the Restoration, and his reputation survived chiefly because he came to stand for the very type of the rugged and obscure, 'conceited' poet.

The excellent edition now produced by the Nonesuch Press (excellent in text and format, containing much material hardly accessible elsewhere, and priced remarkably low) should definitely re-establish Donne's reputation with the general reader – as the keenest-minded of English poets who have written extensively of love; as a fine prose satirist for his attack on the Jesuits – 'Ignatius his Conclave'; and as an astonishing rhetorician in his devotional prose.

. . . .

The Dean of St. Paul's was the last flower of the scholastic philosophy, but he retains his hold on the modern reader by the extreme acuity with which he analyses and transcribes his devotional experience, as in his early years he had done with his amorous experience. In the poems, as in the few sermons, of the Dean of St. Patrick's all that metaphysical subtlety has vanished. Donne's intense preoccupation with the individual at the extreme tension of consciousness – that is, within the aura of love, human or divine – is replaced in Swift's work by an intense preoccupation with man in his social aspect, where his consciousness is necessarily diffused. The misanthropic bias of Swift's creation has occupied the apologists of every generation, and though 'Gulliver' has survived through the sheer inventive richness of its fable, the poems have been gradually shouldered out of popular estimation. That none of Swift's major poems is included in the 'Oxford Book of English Verse', that semi-official standard for poetic gold, is evidence of a contemporary depravity of taste no less pronounced than that of the mid-eighteenth century.

. . . .

The late F. Elrington Ball, whose unsurpassed knowledge of the history of Irish society enabled him to produce the splendidly annotated edition of Swift's correspondence, had, when he died, practically passed for press this study of Swift's verse (now completed at the few necessary points), and it is indispensable to the student of the subject and full of interest for the ordinary reader.

Since the disturbance of romantic ideas as to what is and what is not poetry, Swift's verse has not enjoyed the prestige it had in a more virile age, when men of mind and men of affairs did not revolve, as now they do, in different orbits. Its force and purity of style and its variety of tone, from gay familiarity to obscene vituperation, ensure its admiration by all those for whom literature is of the essence of life, whatever fashion may determine to be the definition of poetry for the moment. Donne, too, has suffered from fashion, and even Jonson told Drummond that Donne, 'for not keeping of accent, deserved hanging'.

. . . .

Since then the charge has been repeated in various forms, but the modern ear has learnt to appreciate in Donne one of our most subtle metrists. But, aesthetic considerations apart, one of the strangest speculations aroused by the accidental concatenation of these two great English writers is whether, in our time, the Anglican church would have been able to hold them in its net, for they are, with all respect, the two queerest fish that ever served that institution with the utmost loyalty.

POETS AND THEIR CRITICS

Baudelaire and the Symbolists. By Peter Quennell (Chatto and Windus)
Dante. By T. S. Eliot (Faber and Faber)
Andrew Marvell. By V. Sackville-West (Faber and Faber)

Although it is more than sixty years since Baudelaire's death there is no sign of his being superseded in his position as Europe's most influential poet during this period. Unfortunately, so far as his fame penetrated English literary circles, it was for long associated with a taint of immorality and decadence, though it is interesting to note that a young critic named George Saintsbury already perceived the essentially classic quality in Baudelaire's poetry, and, some fifty years ago, wrote a lucid essay from this standpoint. But the tradition of his decadence died hard, and it is only since the War that a juster view has been able to gain ground. In these essays on Baudelaire and five of his literary successors (with one on a predecessor, Gérard de Nerval, a Symbolist *avant la lettre*), Mr. Quennell, himself a poet, reveals a critical ability which has two outstanding merits. The first is the capacity for placing his subject in the historic environment, and in this he is assisted by his sense of style which enables him to manipulate the picturesque without overburdening his theme; the second is much rarer, a realization of criticism as an aesthetic, in which, that is, these minute particulars are incorporated but transcended; what Rémy de Gourmont called 'the erecting of one's personal impressions into laws'. Without the impressions, of course, criticism is dull, not to say meaningless; but without the generalizations it must remain only a vague agglomeration of impressions. Mr. Quennell keeps the balance, so that his book, besides being most enjoyable to read, is a coherent account of the relations of the four principal 'Symbolist' poets – Laforgue, Corbière, Rimbaud, and Mallarmé, to Baudelaire, their fountainhead, to each other, and to the poetic ambitions of our own time, for no more seductive masters than these have yet been found.

·   ·   ·   ·   ·   ·

Mr. Eliot's essay on Dante is the more effective because it is restricted to the establishing of three particular points. The most important of these is the demonstration of the necessity of comprehending the *Divine Comedy* as a whole. There is a tendency to concentrate on the magnificent episodes, in which the *Inferno* is particularly rich, to the exclusion of the realization of the poem as 'a complete scale of the *depths* and *heights* of human emotion'. Many admirers of Dante would no doubt plead guilty to skipping a good deal of the *Purgatorio* and *Paradiso*, but Mr. Eliot, with his customary lucidity, convinces the reader that such half measures are an injustice to the poem and an impoverishment of real appreciation.

·   ·   ·   ·   ·   ·

There is not very much to be said about Andrew Marvell. He was such a consummate poet that the content of his poems is all transmuted into poetry, and about that, of course, there really is nothing to be said, except to point to it with such expressions as shall best excite to admiration. In this Miss Sackville-West succeeds, but when she risks generalizations they are often ill-founded, such, for instance, as that 'the faculty of self-criticism has never been the strong point of poets.' The *Dante* and the *Marvell* are the first two booklets in a series called 'The Poets on the Poets'.

MR. VINES'S NEW POEMS

Triforium. By Sherard Vines (Cobden-Sanderson)

A poet would be justified in resenting a little the statement that he represents a 'tendency' in contemporary literature; it seems too much as if it deprived him of his individuality. But as all poetry is an amalgam of the period with the personality, it is rather a sign of vitality than otherwise to exude a strong flavour of the period, more hopeful of achievement, at any rate, than allowing the personality to pine in a timeless vacuum of unidentified regrets, which is what Mr. De la Mare and a host of less accomplished writers have done.

But Mr. Sherard Vines, whether he writes well or badly – and he can do both – always aims at making his statements concrete, hewing them out of the emotional and intellectual here-and-now, and drawing his imagery with equal freedom from the commonplaces of the mechanical age and the paradoxes of world-old fantasy. And it is in this direction that a good deal of contemporary effort seems to have been working; that 'cosy, home-made art which for nearly two decades has debilitated both theory and practice in England' – Mr. Vines so assaults it in his preface – has given place to a poetry in which the immediate, and too often facile, response has been sacrificed to a greater complexity of effect, and so, when successful, to a fuller and more humanly satisfying pleasure.

For it is absurd to imply, as some of the antagonists of modernism do, that the simple and changeless things of life, trees and cows and the countryside generally, are in some unexplained way more 'human', and so a proper subject matter for verse, than the creations of the human intellect and the mad confusion of civilization.

The danger of this technique is that the poet will be unaware when his references are too recondite. He must, of course, postulate an ideal reader whose culture is co-extensive with his own; he will not try to make his verse easy, but he must be sure that his reference comes to life in the verse, otherwise the information in the notes is valueless. When Mr. Vines writes:

> Life that yesterday like old Harry Hunks
> Would growl and peep from blood-shot eyes
> Is at length obsolete

we do not mind turning up the notes to find out that 'Harry Hunks or Huncks was a famous bear in Elizabethan London', but the comparison does not strike us as more than interesting: there is no compulsion about it, the rhythm is weak and the construction of the sentence does not help matters. In many of these poems, indeed, there seems to be little chance of reconciling the detail with any rhythmical interpretation of the passage. This is perhaps only a passing defect in Mr. Vines's verse, there are numerous poems, including the long *Élan Mortel*, which show a controlling power over rhythm.

I have suggested that Mr. Vines is 'representative', and this seems to me true as much of his attitude to experience as of his revision of technique. Some years ago it seemed that *The Waste Land* might dominate the sensibility of a half-generation or so. But there was a definite weakening of influence when Mr. Eliot expressed his vision of the way the world ends – 'not with a bang but a whimper', and since then a search has gone on for a more virile gesture. *Triforium* is at least a contribution towards this. It is disillusioned, naturally, but it has also an heroic quality in it, and can celebrate ultimate annihilation with poems, not because that will be an escape from the ugliness of life, but because it is the only way the finite being can express himself against the background of the universe as it is. In the meantime there is the plastic beauty of the flesh and its works:

> Then, O ye fugues, build swift and true
> Aerial scaffolds all of blue;
> These let the singing masons foot,
> Each aproned therapeut,
> And plaster lapis lazuli
> To staunch and ease this ailing sky.

A MODERN TROUVÈRE

The Set-Up. By Joseph Moncure March (Secker)
The Wild Party. By Joseph Moncure March (Secker)

Verse narrative has played a losing game for so long that the couple of good tricks scored by Mr. March might have surprised even those who watch the literary card-table with some care. Not that there have been no narrative poems published and read, but they were either romantic maunderings in a world of fancy, or, if they dealt with life under modern conditions, as in Mr. Masefield's work, one wondered why this instrument of verse, which has been elaborated to such a pitch of sensitiveness, should be used to do the dirty work that prose has learnt to do so much more efficiently. And another weakness of the pretended revival of realistic verse-narrative was the inability to get the essential colloquialisms to look at ease in their unaccustomed metrical rig-out; the whole affair had the look of a fancy-dress ball when the electric lights are beginning to pale out. Only, in this case, it was the peculiar vice of all pseudo-poetry, 'poetic feeling', masquerading as squalor and violence in an attempt to make itself more 'real'.

· · · · · · ·

Now Mr. March, with two very good stories of modern American life to tell, has the audacity to tell them in verse, and to pull it off. There are several reasons for his success. In the first place, he has no divided purpose; he does not try to add poetry to his subject, but, using rhythm and rhyme, he gets every ounce of effect that these neglected but powerful instruments can give him. Besides, he does not use metre which, rich in its associations with lyric and elegy, gives such an air of factitiousness when used to convey contemporary atmosphere. He has the advantage, of course, of the extremely vivid American idiom, and for his rhythm to get its full effect the American intonation is perhaps essential.

· · · · · · ·

The Set-Up is the story of a frame-up some shabby boxing-match promoters tried to work on an old Negro boxer. The Negro upset their plans by knocking out his man, so the gang got wild and went all out for his blood. They chased him down a subway, and in the resulting scuffle he falls under a train. The simple tragedy is ad-

mirably constructed. So, too, *The Wild Party* (the setting is among
a crowd of New York vaudeville artists) ends in a tragedy, which has
been worked up to with a fine cumulative sense.

. . . .

Mr. March is a modern *trouvère*. His poems should hold a crowd
in the open, for his fundamental gift is that of storyteller. When, as
he rarely does, he generalizes, he is less an individual, but when he
is absorbed in his story he has a flair which literate and illiterate
could alike appreciate, and that is rare nowadays. For his poems
insist on being read aloud, and, once started, on being read to the
end; there may be fine points which the listener will miss at first, but
the important thing is the strong current that sweeps from incident
to incident – there is little irrelevant detail in either poem, but in my
opinion the feeling of impending catastrophe is more intensely felt
in *The Wild Party*.

MODERNIST AND CONVENTIONAL POETRY

Gold Coast Customs and Other Poems. By Edith Sitwell (Duckworth)
The Thracian Stranger and Other Poems. By Edward Thompson,
(Benn)

The Gold Coast customs, which provide Miss Sitwell with much
of the imagery for the title-poem of her new volume, were extremely bloody rites, and she uses them to symbolize the spiritual
barbarity of the natives of that other Gold Coast, Fashionable
Society. On the whole this is too hysterical to be convincing, in much
the same way that Shelley's abuse of kings and priests is, and it also
tends to be sentimental. Poor Lady Bamburgher, with her smart
parties, is featured as a cannibal queen rotten with plague, whilst,
Miss Sitwell says,

> I have seen the murdered God look through the eyes
> Of the drunkard's smirched
> Mask as he lurched . . .

But Miss Sitwell's power of expression frequently overcomes this
intellectual confusion, and there are some vivid passages in which
pain and contempt unite to create a picture of nightmarish reality.

Her other long poem, 'Metamorphosis', though it suffers from a plethora of her own self-sanctified clichés, and though the development of the theme is far from lucid, has essential poetic content and is one of the most moving poems Miss Sitwell has written.

· · · · · · · ·

The bulk of Mr. Thompson's volume is made up of a long poem in heroic couplets on a classical theme. It is, as he says, 'obviously a young man's work, and belongs to a world other than the one which is ours and the author's today'. But, since the poem was written twenty-five years ago, and the author thinks is worth while giving it to this other, contemporary world, he should at least have removed its more obvious infelicities. Athena, surprised in her privacy by Teiresias, expresses herself like this:

> A sight to purge whose guilt thy soul requires,
> Hurled hence to Tartar quick and penal fires,
> · For which that from my anger should befall
> No stroke but in taut death were pang too small!

This is not an uncharacteristic sample. On pages 22 and 23 one finds a verb separated from its subject by five lines, and of the brambles that obstructed some hunters he says,

> Athwart them interposed with horrid let.

· · · · · · · ·

The Thracian Stranger might have been left in manuscript as an unsuccessful derivative from 'The Earthly Paradise'. Of the shorter, and adult, poems there is not much to say, except that the sonnet, 'Memory', is as obscure as anything in the earlier poem. Generally, though, Mr. Thompson can express a simple emotion with the decorum required of conventional verse, though without the slightest quiver of individuality. His epitaph for the men killed in one of the Palestine battles is a good example of this:

> Make of their graves a garden, lest they mourn
> For Lowland heaths and fields of sunlit corn!
> Ay me! Not all your meadows shall atone,
> Waters of Raqquon, for the meadows known!

A THINKING POET

Twelve Idylls. By Lascelles Abercrombie (Secker)

Professor Abercrombie was one of the more interesting contributors to the early volumes of *Georgian Poetry*, for his work had the qualities that the characteristic verse of the pre-War period most significantly lacked – a touch of passion and a measure of intellectual curiosity. His new volume has the same virtues, and it is one of the few published during the last twelve months which the ordinary intelligent person can read without blushing for the exceptional fatuity of that part of humanity which still indulges in the composition of verse.

In most of these idylls, the vivid fable is the vehicle for some philosophical speculation. In 'The Olympians' he depicts the feud between the gods of Being and the gods of Becoming. In 'Asmodeus in Egypt' he succeeds in the difficult task of actually portraying a non-human, daemonic nature, beautifully unconfined, and his story describes the disaster that results when human desire infects this absolute simplicity. In the poems where the subject matter is absolute simplicity. In the poems where the subject matter is 'realistic', 'Witchcraft: New Style' and 'Ham and Eggs', his treatment is less successful. Since Crabbe, there has been hardly a poet who could versify the details of everyday life without staggering in turn from violence to bathos. Since the romantic emphasis on the 'poetic', poets have lost that innocence of eye which enabled them to accept every detail with impartiality and to dignify what was intrinsically uninteresting though necessary to their tale, not by periphrasis, but by its fusion with the current of their verse. So, when there is no great pleasure to be derived from the verse itself, one feels that the short-story form, with its great elasticity, would be more appropriate to such subjects.

The technical merits of this collection are not, on the whole, so indisputable as the interest of its subject-matter. Professor Abercrombie has yet to stamp a style as unchallengeably his. He uses many metres here, and is perhaps most himself in the least usual of them – a variation of the old alliterative line – though even here a sharper definition of the scheme would have been an advantage. But Mr. Abercrombie is not a meticulous craftsman. In 'The Death of a Friar' some of the couplets are rhymed in a most casual way. His blank-verse tends to be unsettled in rhythm.

Colloquialism may be good, especially as a defence against Miltonic mannerisms, and by rejuvenating idiom, but when it threatens the dominance of metre verse becomes a drawl. One of the best sustained passages is Samuel's soliloquy ('At Endor'), when he is hauled from his grave by the witch's spells. There is real imagination in it, and the writing is strong, but unforced.

A SHEAF OF POETRY

Fifty Poems. By Lord Dunsany (Putnam)
Ubi Ecclesia, by G. K. Chesterton; *Dark Weeping*, by A. E.; *Three Things*, by W. B. Yeats; *The Outcast*, by James Stephens; *Inscription on a Fountain Head*, by Peter Quennell; *Animula*, by T. S. Eliot; *A Snowdrop*, by Walter De la Mare. (Faber and Faber)
The Black Christ, and Other Poems. By Countee Cullen (Putnam)

This is Lord Dunsany's first collection of poems, and though it cannot give him so high a rank as a poet as that to which he is entitled as a prose fantasist, it is a pleasant volume. He writes with an economy of decorative effects that allows full scope to the point of each poem, for most of them have rather an epigrammatic quality – here is a reply to critics:

> From little fountain-pens they wring
> The last wee drop of inky spite;
> 'We do not like the kind of thing
> That lords,' they say, 'most likely, write.'

> Beyond the boundaries I have been,
> That dull geography has drawn,
> To bring you light from visions seen
> In kingdoms eastward of the dawn.

The inversion in the first two lines of that last stanza is not graceful, but generally Lord Dunsany is more scrupulous. Among the other poems are some that commemorate the fascinating beauty of travels in the East, and others, pleasantly platitudinous, on man's inscrutable destiny and the transience of his most gorgeous civilizations.

A single short poem by an author does not provide much opportunity for criticism, so one can only say that the new numbers in the *Ariel Poems* are as charmingly decorated as their predecessors. Most of them are marked with that prettiness which is a characteristic of the prevailing fashion, so that Mr. Gilbert Spencer's boldly stylized naturalism comes as a relief, but it quite overpowers the poem by Mr. Yeats, so anaemic in formal quality, which it is intended to decorate.

. . . .

I had read most of Mr. Cullen's volume except the title-poem and the publisher's note on the jacket before I realized that he was either an American or a Negro. I hope I shall not be thought to have a racial prejudice when I say that this seems to me a bad sign, but I mean that I think a good poet reflects in some unmistakable way his racial or national idiom of thought and speech. This is Mr. Cullen's fourth volume, and he seems to have learnt to eradicate all his idiosyncrasies and write like any poetic undergraduate.

The title-poem is a longish narrative in octosyllabic couplets, of which the point is that the Christ allows himself to be lynched in place of the young Negro a mob was hunting. It is written with deep emotion and considerable technical skill, and it enforces a needful moral lesson.

But I have found more essential poetry in some of the naïve songs and animal stories that the Negro slaves invented for their solace or entertainment when they were labouring in the plantations. None the less, such a poem as 'The Black Christ' will make me watch for Mr. Cullen's next volume.

MODERN POETS

A Dream in the Luxembourg. By Richard Aldington (Chatto and Windus)
Adamastor. Poems by Roy Campbell (Faber and Faber)

It was the custom not long ago to deplore the state of poetry, as a reaction, no doubt, from the anthology habit, that most effective of means of swamping real talent under mediocrity's numerical advantages. I do not think there was, or is, any actual justification for such pessimism. Poetry always was, and always will be, rare, and it is too-close contact with perennial banality which induces those atrabilious statements from the unfortunate people who try and sift the annual crop of verse. I am not sure that there were not good grounds for deploring the state of poetry in the age of Shakespeare, at least I should be sorry to have to read ten per cent of the books of verse entered in the Stationer's Register at that time.

If we want to be snobbish about our own times, which is not a bad thing, and claim superiority over less enlightened ages, we can only do it, I think (not on the grounds that more poetry is being written now, or that a new art of poetry, casting off all fetters of rhyme and metre, has been invented), but because we have a greater catholicity of appreciation, are ready to respond to the merits of different techniques—to techniques as immensely different as Aldington's is from Campbell's.

There are a few bigots of the old school left, of course, who would anathematize Aldington because he renounces any formal scheme; there are more bigots of the type Lewis admirably named 'revolutionary simpletons' who would excommunicate Campbell because he both scans and rhymes.

Aldington's long poem is an episode, a crucial episode it is true, yet even so it does not give me an opportunity of discussing his poetry in general. His *Dream in the Luxembourg* is the realization (fancied or actual, he says; he cannot tell us which, but certainly it becomes real in his verse) of a supreme experience of love. And the theme of the poem, as I read it, is the pathos of man under the law, 'the wearisome condition of humanity', that he may have no hold on the moments when he has known himself most surely and purely alive; not merely that he may not keep them, but that he may even have to wonder if they ever happened. So the lover complains after the consummation of his passion:

> Faint, faint are the voices that come to me,
> Fainter and fainter the colours, fainter my dream;
> It is passing like the setting rays from still water,
> Drifting away like the willow leaves on a cold morning
> When they patter so dismally on the frosty ground.
> Fading as the colours fade from the roses at twilight,
> Growing dim like the eyes of a wounded soldier,
> Leaving me, inexorably leaving me.

But it is through art that these moments are given, I will not say immortality, but a longer lease of life, and though I admire the clean, direct phrasing of Aldington's poem, I think that in discarding artifice he is unnecessarily detracting from the vividness of his revivication. But a poem which reflects such sensitiveness, which in construction is so well-balanced, cannot fail to be moving, and its refusal of all adventitious aids to effect, is a challenge to true appreciation.

.   .   .   .

Roy Campbell is the finest rhetorician writing now; I mean, he is a poet who includes a rhetorician, and not that awful thing a rhetorician who is not a poet. If Aldington seems to have what may almost be called moral scruples about exploiting the emotional power of words in metrical and metaphorical formations, Campbell revels in all the possibilities of sound, colour, and movement that these provide. In 'The Albatross', a poem which under the symbol of an albatross struck by a ship's spars evokes the poetic mind in its most fervid experiences and final acceptance of dissolution, he writes:

> I had been dashed in the gold spray of dawns,
> And hit with silver by the star's faint light.
> The red moon charged at me with lowered horns,
> Buffalo-shouldered by the gloom of night.
> The world revolving like a vast cocoon,
> Unwound its threading leagues at my desire:
> With burning stitches by the sun and moon
> My life was woven like a shawl of fire ...
> No more to rise, the last sun bombs the deep,
> And strews my shattered senses with its light –
> My spirit knows the silence it must keep
> And with the ocean hankers for the night.

This poem, the sombre 'Tristan da Cunha', and the beautiful poem 'The Palm', deliciously handled in a metre that might easily have been disastrous, are to me the highest peaks of achievement in a volume which well bears out the promise of the earlier *Flaming Terrapin*.

In one or two pieces which are less successful one may notice a lack of intellectual suppleness, a fixation in a mental attitude which requires the most absolute absorption in the symbolism not to seem theatrical – as, for instance, in 'Mazeppa'. But that is included among the 'Early Poems', and Campbell's later tendencies seem to be away from this danger-area – for which the subtle intellectualism of Paul Valéry's poetry is perhaps to be thanked. Campbell has a peculiar gift of sarcasm which is extraordinarily successful when involved with a lyrical theme, as it is in 'Festivals of Flight' and 'Poets in Africa'; the deliberately satirical pieces are rather out of place in this volume. This lyrical sarcasm, which is quite personal to him, a sonority of line which is at its best so vibrant as to remind one of the young Marlowe, and the spontaneous use of vivid, exotic, or violently familiar metaphors, these are what I should define as the technical characteristics of a poetry which is unsurpassed in its kind today. And it holds this enviable position not because Campbell is a wild and untamed son of the veld, as some of his admirers in the press insist (what the man is, is beside the point, certainly the poet is as familiar with the poetry of the past as a good poet must be), but because he has had the strength to dominate that formidable charger, our traditional verse, which is always trying to amble back to its lush paddock in the past, and force it to career across the plains of his imagination.

HIGH-SOUNDING NONSENSE

Snow. Poems by Humbert Wolfe (Gollancz)

Mr. Wolfe is *such* a poet, and he does not for one moment allow us to forget the fact. He is an adept at high-sounding nonsense. A typical beginning of a sonnet is this:

> Austere, removed, grave as the thought of death
> and whiter than white hands for ever lost . . .

and that, on the face of it, is what so many people take to be really peetic. It provides them with a certain feeling they are used to getting from verse, and what is actually said by the words is practically insignificant. 'Grave as the thought of death' sounds well, and if the suspicion that it is platitudinous crosses the mind, one has the consolation of thinking that all the greatest poetry expresses the commonplace.

But to continue:

> intangible shape of beauty's frozen breath,
> incredible and noiseless as a ghost.

This is rather like a not very good charade, but now Mr. Wolfe puts us out of our misery, and tells us that he means *snow*. 'Snow,' he says, 'be saluted.' And surely, long suffering as our meteorological phenomena are under the assaults of writers of verse in search of a subject, snow can never have been called upon to endure more portentous vagueness.

In spite of the fact that the worst excesses of his style have been thoroughly guyed by the author of *Poems by Pinchbeck Lyre*, Siegfried Sassoon, Mr. Wolfe continues unrepentantly to parody the little spark of individuality he once had, as here:

> How fare it, ghost, now
>   the only stir
> is of quiet becoming
>   quieter?

And though he ostentatiously renounces, in a poem prefacing this volume, the easy flow of pretty words and admonishes himself thus:

> Be mercilessly pure
> with form's uncompromising rectitude,

it would be hard to imagine a style which was more predominantly characterized by a yielding to the cheap and meretricious effect. That explains, I think, the measure of popularity Mr. Wolve enjoys. A not very discriminating audience has been glamoured by this glittering flow of verse which is so very like the poetry they have known and which, largely because of that likeness, is so infinitely remote from it.

THREE AGES OF POETRY

Dunbar: The Poet and His Period. By Rachel Annand Taylor (Faber and Faber)
Jezebel Mort and Other Poems. By Arthur Symons (Heinemann)
Red Roses for Bronze. Poems by H. D. (Chatto and Windus)

In this essay on Dunbar Mrs. Annand Taylor has given us a fine, rich piece of writing, which, though concentrated, evokes the poetic, beauty-loving, yet fervently intellectual Scotland of the time of James IV.

The general reader of verse is probably only familiar with Dunbar's two or three anthology pieces – the lament for dead poets and his eulogy of the City of London – which give little idea of his varied mastery of different forms of verse. Mrs. Taylor certainly does not err by making extravagant claims for her poet; rather, she would damp down the enthusiasm for Dunbar expressed by the young bloods who are raising a national renaissance in his ancient kingdom. But south of the Tweed there is ample room for more knowledge and a keener appreciation of Dunbar.

Dunbar, Mrs. Taylor cogently argues, must ultimately be judged inferior in poetic power to Henryson, James I of Scotland, and many of the nameless ballad-makers, because of a certain coarseness of imaginative fibre, a failure to respond to the height of endeavour that was stirring all round him or to the depth of tragedy when Flodden Field left his nation desolate. He is, perhaps, justly termed a bourgeois poet, for though the term carried some aura of contempt, it is also a definition. He had very distinctly in his mind's eye a snug Church living, and he asked his King for it more than once in verse, with no effect. He might have been a better poet had he got it; how very well he managed to write without it is fully acknowledged by Mrs. Taylor and her essay should send all who read it in search of a copy of his always virile, often satiric, and often charming poems.

. . . .

There is a marked difference in attitude between the two modern poets, Arthur Symons and H.D. Though Mr. Symons is influenced by the Catholic tradition which Dunbar naturally breathed in, he does not accept the authoritative notions of good and evil of the Church. The poet's conceptions remain vague in an amorphous veil of mingled Christian and pagan mythology. The most satisfying of the many poems in *Jezebel Mort*, whose dates show them to be drawn from the work of twenty years, are, to my mind, the simpler ones, some of them written to girls, some of the best to cats. These communicate an intensity of experience in unadulterated language.

. . . .

H.D. is poles apart from either of these poets. Not only has she created her own technique of expression but her emotions, like her pellucid imagery, are free from the conflicts and complexities, the detritus of moral combats inseparable from an anti-sensual creed. In this volume her gifts seem more mature than before, her touch surer because her sparsely-strewn imagery is now more vitally connected with the emotions she expresses. It may be argued that her method of printing her poems is a way of marking rhythm that is only superficially effective, but she does invest it with a personal quality; and not a few of these poems have a sunlit grace, a stainless clarity, unshackled by the chains of fact.

SURVEY OF WORLD POETRY

An Anthology of World Poetry. Edited by Mark Van Doren (Cassell)

There is a touch of the madness of genius in the conception of this volume. Its selections represent fifty centuries of human life, and are the expression of a score or so of civilizations. To have attempted to be exhaustive would, of course, have been to court ruin by filling many pages with faithful or unfaithful mediocrity. Mr. Van Doren's principle was much the better one to work on, which was 'to make an anthology of the world's best poetry in the best English I could unearth, and when I found no good English at all I left the poet out'. There is no Pindar, for example, no Malherbe, Leconte de Lisle or Hölderlin, but that is preferable to their being represented by dull versions, and, as it is, one can open this volume at almost every page in the certainty of finding good English verse. Indeed, brought together in one volume like this, the richness of English in good translations may well come as a surprise, and whilst there is naturally much that is familiar, like the Hebrew poets of our Authorized Version, or FitzGerald's Omar Khayyam, there is even more that will probably be quite new to a large body of readers of poetry, such as Mr. E. Powys Mather's exquisite rendering of the eleventh-century Sanskrit poem 'Black Marigolds', and Thomas Stanley's 'Vigil of Venus'.

Since it is part of a reviewer's business to cavil, 1 must point out what seem to me a few flaws in a volume whose general excellence must be heartily acknowledged. The English section unfortunately starts in the conventional way with 'Sumer is icumen in', followed by Chaucer, though here was surely the opportunity to popularize his Anglo-Saxon predecessors, e.g., 'The Seafarer' and the 'Complaint of Deor', which have both been done into modern English. Among the French poets Baudelaire is unfortunate in being translated into the piteously thin idiom of a fleeting fashion in English poetry, so that his classicism, his fullness in simplicity, is completely lost. Lord

Alfred Douglas, for instance, renders *Nous avons dit souvent d'impérissables choses* by 'We said things wonderful as chrysolites'.

. . . .

Leopardi has for some reason lacked good translators, though Mr. Van Doren might have included an excellent version by James Thomson of *Chorus of the Mummies*.

It is strange, since Li T'ai-po and Tu Fu are rivals for the position of the greatest Chinese lyrical poet, that only one poem by each should be given here. Mr. Arthur Waley has some excellent versions in this section, but we miss the work of Mr. Ezra Pound, whose 'Exile's Letter', for example, is a most spirited piece of translation.

Translators are an unpopular race with poets, since it is axiomatic that the better the poem the more inevitable the order of its words, its echoes of vowels and consonants, the closer it will be to the genius of its own language, and the further off will be any possibility of finding an equivalent in another language for all these complexities of sense and sound. But I imagine the translations least offensive to the creator of the poem are those which are, at any rate, good poems in the translator's own language. Something must be sacrificed, and since, if an exact rendering is ugly it falsifies the original irremediably, it is better that aesthetic considerations predominate, and the equivalence then may actually be closer. It is rarely in these pages that the alien poet will have to blush for the English version in which his poem is clothed.

The book is excellently printed and bound, the page is most agreeably designed, and the price is surprisingly low at ten and sixpence. The texts seem to have been reproduced with great care, but I did notice one misprint which makes nonsense of this famous epigram, *never* being given as *ever*:

> Venus, take my votive glass,
> Since I am not what I was:
> What from this day I shall be,
> Venus, let me never see.

ELIZABETHAN CONTRASTS

The Elizabethan Underworld. A Collection of Tudor and Early
Stuart Tracts and Ballads. Edited by A. V. Judges (Routledge)
The Elizabethan Home. Discovered in Two Dialogues, by Claudius
Hollyband and Peter Erondell. Edited by M. St. Clare Byrne
(Cobden-Sanderson)

The twentieth-century appetite for crook fiction is not keener than
that of our ancestors' was for the mingled fact and fiction of the
'rogue pamphlets'. True, these had a utilitarian as well as an entertainment value, in which they differ from their modern progeny,
but I should be inclined to suspect that before the coming of the
novel they catered largely for the sort of interest the popular novel
now satisfies. Whatever the value of their information to the unwary
contemporary (and Robert Greene boasts that after his revelations
of their tricks, the takings of the coney-catchers were so reduced that
his life was in danger from them) to the reader who is interested in
Elizabethan life either from the point of view of history or literature,
they are invaluable in providing a vivid background to the splendours
and miseries of that mighty age. The Elizabethan was florid in a
way which has since, it is taken for granted, been foreign to the
Englishman, and the villains and even the vagabonds of the time
flourished with a characteristic luxuriance, which is matched by the
vigorous writing of the many exposures their depredations gave rise
to.

   The first of the above volumes contains an excellent selection
from these entrancing documents. It falls into two main divisions:
the first describes the highly-organized society of ruffians who
exploited the highways and villages, the other the disreputable city
crooks, principally those of London and its outskirts. In the first
class Harman's 'A Caveat or Warning for Common Cursitors,
vulgarly called Vagabonds', holds pride of place as an almost
scientifically rigorous classification, drawn from long official experience, yet marked with shrewdness and a certain humanity, though
not humanitarianism; in the second class Robert Greene with his
series of 'coney-catching' pamphlets expounds many of the innumerable cheats by which the unwary Londoner or country bumpkin
might expect to be relieved of his money; a field which Nashe and
Dekker exploited with a greater wealth of fantasy. The profit the

dramatists drew from their knowledge of this side of life was, of course, immense.

. . . . . .

It is impossible to describe all the seventeen items which fill nearly five hundred pages of text, making a pretty complete encyclo-paedia of roguery. In fact, one author has to rebut a complaint that the spreading of the knowledge of these evil tricks will extend the practice of them, and if a modern reader feels tempted to embark on a life of crime he may have some difficulty deciding in which of the numerous 'laws', as the sub-divisions of villainy were called, to specialize. It may be doubted if any of them have quite died out, for the principles they are based on are sound psychology, greed for easy gain being most men's weak spot . . . whether be he a yokel who is persuaded to 'find the lady' or the hard-baked business man in a cosmopolitan hotel who is rooked of thousands by the plausible confidence-man. 'Curbing-law', though, cannot number many ad-herents today; in this 'law' the method of operation was to hook articles out of windows; like the rest of the 'laws' it had its own nomenclature or 'words of art', as Greene tells, 'he that hooks' being the *curber*, 'he that watches' the *warp*, and so on. And the pam-phleteers illustrate the working of each trick with many merry, and sometimes broad, anecdotes.

The writers generally set themselves up as physicians of the body politic. 'Detestable caterpillars that devour the commonwealth' is the sort of phrase that recurs in the admonitory portions of the pamphlets. It seems undoubted that the rogue class levied a much higher toll on the industrious part of the community than is possible now with an organized police system. Greene, who a few months later was to write his supreme 'remorse pamphlet', 'A Groat's Worth of Wit Bought with a Million of Repentance', sums up in simple but moving language one aspect of these petty crimes, for when there is no bank a man might quite possibly have his whole wealth in his purse. A mug has fallen in with some card-cheaters in a tavern, and naturally been cleaned out:

'Perhaps the man is very simple and patient, and, whatsoever he thinks, for fear goes his way quiet with his loss (while the coney-catchers laugh and divide the spoil), and being out of the doors, poor man, goes to his lodging with a heavy heart, pensive and sorrowful, but too late, for perhaps his state did depend on that money, and so he, his wife, his children, and his family are brought to extreme misery.'

The accent of painful personal experience is never long absent from these tracts of Greene's.

. . . . . .

With something like relief one turns to the wholesome atmosphere of domestic respectability which is exuded by the dialogues in Miss St. Clare Byrne's volume. It should certainly be read with the previous volume, for though much less bulky it will restore a sense of proportion that was in danger of being swamped by such an exhaustive acquaintance with roguery. In these dialogues, originally published as language-manuals for Elizabethans who desired to learn French, we are given a quite intimate and delightful introduction to the home-life of the time, first to that of a wealthy burgess, then to that of a great lady. This is the solid basis on which the national greatness was established. And in those days even the naturalized Frenchmen who composed these dialogues could catch that richness of phrase which gives even the journalism of the time a lasting value. The vignette of the lady visiting her baby is charmingly natural; and the enumeration of the dishes served at dinner is enough to make one think that if we have progressed in many things the modern kitchen is a weak and unimaginative descendant of the Elizabethan.

LADIES FAIR AND FRAIL

Harriette Wilson's Memoirs (Peter Davies)
Moll Flanders and *Roxana*. By Daniel Defoe (Peter Davies)

The three ladies whose lives are recorded here must be allowed, in the narrow space of a review, sanctuary from the vindictive hand of the moralist. If they succeeded in obtaining a measure of enjoyment which, no doubt, a stricter conduct would have denied them, it was not without an expenditure of courage and resource, and that in an arena where, having forfeited the protection of society when they disdained its approbation, a single failure meant destruction. Roxana has some very shrewd things to say on the relative advantages of the positions of wife and mistress. Her words are the expression of Defoe's strong common sense, reaching forward to the more equitable vision of sexual justice which society has since done something, though not enough, towards realizing.

The verisimilitude of Defoe's creations is a matter of common appreciation. Harriette Wilson, though far too happy-go-lucky to worry if her narrative has continuity or not, succeeds in convincing one of the reality of her existence. It is immaterial if Moll or Roxana had prototypes in actual life or not, but without the claim of historic fact a good many of Miss Wilson's six-hundred pages would have been better out of the way. What was left would better have shown up the skill with which she portrays the curious little group of which she was a most attractive member and the whole glittering surface of 'high life' during the Regency. That period has not been deficient in chroniclers of its scandals and its pastimes, of which Pierce Egan's *Tom and Jerry* is one of the best, but Miss Wilson shows us her own side of it more completely than anyone else. It was a time when fashionable courtesans, 'elegant Cyprians' was the contemporary slang-phrase, had their box at the opera, with titled ladies for neighbours, and no one attempted to pretend that they were any better than they were. As Mr. Laver points out in his Preface, these women created a definite division in Society. Some men preferred their company to that of the women of their own class, and were always welcomed at their parties. 'Others, who tried to compromise (Palmerston looked in one evening, coming from Lady Castlereagh's) were received more coldly.' A strange reversal of conventional notions.

There is a great deal of detail in this book which will be valuable to those who are interested in the history of manners and in period-colour. Many well-known personalities, members of the aristocracy, are also present in the rôle of lovers or acquaintances. The great Duke of Wellington seems to have been a very wooden lover, and is ridiculed rather cleverly, though he seems not to have been without some delicacy of feeling. When on leave from the Peninsula the first woman he went to see was Harriette. He said: 'I have thought of you very often, in Spain, particularly one night, I remember, *I dreamed you came out on my staff.*' Miss Wilson's stories are generally of the kind that cannot be proved or disproved, but if that last touch is an invention, it is one which a very good novelist might be thankful for.

The two Defoe novels are not easy to come by, *Roxana*, at least, is not, and we are grateful for this reprint. *Roxana* does not quite stand up to its companion, but it has a more romantic colouring. Moll is one of the solidest figures in literature.

RONALD FIRBANK

The Flower Beneath the Foot; *Concerning the Eccentricities of Cardinal Pirelli*; *Prancing Nigger*; *Caprice*; *Inclinations*; *Valmouth*. By Ronald Firbank (Duckworth)

If the autobiography of a contemporary aesthete were to be published, say a modernization of *A Rebours* or its off-spring *Dorian Gray*, no doubt the novels of Ronald Firbank would rank among the books he most appreciated. But if, some years back, Firbank was rather the cult of the few, a pet of the ultra-fashionable, there is no reason why some of his books at any rate should not gain a more enviable reputation. For Firbank, though not a 'serious novelist', was that much rarer thing, a serious writer. He died at an age when writers are still entitled to be called young, and in his later novels there are all the signs of a progression towards a mastery of his peculiar technique of story-telling.

It is this technique which might alienate a reader pulling a Firbank novel from the shelf for a casual glance. Everything that one expects in a novel seems to have been left out, except the conversation, and half of that probably seems missing, too. But on closer examination the loss turns out to be a positive gain. Not that one is merely saved the innumerable paragraphs of the ordinary novel in which the characters are lengthily described in circumstances that we know only too well ourselves, but this elimination of the superfluous permits of the story being developed in an almost poetic way.

Firbank's world is the same as that of most of the great writers of comedy, the cosmopolitan set, the 'cream' of society, but fantastically distorted, often with delicious malice. He was a satirist, though with no axe to grind, and his aristocrats are not ludicrous because they are aristocrats but because they are vapid. He has, too, a very pretty sense for verbal wit, and though that has been common from Wilde to our contemporary dramatists and is not his most distinctive gift, it is generally well worth the laugh it raises.

If Firbank has something in common with the aestheticism of the nineties, and with the 'naughtiness' of that period, that should not prevent the recognition of his unique sensibility. The sentimentalist may talk of his cynicism, but beneath the careful indifference of his style there is a hint of deeper feeling, of which *The Flower Beneath the Foot* is perhaps the aptest symbol. A closer analysis than is possible here would be necessary to define his merits and his short-comings. One can only hope that the present uniform edition, which is as tempting in outward appearance as ingenious designing can make it, will result in a wider admiration for Firbank's really genuine artistry.

MODERNS LOOK AT MODERNS

Dorothy M. Richardson. By John Cowper Powys (Joiner and Steele)
Richard Aldington: An Englishman. By Thomas McGreevy (Chatto and Windus)

Each of these very opportune essays on the work of two living writers refers to the 'Englishness' of their writings. This is not done from any rabidly nationalist prejudice but to define an inherent freedom and variety we find in them, contrasted with writers of races like the Latins, who are more sensitive to external form or style.

Mr. Powys finds Dorothy Richardson specifically English in her 'steady, persistent, undeviating preference for the *sensation of life* at all costs over the sentiment, or the passion, of *the appropriate gesture*'. And this is paralleled by Mr. McGreevy when he says that the English 'achieve verbal felicity on the way to something else' when he shows how the verbal perfection of Aldington's Imagiste ideal has been expanded by him into something less finished in detail but more vital.

· · · · · · ·

'Englishness', of course, is not enough. Many writers among our fellow-countrymen certainly fail to achieve verbal felicity, and still do not get far on their way to the 'something else'. And some French writers . . . but what Mr. Powys says is appropriate here: 'I think it will be along the lines of the presence in the feminine sensibility of something almost Rabelaisian in its unfastidiousness, certainly of something Montaignesque, that posterity will come to find so much grist for its cosmic mill in the work of Dorothy Richardson. Al-though all great writers have had something of the consciousness of both sexes in them, Dorothy Richardson is the first woman to have accepted femininity as the raw material of her art: to have used the peculiar acceptance of the bitter-sweet of all experience without irony (as with the intellectual male) and without rebellion (as with the feminist, who is really a woman who is angry because she is not a man).'

It would be confusing values to expect, or even to wish, Miss Richardson's work to have the enormous numbers of readers that the sensational novelist has; but it must be admitted that by a series of accidents this work is still far from well-enough known to the quite numerous body of genuine readers to whom it would appeal as the revelation of a rich and hardly explored world; and to whom it would bring an invaluable extension of their consciousness of life. To those who hesitate to embark on this exploration unaided, Mr. Powys's essay will bring, if not a detailed chart, at least a compass-bearing or two and a handful of fruit and flower, testifying to this new province's fertility.

· · · · · · ·

There is, fortunately, no need to introduce the author of 'Death of a Hero' and 'The Colonel's Daughter' to readers of the *Sunday Referee*. Mr. Richard Aldington's work as poet, critic, and translator, or re-creator of masterpieces for English readers, is perhaps less well known, and in Mr. McGreevy's essay this part of his activity is excellently described. As an account of Mr. Aldington's emotional and literary development, this short book could hardly, it seems to an outsider, be bettered.

It would, perhaps have made more pleasant reading if the author had resisted the temptation to diverge so often into the exposition that he considers necessary, of his own points of view on questions of nationalism and religion. And if he must think that English poetry has only one example of 'religious exaltation' fit to compare with those in French, at least he ought to have quoted our unique specimen correctly and not ruined its rhythm. These grumbles apart, I think no exception can be taken to his appreciation of Aldington's genius.

Everyman Remembers. By Ernest Rhys (Dent)
Fashion in Literature: A Study of Changing Taste. By R. E. Kellett
(Routledge)

I opened the first of these two books, Mr. Ernest Rhys's reminiscences, in the hope that it might indirectly throw light on the subject of the second. For Mr. Rhys has had his place in the heart of the literary furnace for about fifty years.

What a change in taste occurred during that period we may imagine if we remember that at the beginning of it a poem greatly admired by a large but discriminating public was 'The Earthly Paradise' and at the end of it 'The Waste Land'; whilst Tennyson's 'Ulysses', 'made weak by time and fate, but strong in will', has been re-born, some say, in the plebeian figure of Mr. Joyce's Leopold Bloom. And if Mr. Rhys was present at one of Browning's last appearances in public (it was at a performance of Shelley's *Cenci*), he was also the host at what was perhaps the first public appearance of D. H. Lawrence, who was being exhibited by his discoverer, Mr. Ford Madox Ford. Yet even that incident has already a faintly historical air, so wide is the gulf due to the mere fact of death.

Though a great bookman, Mr. Rhys was never merely a bookman, and, thanks to his range of interests, we meet many of the figures who are responsible for much of that revolutionary change in the arts, in manners, and in our attitude to life for which the present generation sometimes rather complacently takes the credit. Most of the spade work that went to the undermining of what has been well labelled 'the Victorian compromise' was done by men and women whom Mr. Rhys knew in the eighties and nineties.

. . . .

I doubt if there has been in this last decade, when unconventionality has been all the cry, any such courageous affronting of convention as was for many of these people, famous and obscure, the daily inspiration of their lives. I refer, of course, to the causes which these earlier comers were fortunate enough to possess as vehicles for their emotional energy, among which female emancipation, Socialism, Ireland, and the aesthetic life were most prominent, though there were numerous others. Broad, noble, disinterested motives seem to have actuated everybody then; and even the talk about free love, which so perturbed the respectable, was much more often a rather grim testifying to one's faith in the libertarian creed than any actual pursuit of pleasure.

Walt Whitman, Havelock Ellis, A.E., Olive Schreiner, Tagore, Kropotkin, Shaw, and William Morris – that is a random and queerly-assorted selection from among the personalities Mr. Rhys has known, and all of whom, in greater or less degree, have had a share in determining the mental climate of our time. Writers move in even greater variety across Mr. Rhys's pages; it is illuminating to see some of our present great men in embryo and sad to reflect on talents that never came to flower.

It is, of course, as an editor that Mr. Rhys has been able to do most service to literature, and I do not know that anyone can even approximately compute the accumulated debt that the reading classes owe to the organizer of 'Everyman's Library' and to that practical visionary the late J. M. Dent, its originator and publisher.

. . . .

The popularity of 'Everyman's' might have provided Mr. Kellett with some reflections for his concluding chapter, 'Catholicity of Taste', in *Fashion in Literature*. How much of the narrowness of taste of previous ages has been due to the comparative inaccessibility of earlier works? Not all, of course, but under present conditions we should expect epidemics of taste to be less devastating since there is such a variety of alternatives available. Violent reaction from simplicity to hyperbole, from allegory to realism, is less likely when it is seen that each satisfies a particular need at a particular time. But absolute catholicity of taste is an academic ideal rather than a practically desirable attainment.

Mr. Kellett is perhaps not sufficiently curious as to what the act of aesthetic apprehension ultimately implies. By that he misses the occasional unexpected naïvetés of a 'scientific' critic like Mr. I. A. Richards, but he also forgoes all his stimulation and has often to fall back on a hard-run hack like 'intuition'.

I find Mr. Kellett's method a bit dull and tending to repetition; and the most extensive scholarship, of which he once again gives evidence, does not compensate for the virtual surrender of an argument to the mere enumeration of instances. Nor are his meanings always free of the inflated currency of the lecture-room and the literary weekly.

Speaking of the taste for the Precious, he says, 'Two other poets, Donne and Crashaw, show how possible it is to combine absolute sincerity and real depth with a quality that in others would be a sure sign of the absence of truth.' The notion of sincerity in poetry is a complicated one, and as to whether the 'depth' be real or assumed we can judge that only and entirely by the success of the poem.

If his poem pleases us, if it seems to us beautiful, we assume that he really felt these emotions. It is a convenient fiction, it can never be proved either way and does no one much harm. It follows that every poem that does not please us marks the wretched author as a liar and a charlatan; and one may well be delighted to have support for one's belief that all bad poets are morally reprehensible.

Scrutinies I

The first volume of *Scrutinies by Various Writers* was published by Wishart & Co. in 1928. Edgell Rickword, who was responsible for collecting these often biting studies of established contemporary writers, provided a Foreword. Rickword's 'scrutiny' of Sir James Barrie had appeared in the first issue of *The Calendar of Modern Letters* in March, 1925. Subsequent issues of the *Calendar* included Douglas Garman's study of Walter de la Mare; Bertram Higgins on John Masefield; Edwin Muir on Arnold Bennett; C. H. Rickword on Bernard Shaw; Higgins on 'Ancients and Moderns', and John Holms on H. G. Wells. The 1928 collection also contained Dorothy Edwards's essay on G. K. Chesterton; D. H. Lawrence on John Galsworthy; Robert Graves on Rudyard Kipling; T. McGreevy on George Moore, and Roy Campbell on 'Contemporary Poetry'. W. J. Turner supplied a new study of Bernard Shaw.

FOREWORD

This volume is perhaps ten years overdue, for it would be an exaggeration to deny that, by this time, many of the revaluations it suggests are shared by most intelligent people.

There is a sluggishness in the communication of ideas in this country and a lack of curiosity about them which make a response to the intellectual situation slower than it is anywhere else. Such a disturbance as the War, and the consequent economic troubles, undoubtedly helped to aggravate this tendency, increasing the prestige of reputations established before the catastrophe; and the repugnance to modify an attitude once adopted helped – directly, because half a generation of potential rivals and critics was eliminated bodily; and indirectly, since a threatened organism must curtail its expenditure of energy on everything not concerned with immediate ends. So for a number of years the distinguished reputations here discussed have stood like an avenue of cyclopean statues leading to a ruined temple, but, except for a few short-lived protests, the information that it is necessary to travel in some other direction for enlightenment has been carefully withheld. By concentrating a disillusionment which has been in the air so long, it may be possible to realize where contemporary literature stands. That would be an advantage even if it were a realization that no new direction has yet been found.

An account is given somewhere of a Christian martyrdom during which the saint serenely watches his entrails being drawn out and coiled on a windlass. This is symbolic of what is happening today under the general assault on humanistic values. It is perhaps a salutary, perhaps a fatal ordeal, but the peculiar thing is that our martyred society should be so short-sighted as to indulge in light refreshments during the operation; such complaisance is the reverse of seraphic.

It is probable that some reviewers, if they do not read our Foreword will describe this volume as 'the merely inevitable reaction'. But a reaction is never inevitable; it is only necessitated by the incompetence of a previous period of criticism. Nor does it seem correct, though it is often suggested, that criticism of contemporary work can never be so 'pure' as that of a thoroughly dead subject. But it is a critic's business to evaluate his own temporal bias just as he would an historical qualification; and if it had not been so frequently assumed that a critic who cannot deal intelligently with a contemporary becomes, by some queer metamorphosis, intelligent when discussing a classic, literary history would not have become the dust-bin it is.

There is, of course, no sacred line at which criticism becomes inoperative, and it is proposed to compile a second, and if necessary a third, volume in which later developments may be considered with similar freedom. In the absence of much periodical literature of any account, it may be expected that there is a place for such miscellanies.

To prevent hasty deductions, it must be stated that there are no special, or group, relationships between the contributors to this volume, and that no one, by the mere fact of contributing, is committed to any opinions beyond those expressed in his own essay.

SIR JAMES BARRIE, O.M.

The discussion should begin in Thrums, a mountain village north of the Tweed. The idylls and romances Barrie has written around it, would provide the ethnologist with a useful compilation of the habits, customs, and superstitions of a tribe living at a very early stage of culture; and though those works are not the most characteristic Barrie has produced, yet the fact that the later plays must have the same roots gives them an interest which as literature they do not possess. The story of the *Little Minister* is told through the Dominie, a character who has in germ that trick of oblique observation that Barrie afterwards turned to account; whose secular piety also is a frequent constituent of the later atmosphere. The little minister's relation to the Thrums tribe is very much like Barrie's later position in metropolitan society. To the tribesmen of Thrums their little minister is just what the medicine-man or witch-doctor is to primitive peoples, the intermediary between them and the Big Man who makes the crops grow; he brings down the rain. So Barrie brought refreshing showers to the emotion-starved tracts of the big cities, and still, in the cheaper parts of the house at any rate, and perhaps in the stalls too, the detached observer has to protect himself against an intermittent drizzle from overflowing hearts.

The efficaciousness of the minister's petitions, though, is dependent on the possession of certain virtues, and he must keep the traditional taboos with a strictness not essential in the conduct of the lay tribesman. So the peculiar indirect sexuality of the plays, so acceptable to our metropolitan primitives, is perhaps the reflection of an attitude enforced by an earlier repression at the dictation of a less-involved social order. For, though with the city-dweller chastity has degenerated to a question of hygiene, in a village it is still a condition that it would be fatal for a minister to infringe. When Gavin becomes polluted through his attachment to Babbie, he is in danger of being dismissed in favour of a more scrupulous or more cautious minister of the Unseen; he is in danger even of mutilation: 'The very women is cursing him, and the laddies has begun to gather stones.'

The parallel to the primitive tribe is perfect even to the fact that the personal property of the minister is a fetish invested with the virtues that belong to his vocation, a vehicle of power, and so, if improperly handled, of disaster: 'This was not the only time Jean had been asked to show the minister's belongings. Snecky Hobart, among others, had tried on Gavin's hat in the manse kitchen, and felt queer for some time afterwards. Women had been introduced on tiptoe to examine the handle of his umbrella.'

The Dominie, it may be admitted, was more intelligent than most members of that community; at least he was able to observe and describe them with a certain astuteness which is, though always within a distorted image of reality, the only positive merit of the plays written by his successor, Barrie. So, when Barrie came to describe a more sophisticated society, he sometimes introduced a little trenchant maxim, almost a cynicism; a tiny mischievous wriggle not meant to be taken seriously by the Big Man of Thrums, who of course has an eye on a stalk like a snail's for wandering tribesmen. Though his plays are empty of real piety or cheerful faith, one is generally aware of a pendulous Benevolence, from which the characters suck a comforting resignation, for Barrie has the knack of always dodging the irremediable by a flight into fantasy.

The lack of emancipation from local theological concepts reacted on his attitude to sex. Though he outgrew the extreme irrealism of that idolatry of women which the maudlin Dominie expressed: 'All that is carnal in me is my own, and all that is good I got from her' – the sweet and capable creature who appears so monotonously in the plays was turned out of the same incredible mould. Barrie's observation was keen enough to have followed more deeply, had he wished, the ramifications of the desire *d'être un peu l'Homme avec la Femme*, and he has expressed, with an accuracy which does not render the absence of disapprobation less distasteful, the furtive sex-interest of the unemancipated male: 'They were two bachelors who all their lives had been afraid of nothing but Woman. David in his sportive days – which continue – has done roguish things with his arm when taking a lady home under an umbrella from a *soirée*, and has both chuckled and been scared on thinking of it afterwards.'

Love is for Barrie a kind of Benger's Food for infants, invalids, and the aged. His lovers always have the tendency to fall into the relationship of mother and child, or into more involved exchanges of rôle, such as those on which the theme of *Mary Rose* seems to be hinged:

'The loveliest time of all will be when he is a man and takes me on his knee instead of my putting him on mine. Oh gorgeous!' And the reflection of this in the queer entrance of the rollicking sea-dog, who had a face 'that could be stern to harshness,' with his elderly mother-in-law kicking in his arms . . . and the soldier who spent all his leave with a decrepit charwoman. 'The nearer the grave the sweeter the meat' seems to be the working rule with the Barrie male.

The skill with which Barrie handles the half-human material he selects for use on the stage, to some extent dazzles the spectator into accepting a sleight of hand. It is only on drawing closer that a cotton thread becomes visible, running from the puppets' breeches to the showman's waistcoat; for it is Barrie's heart that pumps into them what vitality they possess. He loves them, and wants them to be loved so very much. The way in which, in the printed text, he insinuates his figures on to the stage shows an evident anxiety to win sympathy for them at the start. Shaw's practice in this is exactly the opposite, for by his diagrammatic preliminary directions and the aggressive shove with which he pitches his people into their opening lines, he would seem to repel any sentimental inclination of the audience.

The real dramatist's attitude to his creations may be paternal, he may watch them with curiosity and passion, but he may not intervene in the destiny which his impulse has set in motion. His fertility is everything, the objects of his fertility nothing, to him. Barrie, on the other hand, shows a maternal solicitude in protecting his characters not only from consequence but even from the possible criticism of the audience. He darts here and there, like the Shopman in *Boutique Fantasque*, petting his little people, and displaying their good points to the best advantage. In *Alice-Sit-by-the-Fire*, Alice's maternal instinct requires freshening up (for he has rather emphasized her gay, flirtatious nature), so when she finds her daughter in a cupboard in a man's chambers he puts in parenthesis, 'It has been the great shock of Alice's life.' Maggie, in *What Every Woman Knows*, a prominent politician's wife, must be rehabilitated as a cliché of Scottish industry and domestic virtue, so she 'resumes her knitting'. In what has been hailed as a 'triumph of dramatic *volte-face*', the ballroom scene in *Quality Street*, the author's peculiar prejudice in favour of spinsterdom forces a ten-year-old sentiment into supremacy over the natural attraction of physical youth and vitality; another example of the incipient necrophily which hangs about most of Barrie's characters.

There is an essential dramatic deficiency in this failure of Barrie's to separate his figures from his own emotional attitude towards them, a failure to complete the objectification of feeling which is the condition of art. It has prevented him from presenting a comedy in which there is any real conflict of character, as his hope that the powers may be placated by a little nonsense and a lot of slop inhibited any true realization of the tragic theme involved in *Mary Rose*. Since his characters are all so closely attached to himself, they must all swim in the sweet oily liquor of universal pathos which is his philosophy of life. It results from this attempt to construct a drama without conflict, that to go to see a Barrie play is like going to see a sheep in a cage at the Zoo; the bars, the 'drama', are merely a device to encourage mutual self-esteem.

A dramatist may deny a fact of circumstance at his own risk, he can only contradict a spiritual fact at the cost of his own existence. The law which Barrie has violated is that of the conservation of spiritual energy. Whatever access of passionate life we receive is at the expense of some other individual; if we give it out again it can only be in a lower form. 'Nothing is born except from another's death', is as true of emotions as of things. At the end of a genuinely successful play, somewhere the level of emotion has been raised, somewhere else correspondingly depressed. But Barrie has the peculiar trick, which commended him to his contemporaries, of so confusing the emotional perspective that no values emerge to stimulate the sensibility; like a race in which everyone who runs is involved in general congratulation, and the loser, even, robbed of his distinction. Such tolerance is the shabbiest form of injustice. Loss or deprivation must be valuable when acutely felt, but pernicious when really welcomed as an escape from the consummation of passion; and at the root of Barrie's elaborate system of avoidances may be found the edict of Thrums against the satisfaction of impulse. No one could be less of a Calvinist than Barrie, for he is what is left of a man when Calvinism has done its worst. Frighten a man out of doing wrong, of offending God and his neighbour, and there is the most amenable piece of sentimentality that any pusillanimous populace could desire for its representative playwright.

We are not complaining that there are no villains in Barrie's plays; villains are almost as much discredited as heroes by the contemporary moral inertia, and we will only point out a couple of amusing instances of attempts to supply one. There is Lord Rintoul, a naughty English lord from a *feuilleton*, a foil to a God-fearing monogamous Scot; and there is Lady Sybil, also English, who is so like a vampire of the cinema, and can be thrown aside as soon as she has played the part of temptress long enough to 'bring together' John and Maggie Shand; but these are only literary machines. The nearest thing to a villain Barrie has ever dared to imagine is Captain Hook, and because his existence is admitted, even though merely a fantastic shadow derived from Stevenson's romantic shadow, *Peter Pan* has a sort of vitality that the plays of experience lack. In the language of psychoanalysis, Peter Pan is a symbol of the libido wandering in the infantile world from which it has always been denied an outlet into actuality. For it would be absurd to accept Peter as a valid symbol of joy. He is a dwarfed and clammy imago, the *alter ego* of an adult who has grown up in spite of himself, physically, whilst his mind messes about among shadows. Children may get something out of the play, for they get something out of almost anything, but it is to be hoped that it is not the same thing as their elders get, which is a middle-aged person's idea of their own childish innocence. And that would not be a very good idea on which to bring up a child. It is curious, too, that Peter should have been mistaken for boyish; a boy is actually in a ferment to grow up, to shed his dependencies and ignorances. Mr. Desmond MacCarthy has very clearly pointed out the blind spot in Barrie's attitude to young people:

'Judging him as an artist, he strikes me in general as beautifully unshockable, most wisely indulgent; but there is one thing I think would shock him artistically – a youth who did not take an enthusiastic, trusting attitude towards the world, who was discontented, though not personally persecuted, sceptical, self-withdrawn, world-questioning, disillusioned. I cannot approve Sir James Barrie as a lover of youth, because I have never yet seen in his work that sympathy with pimpled and sullen spiritual gawkishness which, it seems to me, youth's true lover must also possess.'

It is strange that a critic so discriminating as Mr. MacCarthy should not have followed his thought further and seen that it leads to a general indictment of Barrie, his failure to sympathize with any but a few of the most devitalized forms of life.

It is not often, of course, that Barrie's real indifference to human emotions is allowed to peep through the frills. There are even some people to whom his treatment of that case of infantilism, Mary Rose, may seem pathetic and not cruel. But the most brilliant example of the way in which his manner makes fun of pain may be seen in this specially prepared sub-title from the film version of *Peter Pan*:

'When was I born, mummy?'

'At midnight, dear.'

'I hope I didn't wake you, mummy.'

There is a special doom on the apostles of loveableness, by which, when straining after a piece of extra-extra-loveableness, they land themselves in the dirt they had taken such pains to ignore.

The mental conditions which find expression in the plays are also reflected, of course, in the prose in which they are set out. However apparently impossible, Barrie will always avoid an object and replace it with a little bit of his lovable personality. Faced with a char-woman's bonnet, which it would be difficult to make effectively of the Barrie atmosphere by a description in terms of fusty gimp and jet, he slips off at a familiar emotional tangent: 'Such a kind old bonnet that it makes you laugh at once; I don't know how to describe it, but it is trimmed with a kiss, as bonnets should be when the wearer is old and frail.'

Even the stage furniture oozes sentiment. It is doubtful if a single palpable object could be reconstructed from the words in Barrie's plays.

It has still to be inquired how or why a writer of this kind became the recipient of public honours, affection, and the laudations of the literary experts, who, though they were no better, were probably no worse than those who now sing in a much lower key. The answer is connected with the fact that a degenerate society always searches for stimulus and self-expression outside its own experience. Even now one finds elderly critics advising young writers to hunt for material in a life of action, and remaining tensely responsive at home to whatever productions may reach them from the ends of the earth, where the tedious exploitation of our half-settled dependencies is supposed somehow to provide magically efficacious material for creation. That is only one form of the exotic fallacy which has dominated criticism for so long. Barrie owes his reputation to another form of it. It was the response of debauchees to the promise of pure affection. Barrie's incursion into Edwardian London though modest, was in result not so dissimilar from the entry of Heliogabalus and the priests of Cybele into imperial Rome; for the instruments of that modern emasculation were no less drastic in their effects though they were insidious in the operation. Our metropolitan critics, glutted with high living, fell avidly on his simple bunch of seemingly uncultivated sentiment, but unlike *The Golden Ass* of Lucius were by their feast only confirmed in their assininity. But the Barrie salad, which was then all dewy fresh with that essential quality that the critic of a great paper described as 'the infinitely variable cleverness with which he reveals his lovableness', is now more than a little wilted. The apotheosis of Barrie was a social phenomenon, hardly a matter for literary criticism at all, and as a society's criticism of itself hardly to be bettered. When such glamour is at work, the spectator is impervious to any demonstration of the falsity of the creation. The moonlight seems real, and the trees and flowers real, there is a lovely fay dancing for us in the glade. But it is in the nature of this sort of glamour to change its tactics constantly, a Tom Moore for one age, an Arlen for ours, so that its confections follow fast on one another's heels, leaving behind in heaps of debris, on bookstalls and in obscure picture galleries, the rubbish through which it manifested itself.

The process is comparable to the curve of a passion which has a merely subjective origin, unsubstantiated by any real qualities in the object, like that which Hazlitt describes in *Liber Amoris*. When he had at last been shocked out of his obsession, the girl he had been in love with, whose 'exquisite, unstudied, irresistible graces' were ineffable 'unless you can imagine a Greek statue to smile, move, and speak', appears a very different thing in the open air: 'I am afraid she will soon grow common to my imagination as well as worthless in herself.'

This is the fate of all 'lovable' work when no longer surrounded by the halo of its contemporary atmosphere; only the structures in which reason and the senses coalesce can stand the test of age.

Scrutinies II

Scrutinies II was published by Wishart & Co. in 1931. As Rickword pointed out in his Foreword, the second collection did not deal with the Establishment figures of the Edwardian era. Such writers, by 1931, had lost their authority and much of their influence. *Scrutinies II* provided an opportunity to look at the achievements of some younger writers, most of whom were not yet so established as to need 'revaluation'. Rickword contributed a study of Wyndham Lewis, and there were a dozen other articles, including one on the visual arts, and one on 'Contemporary Music' by Constant Lambert:

CONTENTS

FOREWORD

This set of Scrutinies differs from the first in at least one rather noticeable way – the writers criticized are not national figures in the sense that Wells, Shaw, Kipling, and the others were, each expressing the 'conscience' of some numerically important group. And as these reputations are not sacrosanct, as they have not been hallowed by long years of habitual praise, this volume will perhaps be found to be less astringent, to have less about it of that 'chill as of some haunt of Dissenters' which a perspicacious critic observed in the first. As these writers have not been rigged into an orthodoxy, as opinion has not hardened into dogma, Dissent is not present in quite that crude ungraciousness for which it has always been ridiculed by the comfortable incumbents of the literary Establishment.

So the necessity for a revaluation hardly enters into the intention of this volume as it did into the intention of the other. This is an attempt to see the subjects in rather longer perspective than it is possible for a reviewer, poor galley-slave, to do: and nothing in the nature of a *putsch* is intended, no attempt to impose a judgement, though that apparently is the way any attempt at free discussion of literary values is visualized, so inconceivable is it to some minds that there may be a disinterested pleasure to be gained from that kind of activity. It would be ridiculous to dogmatize, since literary judgement is the most complicated thing in the world, involving as it does all the other judgements from the aesthetic to the moral; but the most useful criticism is bound to be biased, because the critic's personal reactions are the only sound basis he has to work on. That is why there should be an immense amount of discussion of these matters, not in order to arrive at the truth, which it would be difficult to define in this relation, but to combat that natural tendency to acquiesce in a quasi-truth, to acquiesce in anything rather than continue in this uncomfortable condition of mental activity. So it is much easier to say, 'These people want to force me to think the opposite of what I think at present', and so to react with some variety of indignation. That was what happened with two journals over the previous volume. The *Spectator* burst into an angry screech and the Literary Supplement to *The Times* administered a dignified rebuke of our low 'standard of literary courtesy'. To a paralytic, I suppose, any man who walks with ordinary freedom must seem to be executing a violent and gratuitously offensive gesture.

This list might have been composed of more popular writers,

but with one or two exceptions there are no writers now who combine a really large following with intellectual eminence in the way the Edwardians did. To express it very roughly, I should say that the talented writer of today inclines to a more intensive study of the individual, whereas much of the literature of the Edwardians consisted in an extensive study of the reactions of not very strongly individualized units to changing social forms. Social re-organization in a multitude of forms was a passion common to most of the reading class before the War, and dictated their preferences in literature. Naturally, with the evaporation of that common emotion and in the absence of anything equally widely distributed to take its place, taste disintegrates, and the only common point of interest must be the individual. At the same time more energy is released for the consideration of technical problems, and a good deal of the work considered in this volume is, as a consequence, experimental.

Two years ago I said that in the absence of much periodical literature of any account it might be expected that there would be a place for occasional volumes such as these. Nothing has happened since to require that statement to be modified. In fact, after the publication of Mr. I. A. Richards's *Practical Criticism* it seems to be more than ever essential that the circulation of ideas should be speeded up, for I can but think that the present stagnation and poverty of means of discussion is partly responsible for the deplorably perverse or meaningless reactions exhibited by the reputedly intelligent readers on whom Mr. Richards worked his experiment.

WYNDHAM LEWIS

For a general description of the subject I cannot do better than quote the cover of number three of *The Enemy*: 'The "Enemy" is the notorious author, painter, and publicist, Mr. Wyndham Lewis. He is the Diogenes of the day: he sits laughing in the mouth of his tub, and pours forth his invective upon all passers-by, irrespective of race, creed, rank or profession, and sex.' The indiscriminate cynicism claimed there has not yet been realized, and in fact Lewis himself has from time to time exposed more altruistic motives. It was perhaps the discovery of the vast extent of the conspiracy to pretend that the Universe *moves* that accounted for his change of temper.

The Caliph's Design contains the germ of much that will be found developed in the more extensive writings of Lewis. That early pamphlet is an admirable example of his mental adventurousness, his energy of style, his fecundity in sardonic abuse. It outlines a workable attitude for the artist in relation to the Machine Age, free from the frenzies of the Futurists as well as from the nostalgias of the mediaevalists, the cult of the savage and other exoticisms. Also, the fable from which it takes its title reflects the problem which is at the root of most of his critical and controversial writings. There, it will be remembered, it was the Caliph himself who designed the new street that transformed his capital; it was his power that compelled his architects to realize his design; and it is, of course, the mating of vision, capacity, and executive power that is the ideal end of any political theory. The Caliph's street was a good one, we are told; if it had been a bad one it would have had to go up, none the less. Hence the necessity of finding a Caliph, a source of power, which shall also be a touchstone of aesthetic and intellectual quality. That is the problem round which his thought revolves in a spiral, with ever-increasing radius as fresh ramifications present themselves.

A period of very hard reading, the evidence of which is apparent in all Lewis's subsequent books, must have followed the writing of *The Caliph's Design*. But each acquisition of knowledge revealed further complications in the problem, whole forests of windmills were observed to be massing for an attack on the unarmed and unsuspecting intellect. So much print, perhaps, dazzled the free intelligence of the earlier work; objects of attack acquired the obsessive characteristic of phobias, and instead of greater definition and concentration resulted only in an extended front.

Besides the pleasure of its comic sarcasms and vituperative energy, *The Art of Being Ruled* has done great service in clearing away many moribund ideas. At the time, I thought this work might become the *Culture and Anarchy* of our generation, trusting that its rather thick and muddled prophetics would be clarified in subsequent pronouncements. This has not yet occurred, and the trend of Lewis's later writings does not encourage me to think that it ever will. He has not that central sureness that Arnold had which enabled him to give the inadequate formula 'sweetness and light', a conception beyond the merely genteel refinement to which in lesser hands it has so comfortably relapsed. But at the moment of positive statement Lewis always breaks down, largely because of his own uncertainty as to what the intelligence, and still more the human being, really is

– at one moment buttering it up with fine phrases, at another belittling it with mechanistic metaphors, as it happens to be Plato or some 'small man'. The fact that they are both men seems repugnant to him. The intelligence is something he would separate from the man (and art, on one occasion, is a 'tapping of the supernatural'). But as metaphor is always nearer the real thought than abstract phrase, we may conclude that the concept of mechanism is very close to Lewis's vision of the human being, and this results in the shallow treatment of the central problem of *The Art of Being Ruled*, the relation of the creator of values to the comparatively inert political mass. He says, 'This greatest and most valuable of all "producers" should be accommodated with conditions suitable to his maximum productivity', as if the artist, the intellectual, was a milch-cow turning out nourishment for the benefit of humanity. Intellectual and aesthetic activity is perfectly selfishly motivated, and society will quite justifiably, refuse to pay anything unless it gets some benefit from the result. Is Bergson, now to Lewis, the 'arch-villain', to be 'accommodated with conditions suitable to his maximum productivity', and, so subsidized, poison all the wells of truth? Besides, those conditions are themselves indefinable. Lewis often writes as if one could snatch an 'intellectual' out of the welter of experience and put him down in a laboratory or studio, where he would go on functioning even faster. But even in the case of a scientist, we do not know that some maladjustment of his social life may not be of more stimulus to him than external calm. And artists have been notoriously successful under conditions that must seem outrageous to the reforming zeal of a social hygienist. Short of giving the 'intellectual' a blank cheque every Friday night, I do not see how he can be accommodated. For, apart from his gifts, he has character as an individual, which means achieving an inner order out of the external disorder. By all means let us have a dole for 'intellects' and not a sanatorium. But apart from constituting Lewis omnipotent umpire, I see no means of refusing Bergson or Anita Loos places on the register. A body of experts might be able to relieve obviously necessitous cases, but the judgement of values is such a subtle matter that any repressive tendency, apart from the right of individual criticism, must be deprecated.

It has been a commonplace for a long time to say of Lewis that he is teeming with ideas, that 'he can start more hares in a paragraph than another man in a volume.' But this facility in starting 'ideas' is only half a virtue; if they are not run down they are mere exhalations of an active fantasy working on a rich mass of miscellaneous information. But to have a lot of ideas is no more to be a good thinker than to have a lot of soldiers is to be a good general. Full of suggestive side-views as his treatises are, it must be observed that he is always free to choose his own ground, he has as large a charter as the wind to blow on whom he pleases. Like the rest of his generation he has no concrete political existence, and his view of world politics is a dream based on the dreams, which he dislikes, of other disfranchised intellectuals. It would no doubt be better for the world if Lewis had a seat on the League of Nations Council; it would also be good for Lewis as a thinker to be obliged to bring his ideas into closer touch with actuality.

'It is my object', says Lewis, 'to carry on a constant campaign for a system of ideas which I wish to propagate. But campaign does not imply a method of activity, or sentiments as regards my opponents, more proper to Marshal Foch [then why use such a misleading metaphor?] than to an artist – compelled, against his will, to clear of refuse a certain tract in order to pursue his way at all.'

Really, this 'against his will' is rather sanctimonious from one who has always shown such a special aptitude for polemics. I suspect that there is more of the politician and man-of-action flawing Lewis the artist than he cares to admit even to himself. The desire to create (though not the will to) is generally sufficient to induce in the artist a sort of anaesthesia to the hostility surrounding him, an interior calm where his creation may flower, regardless of the cost to his temporarily undefended social personality. It is often in the artist himself that the enemy to creation is most deeply entrenched, in distrust of his own intuitions; in fear of, resulting in contempt for, aspects of his own emotional life.

Lewis has effectively shown the disintegrative effect of contemporary philosophy on the unit of personality, but as that could never have happened had there not been a weakening of desire, so it can never be reintegrated by argument, but only by creation in art of new forms of personality, including their automatism, but transcending it in some concept of passionate and conscious action. One genuinely creative work would dispel these miasmas of doubt and self-distrust that resist all the efforts of ratiocination.

In the midst of perplexity it may sometimes restore self-confidence to ruminate on the egregious errors, basenesses, and perversities of the contemporary world. *The Enemy* prosecutes this method on the grand scale, inviting the equally perplexed intelligentsia to follow the development of a critical system which will restore to them the humanly centred values that scientific-determinism through the time-philosophy is supposed to have destroyed; and so reinvigorate the discouraged aesthetic impulse.[1] But so far from leading his pupils to a position from which they can dominate the Flux through their own self-integrity, he is more likely to leave them crowing on a dunghill of irreproachable platitude. *The Enemy* is too much like a Sunday school where it is preached that sensation and various other things are sin; as soon as Lewis leaves off flogging the hostile idea, the preacher supervenes, and the pulpit-tones roll out loud and deep – 'The noble exactitude and harmonious proportion of the European, scientific ideal, the specifically Western heaven' is one example of what might be plentifully illustrated. It is the sort of thing that sets all the glands dribbling their quotas of self-complacence into the blood-stream of the hypnotized (specifically Western) listener.

As a critic of literature Lewis is generally sound in his judgements (and a man of his gifts could hardly fail to be so) when he is estimating the not-very-significant figures of fashionable appeal (or rather, for Lewis they are very significant, because they link up with the Great Time-Space conspiracy). But these judgements are suspect because they are not based on the aesthetic effect of the whole work, the only concrete thing to go by, but on the reputed stigmas of noxious influences. His reaction to a writer of the scale of Proust is lamentably thin and doctrinaire – so blinded by his own doctrines that he can describe the *I* of *A la Recherche du Temps perdu* as 'that small, naif, Charlie Chaplin-like, luxuriantly-indulged, passionately-snobbish figure'.

For Lewis to react to a work of literature at all, it seems necessary for him to find some thesis in it which coincides or conflicts with his own attitude to life. He does not display the critical counterpart of

---

[1] E.g. 'To create new beauty, and to supply a new material is the obvious affair of art of any kind today. But that is a statement that by itself would convey very little. Without stopping to unfold that now, I will summarise what I understand by its opposite. Its opposite is that that thrives upon the *time-philosophy* . . .' Without stopping to unfold that now . . . Caramuel, a famous Spanish bishop, wrote more than two hundred and sixty works attesting to this first principle – that if people would read his works they need read no others. For this purpose his latest work always referred to the preceding ones, and could not be understood till his readers possessed those that were to follow.

that finest type of mind, which 'lifts the creative impulse into an absolute region free of Spenglerian history or politics', in which he asserts his belief. So, in *The Lion and the Fox* he was at ease when he could discover the twin figures of the fable in a play, and on these lines presented a hypothetically interesting Shakespeare (no common feat), but, ignoring the dualism in the creative attitude, a Shakespeare who could never have been a great dramatic poet. Typical of his abstract approach, he lumps all kings together, because they fit his theory of the tragic pathos, though in Shakespeare, at any rate, kings have personal character. But this is a quality which he does not understand. So, knowing that Stendhal was fascinated by Napoleon, he equates Julien Sorel with the Napoleon-idea, a minor truism which dissolves into insignificance in the complete realization of Sorel as a created individual. But, besides seeing human beings as individuals, Shakespeare had a rather strong interest in sex, which required fuller treatment even in a study of the heroic plays, but was perhaps thought unbecoming in a protégé of a philosophy in which sex is restrained to strictly reasonable proportions. Though the basic conception of *The Lion and the Fox* may be a valuable one for the theory of tragedy in general, its preoccupation with the abstract vitiates the complete absorption in the aesthetic image which alone can give a valid reaction to a poetic work. Only when 'ideas of life' are introduced without being transmuted into image is one justified in assessing them against personal 'ideas of life'. So Lewis is on firm ground when he is attacking semi-creative writers like Sherwood Anderson, or Lawrence in his later phase, but his method resembles witch-hunting more than criticism, and a feeling of its irrelevance pervades most of his treatment of modern movements. There is too great a demand for orthodoxy, a tendency to nip experiments in the bud, say, the *surréaliste*; a grandmotherly solicitude for our infant stomachs, threatened by the hard tack of the New Diabolism. An amusing example of this pedagogic complex is his handsome withdrawal in the case of his threatened prosecution of *South Wind*, and the conclusion that it is 'a perfectly harmless production'.

The Enemy promises his readers emancipation from the mental clichés of the time, but up to the present he has done little but provide them with a fresh set of stock reactions; for a champion of the clear outline, etc., the new principles remain remarkably hazy. At a gathering of Enemy supporters I imagine a drowsy summer hum like that which comes through the open windows of the village school. The pupils will hoot whenever the word *Time*,[1] pronounced with a hint as to its sinister significance, falls on their ears; they will eschew the 'gonadal ecstasies of sex' and espouse 'all the male chastity of thought'; they will assert that they are 'on the side of the intellect', and sing in chorus 'I am for the physical world.'[2]

If these are anything more than trite counters, purely emotive trumpetings to herd (though small-herd) action, it should be possible to bring them to clearer definition, to evolve from them some positive and concrete statement as to what might constitute a balanced contemporary human being, instead of being fobbed off with references to 'the chaste wisdom of the Chinese or the Greek'.

When Lewis claims for *his* principle all the remarkable achievements of the past, it is difficult to refuse such an enormous bribe, and easy to overlook the fact that this principle has so far only been described by its effects, not defined in itself.

'I have defined art as the science of the outside of things, and natural science as the science of the inside of things ... A preoccupation with the vitals of "Life" (of the "Up life! Down art!" cry) means invariably the smoking-hot inside of things, in contrast to the hard, cold, formal skull or carapace. The *emotional* of the Bergsonian dogma is the heat, moisture, shapelessness, and tremor of the vitals of life. The *intellectual* is the ectodermic case, the ideality of the animal machine, *with its skin on*.'

This is typical Lewisonian persuasion by rhetoric, but the meta-

---

[1] Among the reckless statements to which this fixation on Time is responsible is a paragraph in which every sentence calls for dispute, but here I can only mention the dogma that literature, though less static than the plastic arts, is more static than an art such as music. I do not see how there can be degrees of the static, but that does not matter, for the material of literature is so obviously a succession of events or emotions that it must be dynamic. The merely hypothetical 'pure lyric' is the exception that proves the rule. Literature has nothing to gain by becoming 'more static', as Hérédia's sonnets show, and Gertrude Stein's success in being quite static is an efficient danger-signal along that road. In Lewis's rhetorical system 'dynamic' is a pejorative. But the speed at which literature can deal with events without 'blurring outlines in a restless flux' is a matter depending on the technical equipment of the writer.

[2] Of the great solace to be found in having a word of indefinite content to lean upon we had an amusing illustration in *The New Criterion*, when the actual meaning of the pet words of T. S. Eliot and J. Middleton Murry (*intelligence* and *intuition* respectively) came up for debate. Herbert Read has staked out a claim to *reason*. Other examples, on less austere planes of thought, abound.

phors should not be allowed to get away with it too easily. A pre-occupation with the hard, cold, formal skull or carapace of things may just as well be emotional as intellectual, may be due, in fact, simply to inhibition, to fear of the emotional; and that is not a very reputable origin for the intellect. Certainly, I should agree, if we must speak as if the mind had separate faculties, that the intellect had better be the unemotional, ordering one. But Lewis wants more than that, he wants to be able to call art intellectual (it follows from the first and last sentences of the above quotation). But granted that the 'intellect works alone' (see next quotation), the aesthetic faculty does not, it must include the emotional, the Dionysian. It is this distrust of the Dionysian which is responsible for all Lewis's distortions, his rationalizations, as well as for the harsh, strained quality of his picture of human life.

'Action (the Dionysiac and dynamical) is highly specialist. But action is impossible without an *opposite* – it takes two to make a quarrel. The dynamical – or what Nietzsche called the Dionysiac, and which he professed – is a *relation*, a something that happens, between two or more opposites, when they meet in their pyrrhic encounters. The intellect works alone.'

He assumes that the Dionysian is merely a relaxation, and not a realization. This is an example, too, of his generally obtuse attitude to Nietzsche.

Lewis admits that the predominance of the Eye in his mentality may give him a fanatical leaning, but this does not make him cautious in levelling charges of the strangest kind against those whose minds are less purely graphic and plastic than he describes his own as being:

'For the mind of Einstein, like that of Bergson or like that of Proust, is not a *physical* mind, as it could be called. It is psychologic, it is mental.'

A simpleton might think that this is a proper characteristic of the mind, but Lewis knows better. A less emotional 'intelligence' than his would have realized that Einstein's achievement is as concrete as anything in the plastic arts. The new view of the universe is one to be assimilated, not rejected, or smothered as the Church tried to smother Galileo's discovery. The human mind has absorbed such shocks before, the sort of shock Donne records in the well-known passage:

> And new Philosophy calls all in doubt,
> The element of fire is quite put out;

The sun is lost, and th' earth, and no man's wit
Can well direct him where to look for it,

but Lewis does not trust it to do so again, and assumes the rôle of a benevolent Canute, protecting the shores of the physical world by a naïve injunction. And his attitude to the 'new Philosophy' is surprisingly pragmatical in one who has indicted William James as a forerunner of the attack on the intellect: 'What I am concerned with here, first of all, is not whether the great time-philosophy that overshadows all contemporary thought is viable as a system of abstract truth, but if in its application it helps or destroys our human arts.'

And a regard for 'abstract truth', whatever abstract may mean there, at least a regard for ascertaining the facts as exactly as possible, is surely a function of the intellect as generally understood, if not of *The Enemy's* elusive principle. Lewis says somewhere that his polemical works are a hasty barrage put down behind the cover of which temples may be constructed. But, as experience has taught us, besides its quantity, the accuracy of a barrage is of some importance. 'Friendly' shells in one's own lines are apt to spoil the *morale* of the troops more than enemy shells, and in his indiscriminate lumping together of real achievement and fashionable mediocrity Lewis comes very near to putting some shells through the structure of the very temple he is so anxious to see erected.

Thomas Nashe has often been referred to as a probable influence on the prose style of Lewis, and it will be found that in their technique of argument, too, they are not dissimilar. They are alike in having a robust, not very subtle intelligence. Nashe, too, was suspicious of the 'revolutionary' thought of his age:

'I heare say there be Mathematitions abroad, that will prove men before *Adam*, and they are harboured in high places, who will maintaine it to the death, that there are no divels.' These seem to have been predecessors of Lewis's Time-philosophers. Nashe also spotted what is one of Lewis's favourite complaints – the competition of the wealthy amateur with the genuine artist. Nashe, however, restrains his grievance to the personal:

'All my thoughts consorted to this conclusion, that the world was uncharitable, and I ordained to be miserable. Thereby I grew to consider how many base men that wanted those parts which I had, enjoyed content at will and had wealth at command . . . and have I

more wit than all these (thought I to myself)? am I better born?
am I better brought up? yea, and better favoured? and yet am I a
beggar? What is the cause? how am I crost? or whence is this curse?

'Even from hence, *that men that should employ such as I am, are
enamoured of their own wits*, and think whatever they do is excellent,
though it be never so scurvie . . . that every grosse brained Idiot is
suffered to come into print, who if he set forth a Pamphlet of the
praise of Pudding-pricks, or write a treatise of *Tom Thumme*, or the
exploits of Untrusse, it is bought up thick and threefold, when
better things lie dead.'

Is not this an epitome of the central contention of *The Apes of
God*?

Under the novel appearance given to Lewis's criticism by his
extraordinary faculty of systematization one can recognize so many
of the stock themes of the satirist, that one is inclined to think that
in spite of its philosophical pretensions, it has a source nearer 'the
hot vitals of life' than calm judgement. Only having as it were, too
queasy a stomach for satire, we have to have it wrapped up in an
edifying pastry. The only other equally comprehensive effort to point
out that the intellectual world contains numbers of mugs and
charlatans was attempted by a syndicate, the Scriblerus Club, who
parcelled out among themselves the several provinces of Dullness.
Lewis is the whole Club in himself – Arbuthnot for the fantasies of
the scientists; Pope, if we equate the Rue de l'Odéon with Grub
Street; Swift, only portraying mechanical Robots instead of bestial
yahoos. But the product so far, owing to this attempt to double the
function of satirist and teacher, has been too discursive, only in rare
sections achieving plastic unification, even in *The Childermass*, which
should have been wholly that.

It is obvious that at the basis of the satirist's sensibility is the
feeling that this is, in certain aspects, the worst of all possible
worlds; it is not necessary for him to justify that feeling to anyone
else's satisfaction, the images he creates should be powerful enough
to induce a similar (if only momentary) conviction in the spectator.
But Lewis seems to be uneasy in his distaste, and to seek all kinds
of extraneous justifications for it. He even, it appears, visualizes
himself rather as a redeemer than a castigator. In a remark which
contains an amazing *nonsequitur* he says, 'supposed as I am to be a
kind of almost professionally "aggressive" person (which plainly I
cannot be or I could not do so much work) . . .' Substituting 'writer'

or 'artist' for 'person', I should say that the only proper evidence, the most characteristic style, goes rather against his repudiation of aggressiveness. In fiction, criticism, or drawing his most characteristic style is reached when he is antipathetic to the subject; when he is sympathetic, as he claims to be to the Greek world, his style is as trite as that of a Classics don.

For in *Tarr* and *The Wild Body* the spectator or narrator is on a superior plane of consciousness to the actors. They are given certain stimuli and obliged to react by a sort of conditioned reflex, but Tarr or Ker-Orr move with a godlike autonomy. So judicial an eye for the folly, error, and sensual chaos which makes up the greater part of existence results in a weakening of consciousness and produces a technically adequate, but thin achievement. This acting the naturalist to characters, too, produces a sort of priggishness, since Tarr and Ker-Orr are so neutral themselves. Tarr is so afraid of Life getting in the way of his art that he reduces its significance to a minimum. What he calls the 'curse of humour' in him results in an 'inverted Quixotry':

'Instead of having conceived the world as more chivalrous and marvellous than it was, he had conceived it as emptied of all dignity, sense, and generosity. The drovers and publicans were angry at not being mistaken for a legendary chivalry, for knights and ladies. The very windmills resented not being taken for giants!'

There has been a tendency from Taine to Watson which has led to doubt as to whether human beings are quite so individual as they once thought themselves. The forces of environment, occupation, and glandular action have been admitted to account for much. For Lewis, at one time, I judge from 'Inferior Religions', they accounted for a great deal, that view has certainly influenced his fiction. Against its absolute implications he has struggled rather desperately in his critical work. His fiction has been praised because it is 'stripped of sentimentality', which means, I suppose, that he does not allow any humanistic concepts to blur his vision of the creature's 'ectodermic case'; and it is perhaps in this sense that Lewis calls *Tarr* 'in a sense the first book of an epoch in England'. For the novel does not innovate in form: the objectification of mental processes in a humorous and highly metaphorical prose is what most characterizes it. *The Wild Body* consists of studies of simpler organisms than those in *Tarr*, vividly grotesque, and written with a complete mastery of the intention. They exist as the record of a peculiar vision. Whether, as aesthetic achievement, they correspond to the expository essays may be doubted.

As only one-third of *The Childermas* has yet been published, much cannot be said about it. Certainly the first volume does not generate any high degree of dramatic tension; the conflict remains abstract in spite of its projection into an admirably realized landscape of desolate, shifting time-tracts. But the Bailiff's court is tediously lengthy. The objects of satire are so familiar from Lewis's critical writing, that to have them rather vaguely personified is an inadequate gilding of the pill. '*Where any sex-nuisance is concerned*,' Lewis once wrote, and italicized, '*the Greek indifference is the best specific*.' If he had taken his own medicine he would have spared us the bleary pathics who draw so many of his shafts. The shade of Joyce, too, is strangely prominent, being not only laid under contribution for technical effects, but stimulating the flow of animus to an extent for which, even as symbol, it seems inadequate, to a detached reader. Both *Ulysses* and *The Childermass* are largely works of exasperation; the first named has an effective coda which does resolve the Bloom-theme, though the Stephen-theme is left up in the air. *The Childermass*, has yet to be seen in its totality, but its exasperations, being less concrete, are less general than those of *Ulysses*. In *Ulysses* it is any body and any mind that suffers, in any city on any sweltering day (its particularity has precisely that effect, unexpectedly), on the lowest common level of humanity, the sensuous one, just capable of sexual jealousy and parental affection. The panoramic phantasmagoria of *The Childermass* is a description of the world under the disintegration of Time-philosophy and its subsidiary influences, which, to put it briefly, make everything unreal. But to us the conflict itself seems unreal, since the Bailiff is so obviously an Aunt Sally (for instance, he is made to say, 'I prefer hot blood to your beastly intellects'), an abstract invention adequate to support the dialectics of *The Enemy*, but not an aesthetic creation. The volume ends on the claim of the anti-Bailiffites to *reality*.

It is up to Lewis to make them real.

In *The Apes of God* the antipathetic artist I postulated has magnificently found himself. If there could have been any doubt, after *The Childermass*, as to Lewis being the most forceful and resourceful prose-writer of his generation there can be none now. That *The Apes of God* is a work of great technical power is certain, but it is not so easy to decide whether it is equally considerable as a work of art. For that, the value of the underlying conception has to be assessed. The triviality of the subject-matter is no more against it than it is against the *Dunciad*, which *The Apes of God* most resembles; but no one could say that the *Dunciad* is intellectually absorbing. It is like an action brilliantly transmuted into the plastic of gesture. And when, in *Satire and Fiction*, Lewis suggests that the greatest satire cannot be moralistic, he is asserting what seems to me a flaw in his work. In the crude, prohibitive sense of moral it certainly cannot be, but there must be somewhere in the satire, implicit or explicit, a standard or ideal of conduct from which the victims are observed to deviate. So the fine reasonableness of the houyhnhnms was necessary to the crapulousness of the yahoos. This standard the hazy lucubrations of the absent Pierpoint are inadequate to supply; and though Dan, in his utter negativeness, may be realistically true to a contemporary type, artistically he is a heavy liability. He is largely responsible for the stickiness of the action, since his character precludes any clash of personality, a lack emphasized by the failure of the characters ever to stand up for themselves. But there are numerous episodes, such as the climax of the Klein luncheon party or the meeting between Mr. Zagreus and the Split-man, which show that the creator of Kreisler is capable of more general and therefore more interesting satire than that arising from indignation at the presence of minor artists in the social limelight.

Without Lewis contemporary literature would be very much less alive, and in a less promising condition, no doubt, than it is. He has been a great ice-breaker, and his ridicule has scorched up many pretentious shams. But latterly his energy has been spent in a reckless way; one is reminded of a powerful man tormented by gnats. The apostolic fervour which the campaign for their extermination develops, threatens to become a breathless pursuit of the insignificant.

ARISTOPHANES AND A SOBERED WORLD[1]

Aristophanes is one of the few poets who have treated women naturally, without idealizing or romanticizing or traducing them. He would have found it as difficult to follow the steps by which Dante convinced himself that his love for Beatrice prefigured his

[1] *Women in Parliament.* (*Ecclesiazusai.*) Translated by Jack Lindsay. Drawings by Norman Lindsay. Foreword to . . . Fanfrolico Press, 1929.

later aspirations, as to have blasphemed creation, in the spirit of some of the Early Fathers of the Church, by appointing Woman the selected instrument of eternal damnation.

It seems to have been only in specific periods or social groups that sexual relationships become intensely selective. To realize the possibility of a uniquely personal relationship is a gain to the sensibility and so to poetry; without it the work even of Shakespeare or Catullus would be depleted and of all those who have cultivated its strange off-shoot, jealousy. But a peculiar species of cant was current in nineteenth-century Britain, to the effect that all sexual relationships are of this kind, and that any other was reprehensible. To keep a balance between hectic promiscuity and drab coerced fidelity is possible only where the choice freely exists.

The Victorians invented a woman who was supposedly devoid of sexual feeling and who meekly, from the sense of duty, submitted to whatever indignity her lawful-wedded husband chose to put upon her. This type gave rise to the over-emancipated feminist in whom repressed energy of sex emerged as a lust for dominance. A draught of Aristophanes is the liquor to clear the mind of such haunting monstrosities.

The women initiate the theme in all three of Aristophanes's comedies, Lysistrata in the play of that name, Praxagora in the *Ecclesiazusai* whilst in the *Thesmophoriazusia* the leading woman character is not personalized, she remains simply 'First Woman'.

Praxagora, the heroine of *Women in Parliament* does not dominate the action so completely as does Lysistrata. We see her efficiently stage-managing her *coup d'état*, and again, triumphant and acclaimed by her fellow-rebels, but she drops out of the play before the end. Had it been as fully elaborated as the *Lysistrata* we should surely have seen her grappling with the situation created by the type of citizen who refuses to bring in his personal goods to the common stock, or by the obvious discontents arising from her excessively egalitarian sex regulations.

It may be that some scenes, as well as some choral songs, have been lost, and that these would have rounded off her character. Or that Aristophanes was content with the uproarious laughter he knew must greet the extravagant farce of his concluding scenes.

If Praxagora follows in the wake of Lysistrata it is because she answers the question: What shall we do when we've got peace? They make a charming pair of sister-strategists, witty, frank, energetic and pleasantly addicted to the delicacies of love-making; witness this little exchange between Praxagora and her jealous husband:

> *Blepyros.*   Can't a woman be embraced
> Without having some scent curling her hair?
> *Praxagora.*   I don't choose to be, anyhow.

In her capacity as Governess, Praxagora is naturally shown as rather more dignified than her companions, whom we may imagine to have been the libidinous wine-bibbing females Aristophanes loved to depict – a type he left Chaucer to elaborate and Skelton to lyricize.

But there is a sinister aspect to the Wyf of Bath which the Athenian women escape, and which was called into existence perhaps by the repressive ethics of Christianity and the corresponding property-laws. There is no spite, no itch to humiliate the male, in these women of Aristophanes. Even in the *Thesmophoriazusai*, where the females' crimes are expatiated on with a satirist's loving care, these are all the peccadilloes of self-indulgence. Had they been accustomed to tyrannize over their men there is no doubt that we should have heard of it. This peculiarity apart, and in spite of her Christian oaths, the Wyf is a good example of the paganism that Christianity could only whitewash, not pluck out:

> But, lord Christ! when that it remembreth me
> Upon my yowthe, and on my jolitee,
> It tickleth me aboute myn herte rote.

And none of Praxagora's companions, in their later years, could have said better than that.

. . . .

So much for the kind of woman Aristophanes, on two occasions, envisaged as having control of the State. For the *kind* is all-important.

A House of Commons of frustrated women would be more deadly to the joy of life than even the ordinary assembly of mediocre males. Aristophanes luckily could not have been acquainted with our earliest example, the ardent Prohibitionist lady-member for Plymouth. Indeed the restriction of other people's pleasure on grounds of high moral principle was a species of perversion his world was mercifully spared. But unfortunately the good-humoured type of man or woman is not one that hankers after political influence: the machinery of government generally falls to the earnest busy-bodies whilst the power, in the usual manner, goes to the Cleons of the day.

A wholly be-skirted Parliament, in our own lifetime, even, is not beyond imagination, but chosen by the present indiscriminate methods it is unlikely that the women would use their power to further any such Dionysian programme of reform as Praxagora's. To bring that about, to ensure the election of the Aristophanic woman, some method of sifting out the candidates would be necessary. For one thing, the register of electors would have to consist solely of those who were active lovers, which would ensure a certain temperamental generosity in our elected rulers.

. . . .

It is too readily taken for granted by some commentators that Aristophanes was *attacking* the communistic notions afloat in the Athens of his time. If we compare this play with almost any other of his we are struck with the good-humour which almost entirely pervades it. If this is an attack, then the arm which had so often castigated the demagogues, the sophists, and Euripides was by then incredibly weakened. The error comes from failing to distinguish between his attitude to Praxagora's 'platform' and his opinion of the practicability of carrying it through. There is nothing he would have found inherently objectionable in her proposals, for he was always willing that the true citizens should have as good a time as possible. In fact, in *The Wasps*, he suggests more or less seriously a generous pension scheme by which the dicasts may live in comfort and be weaned from their eternal vindictive litigation. As the old dicast's son, who is the mouthpiece of the proposal, says, if, in each of the thousand cities paying toll to Athens, ten of her dispossessed citizens were to be billeted, then:

> Of Athenian men thus might thousands twice ten
>   banquet bravely on good cheer and plenty;
> On rich milk and whipp'd cream, life away they might dream,
>   neither chaplets nor flesh of hare sparing . . .

If such a large proportion of the citizens of Athens was on the dole when *The Wasps* was produced in 422, thirty years later, after the crushing defeat of her imperial ambitions, the audience that witnessed the present play must have contained a large majority of spectators who had good reason for desiring a redistribution of the wealth that was left. Perhaps there had been some talk of a decree for effecting this compulsorily. At any rate, Aristophanes, accepting the idea for its dramatic value, simply portrays a typical example of what might be expected to result. In the scene of the Two Citizens he personifies the crafty, hoarding type, the Nepman of contemporary Russia, planning to outwit the state; but it cannot be said that he holds up the champion of private ownership to particular admiration. In the scene of the Three Hags the sheer comic possibilities of the situation run away with him; it is pure lyrical comedy and if it had any political significance the reference is so faint that now it may fortunately be enjoyed for its own sake.[1]

It is significant that in the *Ecclesiazusai* and in the *Plutos*, the latest of his surviving plays and written when he was nearing his sixties, Aristophanes no longer simply looks to the political situation in Athens, but takes account of the economic factors as well, to find a remedy for the unsatisfactory condition of the city. As always after a period of warfare the discrepancy between wealth and poverty had been accentuated. In these circumstances the Utopian visions in which the Athenians indulged no less than more credulous communities, would have become more pressing in order to compensate the unfortunate citizens with phantasmal hopes. No doubt that thousands of the Athenians present at the production of the *Ecclesiazusai* licked their lips at the list of Praxagora's succulent promises and played with the idea that after all they might by some such simple means transform their miserable diet of bread, garlic, and olives into a sumptuous repast. Perhaps the *dénouement* of the play was designed to damp this naïve optimism with a touch of realism.

That the Athenians were in the habit of letting their fancy run riot in regions of improbable luxury is evident from some fragments of the Old Comedy which, though probably designed to burlesque the more outrageous of these visions, might yet be taken at their face value by the more simple-minded spectators. As always, the unsatisfied appetites of a community are built into a coherent structure which is variously located, in the past as a Golden Age, in the future, or in some extremely inaccessible locality like the

---

[1] On the available evidence it seems more likely that he was aiming at some popular theory of sexual communism, rather than at the breeding-arrangements outlined in the *Republic* (which he may have heard about before writing the play) which were not of a kind to be enthusiastically received by the ordinary citizens.

Land of Cockaygne. Here is the speech of Nature from Telekleides, written when hopes were forming that the policy of imperial expansion might enable the humblest citizen to live in luxuriant ease:

> I'll tell you now the life I gave the dead,
> in the first days there was peace for all
> easy as scooping water with the hand.
> Earth brought forth then no fear and no disease
> but everything desired broke blossoming.
> The mountain sides were cleft with hurrying wine
> and barley-cakes were quarrelling with loaves
> which got the first bite from the mouth they wooed,
> bouncing about it, if one liked white bread.
> The fishes, gliding homeward, then would leap
> fried from the water, flopping on the tables –
> a stream of soup, with joints and chops still warm
> and bobbing amid its savours, wreathed along
> past the couched diners, while from pipes there dribbled
> perpetual fronds of mincemeat richly spiced
> for all to lick the luscious stalactites;
> and everywhere in fragrant dishes rose
> confectioneries. And there were roasted thrush,
> and rissoles kneaded out of bread and milk
> spontaneously in any opened mouth
> insinuated their warm succulence.
> There was a champ of cheesecakes, and the lads
> played round with nice titbits and knucklebones –
> Those were the days when men were properly nourisht
> and thewed like giants!
>
> *Transl.* J.L.

Athenaios quotes similar passages from many other comic poets, from Pherecrates (twice), from Nicophon and Metagenes, and refers to the lost *Tagenistai* of Aristophanes. He further quotes a passage from Crates' *Theria* which is even more pertinent:

> A. Then no one shall possess a slave at all,
>   female or male. He'll do his own work now
>   however old he is.
> B.   No, not at all.
>   I have a capital solution. Listen.
> A. And what will all your notions do for us?
> B. Why everything you summon will come forth

and no more effort needed than a word.
Say: Table, lay yourself! – and lo, it's laid.
You kneading-troughs prepare some dough, and you,
cyathos, pour out wine – and where's the cup?
Come here, you cup. Empty and wash yourself.
Trot up, you cake. And you, you loafing dish,
get busy, sir, and bring along some beetroot.
Slidder this way now, fish. *O but I can't!*
I'm only fried on one side yet. You fool!
flop round there in the oil and fry both sides.

Transl. J.L.

I am tempted, in order to demonstrate the immutable characteristics of the phantasy of ordinary folk, to quote from an early
fourteenth century description of the land of Cockaygne. This land,
it appears was situated by the popular imagination in the western
ocean beyond the Pillars of Hercules and its merits, it is curious to
find in the heyday of Christianity, exceeded those of Paradise: for
in Paradise, the poet complains, there is nothing to eat but fruit or
to drink but water. In many ways Cockaygne bears a close resemblance
to the reformed Athens of Praxagora's administration:

> In Cockaygne is meat and drink
> Without care, how, and swink. . .

that is to say, without working for it.

> There is no lack of meat nor cloth,
> There is no man nor woman wroth –

none of that petty litigation for which Aristophanes trounced the
Athenians and that Praxagora abolished. Such water as there is
is merely to look at or wash in, for most of the rivers are of oil,
honey, milk, and wine. There is an abbey, too, built of rich pasties
and many other marvels, the fauna there having the same eagerness
to be devoured as in the times Telekleides described:

> The geese irostid on the spit
> Flee to that abbey, God it wot,
> And gredith: 'Geese all hot, all hot!'

and, most important feature of this earthly paradise:

> All is commune to young and old,
> To stout and stern, meek and bold.

Altogether this poem is a curious stepping-stone between Tele-kleides and Rabelais, to whom no doubt it was known in some form or other since there exists an Old French version of it. And there must still be a great repertory of such visions in the day-dreams of the tired and badly-fed populace if only there were some means of getting at them, if there were but a poet among them to bring them to life in the aesthetic image. For the great weakness of the modern world is its poverty of images; it has no power to visualize its desires. All its so much-boosted miracles resolve themselves into a speeding-up of communication, but the message only grows more trite and meaningless with each improvement. Even the cinema, which on the face of it would seem to be a repository of images, is in actuality merely an easier form of communication than words. It gives the spectator no more than the novelette used to in which the duke marries the servant-girl. It is sheer realistic wish-fulfilment; there is no plastic image.

England in the sixteenth century was more akin to Greece in its great days than it is now, for all its pretentious architecture, classical dancing, etc., for then on the village green, in the city pageants, and on the waggons of the Miracle plays the people projected their ideas in concrete form – the Devil was grotesque, if not perhaps very terrible, and God Almighty was distinguished by his gilded cheeks. The great festivals, Easter and Whitsun, were the excuse for this outburst of aesthetic enthusiasm just as the Dionysia were for the Athenians, only their fun was much more unrepressed than ours. And it is this faculty that we envy in our forebears as we admire it in Aristophanes and his contemporaries. That it is dependent in some way on the solidarity of the community seems certain, since the intensification of capitalism with its consequent splitting of the community into self-conscious sections was accompanied by a decline in popular art in both Athens and England – that is, a distinction grew up between good art and popular art which had not existed before. With the increase of private wealth comes an increase of privacy – almost unknown when the master, his family and dependants lived all under one roof – and a consequent impoverishment of the communal life. Hence, too, the rise of notions of modesty and obscenity which would have been meaningless before.

The relations between the aesthetic fertility of a community and its economic system are too complex for dogmatism. About the well-being of its citizens there can be less discussion and that is always a favourite theme with Aristophanes. His admiration for the warriors who defend the State when it is in danger from aggression is not the result of a belief in the State as an actual entity above the well-being of its individual citizens – he was too concrete-minded to fall into such an unfortunate abstraction.

For why, after all, should not politics be poetic and humour grease the easy yoke? Why do men, without a qualm, entrust their bodily well-being, their only pledge for the delight that is their birthright, to those acquisitive or censorious individuals who make up the major part of the politicians of the world? The politicians, naturally, support the legend that the aesthetic type is universally incompetent and dissipated, and its people have not the gumption to make out a list which would go a long way towards reversing this accusation. But the laws and restraints which the politicians live to inflict and enforce and by which they justify their existence are bogeys at which the poets only grin – that is the real charge against them. For they see that nine-tenths of human frustration is artificial – man-made – and to be swept away in a breath of Aristophanic laughter, like foul clouds, showing the clear ecstatic sky above. As for the other tenth, that which makes tragedy and heroism, it is Nemesis and its stroke is clean. It is by keeping this distinction clear that Aristophanes and the great humorists enrich the quotidian scene and lay their laughter like a scarlet mantle over the hairless ape who created the libidinous gods in his own immortal image.

APPENDIX
Articles from the *Daily Herald*
1920

Appendix

WILLIAM MORRIS
(1834–96)

Becoming conscious of the world around him at the time of the Great Exhibition, when Victorian England cried 'Eureka!' amidst the squalor, ugliness, and snobbery it had erected, Morris turned back to an age he believed nobler than his own preserved in the epics and chronicles of the Middle Ages. In the *Defence of Guenevere*, his first volume of poems, he invests with a personal and passionate life the steel-clad dummies and high-coifed dolls of the history books. But his strength lay in a simplicity and singleness of mind, characteristic not of the dramatic, but of the epic poet, who must consider the size rather than the subtlety of his persons, who are 'cloudy symbols' of the struggles of the race.

It is only by thus regarding Morris, as a man of little complexity and immense energy, that one can reach a true appreciation of his work as a revolutionary and as a writer. For a man who was only sixty-two when he died, a Collected Edition of 24 volumes represents considerable industry, especially as these include very literal translations of the *Aeneid* and *Odyssey* in verse, and of long Icelandic Sagas. Yet besides this, in his spare time he overthrew the Victorian dread of colour with the bright dyes of his wallpapers and upholstery stuffs; wove tapestries and made stained-glass windows; shamed the meanness of contemporary book-production with the magnificent volumes of the Kelmscott Press; and married, Watts Dunton says, the most beautiful woman in England. He became convinced that nothing short of revolution could cure the rottenness of society, and made speeches at street corners on Sundays; he was one of the founders of the Socialist League, and for some years edited its organ, *The Commonweal*, to which he contributed many propagandist articles and poems.

This may not seem the work of a simple mind, but one cannot help noticing that he solved all his problems with a single formula,

that of looking backward. In his Utopia he scrapped all except the
most ancient mechanical devices and created beyond the fretful
modern world a pleasant Arcadian existence. Such a life does not
coincide with our present notions of our destiny, but the courage and
enthusiasm with which he worked for the universal happiness he
dreamt of are qualities for ever admirable in a character free from
all meanness or self-seeking.

THE HEART OF ENGLAND

Collected Poems. By Edward Thomas. Foreword by W. de la Mare
(Selwyn and Blount)

There was surely never a poet so direct, so free from hyperbole
and periphrase as Edward Thomas. To read him is like listening to a
friend in the completest intimacy, in which nothing is said for the
sake of mere brilliancy, but simply as a statement of what has moved
him to interest, to wonder, and, more rarely, to ecstasy. Time and
again his poems begin with the spontaneity of fireside talk: –

> Yes, I remember Adlestrop . . .

or

> They have taken the gable from the roof of clay
> On the old swede-pile . . .

And the rhythm of his verses is not that of the bard's who is rapt
from earth and ordinary speech by the immensity of a sudden glory,
but that which a man might use, a man with the keenest sense of the
harmony of words, recounting an incident that happened in the
course of his day, and musing quietly on its significance; so to
Thomas the owl's cry that broke in on his refreshment and repose
seemed to be

> Speaking for all who lay under the stars,
> Soldiers and poor, unable to rejoice.

Though there was never anyone farther removed from Jingoism
than Thomas, neither is anyone's verse so unmistakably English. It
is of the country of the deepest country where they call

> . . . the wild cherry-tree, the merry tree,
> The rose campion Bridget-in-her-bravery

and in this green heart of the land he finds the type of all Englishmen, old Lob-lie-by-the-fire, called also Hob, Tall Tom, Jack-in-the-Hedge, and many other names; who

> . . . was seen dying at Waterloo,
> Hastings, Agincourt and Sedgemoor, too.

Who lives yet, in spite of four years of battle and the growth of cities.

There are no cities in this book: it is written, if ever any were, with a rural pen, compact of ploughland and orchard, river-meadow and down. It is like the 'touch of rain' to read it, so vivid and fresh are the descriptions, too vivid to be called by that prosaic word 'description', creation rather of a world in the poet's mind, yet true to the England that we know, and 'trust is good and must endure, loving her so'. We have the same trust about these poems of Edward Thomas.

PREACHING AND PRACTICE

The Wooden Pegasus. By Edith Sitwell (Blackwell)
Otherworld (Cadences). By F. S. Flint (Poetry Bookshop)

The best way to make a splash with an indifferent volume of poems is to give it a preface setting out some untenable thesis. There will always be a few fools to support it, and some other fools who will waste their breath in denying it. We belong to the latter category, and as Mr. Flint does not condescend to the level of our reason, but supports his theories with only the most unfounded statements, we do not propose to waste time in argument. Mr. Flint considers that rhyme and metre are outworn and have become contemptible and encumbering because so few people, at present, can do anything with them. He seems to forget that in no particular twenty years of our history have there been many poets writing the best poetry. He forgets the foreshortening that makes the Lyrical Ballads appear almost contemporary with the 1821 volume of Keats. If any poet has ever found metre encumbering (and some have) it is not probable that he will wait for Mr. Flint's preface before discarding it.

Mr. Flint also thinks that metre was invented by poets to show how ingenious they could be, a remark which implies a pitiful callousness of the ear that does not recognize how essential and integral a part of a poem its metre is. Perhaps Mr. Flint invented cadence (strongly accented prose) to show how ingenuous he could be.

> And I came away
> Full of the sweet and bitter juices of life:
> And I lit the lamp in my room
> And made this poem.

We think that theories about the way to write poetry are utterly useless, and when borrowed from the French (whose material requies handling so differently), positively a nuisance. It is so obvious that poetry may be written in a hundred ways, in the rhythms of normal speech, of prose, of a merry-go-round, or even in cadence, though Mr. Flint rarely brings it off, except in his exquisite and altogether delightful 'Swan'.

Talking of merry-go-rounds reminds us of Miss Sitwell. She has not abandoned the poetic conventions so thoroughly as Mr. Flint, retaining, in her own personal way, metre and rhyme. By never forgetting to use all her mannerisms in every poem she sometimes achieves a style at once congruous to her subject, and vivid and refreshing in its imagery. Unfortunately, she seems to parody herself rather over-frequently. Self-parody is a joke which should not be kept up, but it is worth reading many bad jokes for the sake of 'Eventail'.

> Lovely Semiramis
> Closes her slanting eyes; . . .

Miss Sitwell has expressed in her title the limitations of her artifice. A wooden Pegasus cannot be expected to soar, though never so gilded and glossy, but he makes a pleasant figure standing stiffly in the 'fruit-ripe heat of afternoon' that glows continually over her poetic suburb, whilst the circus blares shrilly and insistently from a neighbouring meadow.

ONE IN THREE

The Waggoner and Other Poems. By Edmund Blunden (Sidgwick and Jackson)
Poems. By G. R. Malloch (Heinemann)
India. By Esmé Wingfield-Stratford (Books, Ltd.)

When Mr. Blunden writes of the country, which is most of the time, the rest of our modern landscape poets seem rather urban; their flowers pressed flowers, and their birds stuffed. Their poetry may be none the worse for that, but it does prevent it being of that peculiar kind we call Nature poetry. It is a matter of living *with* things, and getting to know them inside as well as outside, as Edward Thomas did. Mr. Blunden has this interior knowledge, even of fish, which we had thought the most callous and unemotional brutes in creation till he wrote about a perch. 'An ogling hunch-back perch, with needled fin,' had been hooked, and his companion of twenty summers follows him to the surface, careless of danger, and when all is over sinks slowly away. Then

> What agony usurps that watery brain
> For comradeship of twenty summers slain?
> For such delights below the flashing weir
> And up the sluice-cut, playing buccaneer
> Among the minnows . . . and with new wonder
> Prowling through old drowned barges falling asunder.
> And O, the thousand things the whole year through
> They did together, never more to do.

And this is not fish in the abstract, but definitely perch, and we venture to think that Mr. Blunden would not have written it about any other kind of fish, for he knows them not only by their fins and colouring, but by their very souls – the ferocious pike, the sage and deathless bream, the fierce, unfaithful eel. And he understands not only fish, but other creatures, brute and human, that most of us ignore – the malefactors of the countryside, snake, stoat, and kite, and almswomen, and the old soldier living his solitary last years amidst the richness of his garden. The companion pictures, 'Almswomen' and 'The Veteran', are splendid examples of Dutch painting in verse. The first is well-known already, and the second not less worthy. The fighter of forgotten battles sleeps in the fragrance of apples and honey, and of old-time wines:

> And if sleep seem unsound
> And set old bugles pealing through the dark,
> Waked on the instant, he but wakes to hark
> His bell-man cockerel crying the first round.

Description is not often poetry, but Mr. Blunden, in spite of his pictorial qualities is never merely superficial. Without dragging a moral out of everything he makes all his detail significant and contributory to the meaning of the poem. Which is as much as to say that he treats his material imaginatively and can transmute the ordinary into something strange. Besides the everyday atmosphere of 'Almswomen' there is the pure fantasy of 'Chinese Pond', and in contrast to the mellow richness of the veteran's garden, weird desolation in 'A Country God'.

It is a nasty shock after the beautiful accuracy of Mr. Blunden to read:

> The birds are whispering about the dying bed of summer.

At times the poet may transcend appearances in order to create something on a higher level of truth, but never, we believe, to talk nonsense. Haphazard and inappropriate imagery is the usual mark of derivative verse, and we cannot find anything else in Mr. Malloch's volume.

India, says the dust-wrapper, 'is a scathing attack on Anglo-Indians and their ways, and reveals the greatness, beauty, and invincibility of Indian civilisation'. Actually, *India* contains three poems mildly sarcastic to Anglo-Indians, who, it is stated:

> Walk about at noon-day in the dark,
> And then play bridge, because they lack the vital spark;
> And if they talk discuss some bunker-guarded hole . . .
> O Lord, deliver me from Mrs. Pogson-Clarke
> And Sir Pontius Pilate, and Colonel Moale.

It is ridiculous to talk of poetry 'attacking' anything, and even Anglo-Indians are capable of poetic treatment, as a living poet has shown. The subject matter of this book is so interesting that the absence from it of that peculiar and indefinable quality called poetry may be overlooked.

WEED KILLING

The Sacred Wood. Essays on Poetry and Criticism. By T. S. Eliot (Methuen)

The admitted flabbiness of present-day reviewing is a condition which extends, more regrettably, into the region of serious, or pure, criticism. It is a disease which this volume of Mr. Eliot's should do much to cure. He commences by discussing what must be the qualifications of the perfect critic, and in his first essay, where the conclusions are so admirable, we can but wish their exposition had been more lucid; but the attempt to destroy the Philistines and re-build the Temple at one blow has resulted rather in the obscuring of his arguments. The Philistines, in this case, are those even now dwelling in the very heart of the sacred wood, the sheep wearing the critics' wolf-skin, some of whom go about and say, 'Such-and-such is the most wonderful poem of So-and-so's.' They may be right, but to display an impeccable taste is only the first, not the most important, of the critic's tasks. Even less appropriately may those be called critics who recount their emotional adventures when confronted with a work of art. These 'appreciations', so much in vogue a few years back among the disciples of Pater, are probably, Mr. Eliot suggests, the back-wash from a thwarted creative faculty.

Mr. Eliot's essays are full of such suggestive signposts, and two of them particularly important as pointing the foundations of a pure criticism. The first of these is summed up in the statement that 'the difference between art and the event is always absolute.' This is to say, if we have not misunderstood the critic, that the feelings aroused by a play, for example, are of a totally different nature from those that would be aroused by the witnessing of the same events in actual life; and hence it is using the wrong measuring-tape to judge a work by the height to which one's feelings, in one's capacity of lover, parent, or what not, are raised.

The second signpost is this – that the art of the past and of the present forms a structure, not a formless mass; and that criticism is a verbal statement of this structure, and shows the position with regard to the whole of the work of art under consideration. It is from this kind of criticism that one returns to the artist's creation 'with improved perception and enjoyment intensified because made more conscious'.

With an agreeable abstention from irrelevant gossip Mr. Eliot gets down to the imaginative creation, and operates most effectively on Ben Jonson, on Swinburne, on Blake, and on Marlowe. Equally illuminating are the essays on 'Tradition and the Individual Talent' and on 'The Possibility of a Poetic Drama'. Were there a few more writers like Mr. Eliot we would no longer concede to the French the superiority in this kind of literature; but it is so long since these qualities have appeared in a writer in English that we are obliged to hail him as a lonely star shedding light into the dark places of our luxuriant, but tangled poetry.

MORE ARSENIC

Aspects of Literature. J. Middleton Murry (Collins)

A week or two ago, in our delight at his book of criticism, we hailed Mr. T. S. Eliot as the unique exception in the fuddled ranks of contemporary critics, forgetting for the moment (though this detracts nothing from the former's excellence) the work of Mr. Middleton Murry, under whose editorship the *Athenæum* has become the most generally sound of our critical journals. Mr. Murry's philosophy of criticism is the more complex because he considers the relation of the work of art, not merely to other creations of the aesthetic faculty, but to all the activities of life. Hence his scale of values has a moral annotation, or, rather, for him the ultimate moral and aesthetic standards are identical. The ultimate morality, that which is something more than mere subservience to the behests of expediency, is the attainment, or the desire for the attainment, of truth: and if we accept Mr. Murry's identification of Morality and Beauty, we must consider as aesthetic all those efforts which are directed towards the attainment of truth. Such of these efforts as achieve any degree of success (and we can only judge of their success or failure by our aesthetic sensibility) are immediately entitled to be considered as works of art, and the function of criticism is to rank these successful efforts in their order of importance, according to the percentage that they express of the truth, or, one might say, the ideal.

The adequacy of this conception, admitting the distortion occasioned by condensation, to embrace and assess the whole of art, is a matter impossible to be discussed here; whether or not it stand the test, it is one which marks a definite break with the impressionistic criticism of the last fifty years; and one which, though hardly likely to increase the number of our poets, will yet help to expose the more idiotic amongst those who hoodwink their contemporaries. Indeed, if Mr. Murry is really the leader of a school of criticism, as the dust-wrapper suggests, there's a bad time coming for someone. Even now the garden is strewn with wilted Georgian poets, and Mr. Yeats, in what Mr. Murry calls ironically (or considerately) his swan-song, is heard to emit the faint groan of a dying duck.

With the justice of these judgements we are not concerned; of the necessity for the application of some such rigorous standards there cannot be two opinions. We do not think that Mr. Murry has said the final word, not even his own last word, but he has cleared the ground, and, what is more, has raised a fine mass of constructive criticism. After this there can be no excuse for continuing to cultivate such a profusion of weeds.

Index